Concern/s: essays & reviews 1972-1976

Concern/s:
essays & reviews 1972-1976

Tom Montag

Pentagram Press ☆ Milwaukee, Wisconsin

Certain of these articles were first published by
Book Magazine, dodeca, Margins, Mojo Navigator(e), Pentagram Press, Second Coming, Small Press Review, and *Triquarterly.*
Thanks to their editors for permission to reprint in *Concern/s.*

Pentagram Press
Michael Tarachow, editor
PO Box 11609
Milwaukee, Wisconsin
53211

Concern/s: essays & reviews 1972-76

CONTENTS

1975-76

CONCERN/s

There comes a time—for every writer, I expect—when one begins to search through his past work to see whether or not it has achieved anything of substance, whether the work has been worth the time and effort it has demanded. Taking stock is something writers do periodically if they are to understand what they are about. *CONCERN/s* arises from an examination of my critical-reviewing work over the past four years or so and is intended to convey a sense of the territory covered by one commentator confronting literature and publishing in the seventies. The irony of *CONCERN/s* , perhaps, is that it has been written at all: in my own mind, I see myself as a poet—or, perhaps, as a poet who stumbled onto other tasks that needed attention and set about doing them. Completing a good poem of one's own is always more exhilarating than writing about another's work. Yet, over the past four years, I have had the urgent sense that my responsibilities extended beyond my own poetry; that what the world needed was not 'another poet, another poem' but a review journal such as *Margins;* that my best efforts ought to be directed towards understanding and making some sense of the alternative literary publishing happening across the country. It is sometimes distressing to see one's time and energy consumed by editorial and reviewing duties—however self-imposed—while one's contemporaries continue to produce their books of poetry. The more urgent task has constantly presented itself, however, and as a result many of my peers don't even know I write poetry. I am seen, instead, as a reviewer, as a critic, as the editor of *Margins.* Whatever my self-definition, the world has cho-

sen to see me differently. It may be precisely because others have identified me in a role I consider secondary that such a collection as *CON-
CERN/s* is needed—if this is the role I'm to have, it is time to take stock.

Perhaps *Margins,* and my reviewing and criticism with it, has had some
small measure of influence on the alternative literary audience of the
seventies; if so, *CONCERN/s* can stand simply as a gauge of my interests
and enthusiasms as an editor and commentator. The gathering of these
pieces here may afford those who have followed small press publishing
generally, and *Margins* in particular, a fuller sense of the intelligence behind one of the scene's primary review journals. The audience for small
press literature, I think, ought to be able to examine at length the streng-
ths and weaknesses in the commentary of such a journal's editor.

That my interests since 1972 have expanded while certain ideas have
remained central—developed and reiterated in varying contexts—should
be obvious to any reader of *CONCERN/s.* The reiterated themes, the
central concerns, became immediately visible once I began gathering
these pieces and putting them together in logical fashion. The articles
appear here in roughly chronological sequence—those written in 1972
are kept together and constitute the first section, those from 1973 form
the second part, and so on. Within each of the sections, however, I have
dispensed with chronology and have clumped articles of related interest.
The final section of the book collects pieces written over the course of a
year and a half rather than a year—1975 through the middle of 1976.
During the first half of 1976 I completed two long articles—'The Little
Magazine/Small Press Connection: Some Conjectures' and 'Small Publishing, In Your Blood'—and some shorter pieces which add considerably to the collection; these and other of my work from January-August,
1976, are included for that reason.

It will be obvious, as one reads *CONCERN/s,* that since 1972 I have
become increasingly interested in examining larger literary/literary-poli-
tical problems and somewhat less concerned about discussing particular
books. This tendency, I think, is the result of my position as editor of
Margins; the task of reviewing many of the books I might be interested
in could be assigned to others, but as editor I have felt a certain personal
responsibility for making some larger sense of alternative literary publishing. The result is that many of the later pieces in *CONCERN/s*—even
those dealing with specific books—contain a good deal more speculation
than some of the earlier ones.

That my prose is not stylistically exciting will be immediately apparent; this is the work-a-day prose of a writer who finds little time for sustained stretches of writing, who is interrupted—frequently in mid-sen-
tence—by the need to take care of other responsibilities. Even when
considering entirely 'literary,' non-journalistic matters, I have felt like a
journalist—constantly writing for deadline, under pressure. This is said
not to excuse the flaws in some of these pieces, but to give evidence of
what seems to be a general problem facing small press commentators

today: the difficulty of finding time, energy and incentive to practice the trade. The critics of the literature being published by small presses very seldom get paid for their work; the critical task is self-imposed and the reward is almost entirely personal satisfaction: the writing gets done between the gigs we have to take to make a living. And the prose undoubtedly suffers for it.

At best, *CONCERN/s* uncovers only a part of 'alternative' literary publishing today. This is not a systematic survey of the literatures or the presses of the seventies. The pieces here were conceived piecemeal, in response to particular books or problems I have dealt with. *CONCERN/s* of course, could fail to excite the reader enough to send him exploring the various literatures that appear courtesy of the small presses; trust that the failure belongs more to my writing than to the literature itself. As much as I hope *CONCERN/s* will help elucidate some of the problems and prospects of contemporary literature and literary publishing, I hope even more that the book will be viewed as an open invitation to readers of all sorts to seek out and enjoy the rich, 'invisible' literature currently available though sometimes not easily accessible. To my mind, *CONCERN/s* need not be a convincing argument if it helps to introduce new readers to the literature of the seventies. The literature itself is its own persuasive argument.

* * *

Grateful acknowledgement and sincere thanks are due these editors: Len Fulton, who published 'Considering Poetic Language & Technique,' 'Buffalo, Insects, A Salesman' and 'A Sense of Place' in *Small Press Review;* Jay Bail, who commissioned and published 'John Barth: A Critique' and 'Journalism: Looking for the crusader' in *Book Magazine;* A. D. Winans, who commissioned and published 'Five Books from Caveman Press' in *Second Coming;* Maurice Kenny and the other editors of *dodeca,* who commissioned and published 'Milwaukee Literary Activity: A Lot of Energy in One Place'; John Jacob, who commissioned and published 'Passing On the Literature: Some Reminders' in *Mojo Navigator(e).* 'Some Notes on Freedom and Form' first appeared in *Mississippi Review.*

'The Little Magazine/Small Press Connection: Some Conjectures' was commissioned by *Triquarterly* for *The History of the Little Magazine in America since 1950* (No. 41, Winter, 1978); special thanks to the editors of *Triquarterly* for permission to include the article in *CONCERN/s.*

'Small Publishing, In Your Blood' was commissioned by Michael Tarachow for inclusion in *Toward A Further Definition,* forthcoming from Pentagram Press.

'J. D. Reed: Whiskey Profiles,' 'Moving Beyond the Borders/some notes,' 'Little Mags/Small Presses: to shape our literature,' 'Small Press:

accepting our role,' 'Literature & Place: Touching the Landscape; Reaching Beyond' appear here for the first time. The balance of the articles collected here first appeared in *Margins.*

I am grateful to Michael Tarachow, the energetic editor of Pentagram Press, for his advice during the selection of these pieces and for his enthusiasm, encouragement, and patience with me at all stages of the project. *CONCERN/s* has been on Pentagram's 'forthcoming' list a long time; the delay has been mine, not Pentagram's.

The final acknowledgement is to Mary, who helps make this (and more) possible.

Tom Montag
Fairwater, Wisconsin
August 31, 1976

※

1972

JOHN BARTH: A CRITIQUE

In a sense, I am John Barth.

Does that astound you, reader? Do I shock you to speak to you directly? No matter, for now. We must get to our story. I would have you step gently into it, dip an elbow in, your toes perhaps, then your whole foot—both feet, ease your posterior in, sink slowly into the warm, sudsy water. I would have you do this: for my story will work much as a warm bath.

You see, reader, my main literary activity since 1955 has been the framing, rather perhaps the construction of increasingly complex and intricate novels dealing with increasingly complex and intricate matters. Not at all the usual matters of the novel, mind you, nor the usual themes—though I must confess, bear with me, I do use all the old tricks and ruses and my first aim is to entertain, though (you, reader, are the judge) I may go amiss, amuck and run afoul at times. And, I admit, I do send you, often enough, on wild goose chases.

My novels have been becoming also, I fear, more than complex and intricate: long and boring. Oh, you know, I throw in a brutal scene here and there, just to perk up the action and sell the book. But in the main my novels are like warm baths: they put you to sleep pleasantly. But life is like that: long and boring. Yes. I do not want you to think, however, that I am not a great novelist. I am. Even the greatest of critics can make mistakes and I forgive them that. I am not just a good, but a great novelist: as you, reader, shall see as soon as I return from my afternoon bath. . . .

J.D. REED: WHISKEY PROFILES
(The Baleen Press)

Gather round the bar, boys. Get yerselves a drink. I got some people I want ya t' meet.

Okay now first this is *Tom Foley, Irish/man and damned sinner/ with the rest of us.* His *Visions of priests and world-wise mates/fill him like a bilge. He loves/salt, itself.*

And here, this here is Mary the Duck. *She's got ankles to raise the dead,/no teeth to speak of here;/her laugh's a dark tornado-mouth./ They say she owns Greyhound lines,/probably whored for the hell of it/(but maybe not: too drunk)./Anything goes in a town/where every seventh bum/is honorary mayor. She's one.*

And here I'd like ya t' meet Bunt. He kin swear *to Maine lobster-men/with vowels shot from guns.*

Over here, this here's our veterinarian. He has *A life of cracked hooves,/mange, removing nuts and horns. . ./It takes a little rye/to*

*walk in warm barns,/going to needs and aches/that don't speak, or
write/on headstones.*

And I wanted ya t' meet Chicago-tough Sally, but she's sick. I told
her, though, I said t' her *you must/get out of that hospital,/and back to
your best bad house/in Livingstone County.* 'Cause ya know *cowboys
need something more/than lanolin on their chaps.*

Oh hell, boys, I guess ya kin meet the resta these characters fer yerselves. They all like ther whiskey. They'll drink with ya. Get t' know
em. Some of em are maybe a little strange, or sad and hittin the bottle. But get t' know em. Might find ya know em from someplace. Or
somebody like em.

DUNCAN: THE TRUTH & LIFE OF MYTH

I have no doubt that Robert Duncan is, and will remain, an important American poet. Though his more flamboyant and more popular
contemporaries may burn brighter, Duncan's glow is steady, warm, and
will bring us back again and again. Duncan's *The Truth & Life of Myth*
(The Sumac Press) gives evidence why. Subtitled "An Essay in Essential Autobiography", it is a book that can, perhaps, be read two ways—
both of them valuable.

We might, first of all, read it as a general philosophical essay on the
role myth has in our consciousness today, and on its role in contemporary theology, philosophy, anthropology, even science, generally. Duncan opens the book: "Myth is the story told of what cannot be told, as
mystery is the scene revealed that cannot be known. The myth-teller
beside himself with the excitement of the dancers sucks in the inspiring
breath and moans, muttering against his willful lips; for this is not a
story of what he thinks or wishes life to be, it is the story that *comes to
him* and forces his telling." Thus Duncan sets up to argue the contemporary role of myth; and in so doing, he sets down some of the most
lucid, insightful and concise commentary on contemporary intellectual
trends I have seen. Further, I find his assessment of the place of Plato
& Freud interesting and valuable.

But *The Truth & Life of Myth* is more than a disinterested intellectual essay: it is also "essential autobiography". Duncan is no name-drop-
per in the sense most autobiographers are; the names he drops are those
of Shakespeare and Dante; his essential autobiography is the canvas his
life-work is painted on. For Duncan is talking not only about myth,
but about himself: "My thought as a poet has grown in the ground of
twentieth-century mythologists like Cassirer and Freud, found a key in
Jane Harrison's definition of the dithyramb as 'the song that makes
Zeus leap or beget, and followed the mythopoeic weavings of Pound's
Cantos in which 'all the ages are contemporaneous'. My sense of the

involution of any idea with a story or stories it belongs to, of a universe of contributing contingencies, is such that my sentences knot themselves to bear the import of associations." He is discussing "poetry" and yet must be coming to terms with the shape of his own poetry: "The mythic content comēs to us, commanding the design of the poem; it calls the poet to action, and with whatever lore and craft he has prepared for himself for that call, he must answer to give body in the poem to the formative will."

Whether we value *The Truth & Life of Myth* as an intellectual discussion of myth in our culture, or as an exploration of the shape of a particular poet's mind, we must find it important; the more interesting, I think, because it is a major statement by a major poet.

CONSIDERING POETIC LANGUAGE & TECHNIQUE

There is something about an obviously poetic language and style that bothers me: perhaps it is my own guilty conscience stirring around, reminding me that I too have used the finest "poetic" words to weasel my way out of real meaning/feeling in a poem; perhaps my reactions is the usual defense mechanism—proclaiming loudest the faults in others most like my own. Whatever the case, Gary Von Tersch's *This One Is For Janie* (Second Aeon Publications) and Charles Haseloff's *Ode to Susan* (Penumbra) seem that kind of poetry, relying too heavily on traditionally poetic words and ways of moving in a poem in order to give a sense of fullness throughout and of completion by the end.

Of the two books, *This One Is For Janie* is superior. Von Tersch handles his poetry competently and comes closer to success. He can make the leap of imagination from "The stanzas of our flesh" to "a galloping snowfall that chases/the dreaming sunlight down into/row after row of bent branches"; but I wonder why he bothers—though "row after row of bent branches" rounds and completes the poem, it says little more to me than 'here is a good technician'; it doesn't say that this poet is a man who has lived and felt.

Even when he sets down a feeling and situation with the sharpest precision, as in "minor chords", he settles, in the end, for too little: the blind man ". . . starts/singing the/blues, his/voice a circle/ of light" brings technical but not emotional and intellectual conclusion to the poem. Likewise, in another poem, "arched theorems/& electric equations" seems too patent. It seems strange that Von Tersch can juxtapose lines as sharp and tight as ". . . we walk/high as rain &/wide as hills" and the irksome "to prowl/the neon-stung/shelves in comic-/ book dotted ecstasy". The wrenching of reality in the latter lines seems purposelessly incongruous with the quiet lyricism of the former.

Sometimes such a poetic can be highly effective, as here:

The
distance
between
yr legs
as you
stand in
the shower
is sunshine
clapping its
hands,
the space
that hum
mingbirds
vibrate
in

but such instances are too rare in *This One Is For Janie.*

Though there may be some of Portnoy and more of surrealism in *Ode to Susan,* it seems a step backward as far as language and technique are concerned. Merely listing some of the words and phrases Haseloff uses can almost serve to indict him for purposeless intimacy with the 19th century: "the beauty temple", "your categorical imperative/ of false hopes", "lullabies/fleece my temples into pillows of Lent", "eternity's bloodletting", "hymnal of devotion", "silkspun equestrian statue of love", "to iron out folds of wrath/in swaddling clothes", etc. This language might be more palatable if it didn't come on quite so seriously, as if we are expected to believe that

Baroque lips. . .
reach out and. . .
gently kiss my cheeks which wither. . .
like parchments in a monestary
. . . discovering
they have just become archeology—
part of the powdery odor of age.

Even "the river/filled with marmalade" and "the women in the world/whose legs are like wasps" do not brighten the 19th century shadows in these lines. Haseloff's poetry makes me think almost that a whole flock of 20th century poets haven't written at all, or haven't been read.

Both *This One Is For Janie* and *Ode to Susan* make me think it's time again for someone to ask that "poetic" language and "poetic" technique be abandoned in favor of those which can be gleaned from the manifold possibilities we face, now.

BUFFALO, INSECTS, A SALESMAN

> "Strut where spirit
> Falters"
> —Louis Phillips

When you make use of a gimmick or a trick to give structure to a work, you have to fill it out, flesh in the skeleton, complete the parts; and when your spirit falters, when inspiration runs thin, you can end up glib or academically pretentious—unless you strut well enough to fool all the people most of the time. Joe Ribar and Louis Phillips have not been able to do that. Ribar's *The Book of the Buffalo* (Figtree Press) and Phillips' *The Emancipation of the Encyclopedia Salesman* (Prologue Press) and his *The Insect Trials* (Prologue Press) are evidence that a good enemy should be a poet's best friend: one to tell you straight out what poems are weak and detract from the others and should be discarded. *The Book of the Buffalo* and *The Emancipation of the Encyclopedia Salesman* both have some fine sections, but both fail trying to fill out their structures. *The Insect Trials* likewise has some good pieces, but loses much of its impact for other reasons.

The Book of the Buffalo is what you might call a book of an obsession:

> I can't forget buffalo
> sometimes I try
> but there they are again
> grazing on my brain.

Ribar's poems remind me of a night when, unable to sleep, I sat up until near dawn writing poems, all of the same theme: after some sleep I was able to salvage two poems. Ribar does something like that, looking at the buffalo:

> I didn't know any
> of those early buffalo
> I was born too late
> to do anything more
> than run my hand over
> a worn white buffalo skull
> and write these poems.

"Buffalos are big grazing motherfuckers", Ribar says, and "The tree stood in the shade of the buffalo", "When I'm asleep/the buffalo/run very slow/waiting/for/me to catch up".

But in striving to view buffalo from every angle, Ribar sometimes ends up with flat statement and little more: "you ask me why buffalo?/ I'll tell you why/because they're strong/and they protect me/from the cold" and "it didn't make any difference/how many buffalo there were/every one of them/had enough to eat/except when it snowed/and then/some of them died". Lines like these undoubtedly add important information and push the theme along, but I find it difficult to say that they are poetry.

In the course of the book, the poems take on added dimensions: "23 buffalo got drunk/in a bar/but they didn't/break the place up"; "I met a buffalo heifer/she was thirteen/and about to freshen/love came to us". There is something of allegory at work here. Or, who would think, for instance, to take out a want-ad for one used buffalo with good rubber; or to note that "in 1913 buffalo/became nickels/and opened the way/to pay toilets/across the country"; or to pray to "Our buffalo who art in buffalo"? Ribar uses buffalo to look at some of the myths and quirks of our society: a strange way of seeing, but some of the poems work.

And despite the flat and mechanical pieces in the book, some of the spirit Ribar wants to set down comes through, line after line adding weight until Ribar can say, in the best piece in the book:

I've seen it all
where once great herds grazed
at sunset
someone has built a public
school
and children
swing on swings
dreaming at night of sugarplums
in houses built
on buffalo dust

For the sake of the mood or spirit of the book, though, I would like to have seen someone cull out the bad poems here, thereby increasing the force and impact of the whole book.

Phillips' *The Emancipation of the Encyclopedia Salesman* is "a narrative poem" structured by volumes of an encyclopedia: some poems, indeed, are titled accordingly—Volume 2, Volume 3, Volume 8. Other poems take their inspiration from something in a particular volume, e.g. the poem under DUM-FIR is entitled "p. 1682—Johann Faust". This is a 20 volume set of encyclopedias and there is one poem to a volume, like nuts to bolts.

Some of the sections here stand independent of the structure imposed upon the book; some, however, depend upon the gimmick of the book—poem related to volume—and seem weak or too harshly wrought. Others are bad poems entirely on their own; this glibness of "Sibyl" bothers, for instance:

I never wanted
Reason, but reason
Unbuttoned her blouse,
Leading me upstairs to her room
Where I was an overnight guest
& came down with a bad disease,

Something I couldn't tell
My parents.
It seems too easy, too prosaic, and even cheap, to end up saying:
I wanted to know my future,
But what that bitch
Wanted to charge me
Was highly unreasonable.
Even the joke hurts.
In "LAB-LUD" the lines work smooth as a well-oiled machine, but
do not satisfy:
I have a hunch that when man left
Paradise (glossing Milton's verse)
He carried immortal fruit
With him, but made a farce

Of planting it.
Phillips is waxing academic while glossing Milton; there is little poetry
in these lines, for all the easy theology.
Still, Phillips manages some good poetry; in the final poem, for in-
stance, the salesman speaks:
I am
Born to a world
I cannot shape,
To a mind
I cannot catch,

To a light
That will not fade.
I sell it in the form of books.
As with *The Book of the Buffalo,* however, *The Emancipation of the
Encyclopedia Salesman* would have been improved by some heavy
pruning: this could only serve to refine the book as a social document
and reshape its gimcrack structure, thereby clarifying its direction and
increasing its power as a work of art.
Phillips' *The Insect Trials* is in ways both better and worse than his
The Emancipation of the Encyclopedia Salesman; better, in that it is
not tied to over-bearing and unnecessary structure; worse, in that many
of the poems do not seem to be the product of a serious 20th century
man, or comedian, for that matter. Where but on the joke page of some
magazine does "Duns Scotus Writes His Love Letter" belong:
Yet I am not charmed
By your temper or your fatness.
I love your thisness,
I adore your thatness.
There is a modicum of wit here, but little evidence of 20th century experience—unless it is 20th century "literary" experience of the type

that the academic technicians have set down so well.

Other poems here are likewise of the "literary" experience; it is a weakness of imagination rather than of material, in some cases, which pull the poems down. But, for instance, in "Bird-Watching" Phillips almost breaks free:

>The wind is going some-
>Where, but what
>Flutters through branches
>Is not wind,
>But a polished flit
>Of blackbirds handsome
>As boots.

In "Hail to the Chief", however, forty lines of talking to Nixon about

>A flanker reverse
>Around Frost & Eliot,
>
>Maybe even a tight-end sweep
>Against those
>Free-verse guys

can wear patience and humor thin: it sets me to thinking that maybe Ribar's obsession with buffalo is closer to at least my experience of our age—and that, therefore, even Ribar's weaker pieces have something to recommend them.

GOAT SONGS

In *Goat Songs* (The Giligia Press), Ray Drew sets down poems of a mood. These are short and almost Oriental non-statements; they get at the tension beneath the surface of what we see, touch, taste: common scenes, expressed uncommonly.

Drew's poems are, generally, well-worked mosaics with this quality: they end, finally, more than the sum of their parts. In the opening poem, for instance, we are left with mood more than anything; it is not the result of language only, nor only the commonly-shared ritual, nor the sure movement from abstraction to concrete object: it is these in delicate balance, but superimposed on halfdreams and intimations of our own:

>Something sacred
>Has occurred
>If an old scarred goatherd
>Of a youth
>Has broken bread with me
>And told me how
>The moon goes,
>And admired

My river wood.
The various elements which shape the poem fuse with our reading:
Drew is able to achieve the verbal, intellectual and emotional equivalent
of making gold from dross, transforming language, experience, and insight.

Drew at times delineates links in this world that we have all seen,
but his poems manage further explorations:

> Either the wet creek-wood sticks
> In the fire or people outside
> Whistle and sing.

and

> Charlie left
> This plot of stars
> These pink daisies,
> Didn't mow them.
> New moon
> Cuts the sky.

We face, in these poems, not the simple link of the *like* or *as*, of analogy; the shape of each poem is closer to that of separate pieces of
cloth, woven together, a single garment.

Not all the poems in *Goat Songs* work in this fashion, however;
some fail in what they attempt, trailing off like a tired voice, rather
than exploding with sudden insight:

> The first lightning bug!
> How many mint-eating nights
> Without your coming?

and

> Three quarter moon
> Pretending you are egg-
> You cannot hatch.

Despite such failings, though, the total effect of *Goat Songs* is forceful:
insights accumulate to create a mood and a reality beyond the merely
verbal, a tone pervasive as life. The final poem ends:

> In the pines
> Across creek
> Some small animal
> Dies crying.
> Falls and wind
> Sing on.
> I stir the fire.

And, as the poem moves from our brain to finger-tips to our viscera and
back again, we know that it is enough, the power of the vision, and
more than enough.

IMAGERY: ITS CAREFUL USE

Both Victor Contoski's *Stroking the Animals* (Albatross Press) and William A. Roecker's *Willamette* (Baleen Press) rely heavily on the careful use of imagery, not for its own sake, but for the shape of the poem, for the associations the images provoke in us, for the wider possibilities they present. In an age when the image has become baked in a verbal wasteland, there is a certain joy in finding lines such as these from Contoski's "3 Saw":

> High above the sound
> of its voice
>
> it hears the wood weeping.

Though often it is easy to find this kind of personification repugnant, in Contoski's poems there is a softness, a whimsy almost, in its use. Contoski's is a gentle, rather than a jarring, surrealism: "The tongue of the plane/falls silent":

> In the service of Jack
> it shaved the legs of the princess
> caressed her
> without tenderness
> lopped ten pounds off her hips
> smoothed the backs of her hands
> to make her worthy
> of a blacksmith's son.
>
> Now
> it licks
> air
> water
> rust
>
> and dreams
> of the flesh of a girl.

In "Elegy for My Name", even *name* takes on life and qualities of its own:

> My name has gone into the forest
> leaving its trail of bread crumbs.
>
> It has walked naked
> into the camp of the enemy
> trusting a flag.
> And in the end,
> Tortured, it told nothing.

It died
calling
me.

Such is Contoski's surrealism; it pulls diverse materials together, creating links between them; as we read the poems in *Stroking the Animals,* we are struck by the naturalness of the conjunctions he makes. Contoski's imagery, the setting of that imagery, and his poems as whole units, look almost as if they come out of distant, though familiar, levels of our own consciousness, almost as if Contoski has found something strange/familiar that is common to all of us, and has set it down for us to examine at our leisure. In this context, the imagery and linkages have multiple ramifications for our own experiences, and become finally the most forceful feature of *Stroking the Animals.*

Roecker's poems in *Willamette* work in a different way. Roecker aims to achieve a more literal transcription than Contoski does: yet Roecker's poems are not mere pictures of the Willamette River's backwaters and wildlife; he does paint the pictures, and accurately, but he adds colors & lines we might not see:

My life has always been here in the water.
Home can never be in dry places, for I have grown
in the colors of dusk and fog.
River nights own me like Indian parents
and when the water is clear in season
I have seen what it keeps for itself.

Roecker exalts hunting in "this place of reeds and alder/. . . made by the river" in "Hen Steelhead":

We chased her a long way
up Hosmer Creek, John, and you
jumped on the water like
a lover, came out, wet hair
in your eyes, slipping on rocks,
holding her, laughing like winter air
while she kicked silver, dripped her eggs,
you holding her tight as a new bride.

He is aware, however, of other levels of existence, even in this.

There are places in the river
that hold the souls of fish

. . .

The wind vees across the surface
like fast curving fish.

Corpses of salmon come here
tail up, ready for cleaning and burial.
The only sound I can hear
is the rising sand, working
on the bottom of my boat.

Roecker has a clear sense of the place's history, of its meaning in a larger context; this realization is essential to the expansive nature of his imagery. The river is vibrant with ghosts—of Indians, waterfowl, fish: the imagery reverberates, the literal resonant with suggestion.

Both Contoski's and Roecker's images transcend verbal picture-making; in different ways, *Stroking the Animals* and *Willamette* give evidence of some of imagery's best possibilities. What they set down moves in recesses of the reader's consciousness as something his own, and yet reaches out to the world we see everyday.

HISTORY FALLS APART

A number of poets today are turning, for material, to the historical past: not only to put the "facts" into personal perspective, but to relate them, by analogy, by metaphor, to the present and to draw out of them something of universal significance. Eugene McNamara's *Dillinger Poems* (Black Moss Press) and Jim Orvino-Sorcic's *One Day. One Long Day. A Child Looked Over All That Was. & Was Not Pleased. At All* (privately printed) are two such attempts. Each is fairly successful. McNamara is less intimate and looser than Orvino-Sorcic in his treatment of history—viewing it almost as one would view a saint's relics or a trunkful of keepsakes in the attic, little more than something to stare at. Orvino-Sorcic's poems, on the other hand, use history almost ritually, as some primitive medicine man might chant his tribe's past.

The *Dillinger Poems* lose, I think, by their looseness, the texture, the blood and bone of the central, "mythic" John Dillinger, and leave only a faint sense of the man, much as a dried leaf in a book only faintly resembles a leaf. And this may be just what McNamara means to do:

an old man. . .
. . .
says to his grandson   that's
where Dillinger was in prison

who's Dillinger says the boy
. . .
we don't want to lose some
things.

The irony: so much has been lost already. History is a dried leaf. In his grave James Whitcomb Riley "sulks because no one/. . . tries to steal his body/to show at carnivals". Dillinger is our keepsake, our sideshow, our something-to-stare-at.

he leaps and history
falls apart lies
at his feet as he

jumps high there
a figure in the air
higher than death

And there Dillinger remains, higher than death, not flesh and blood, not moving in our world.

In Orvino-Sorcic's *One Day &c.* the central character, General George Custer, lives not in the past but today: the history is stylized enough that with few changes "Custer" can read "Calley" or some such; the poetry moves not as narrative so much as ritual, reaching its most intense moments in the final section when "the child speaks/of what she sees"—Custer's actions viewed through the suffering of a child-victim:

my face opens
& makes the noise
of many hurts .

the noise
of a hundred falling rocks
hit me
every/where .

This, certainly, is not the version of history that ". . . the 11th/edition of the encyclopedia britannica/invites you to believe". This is not "a crushing defeat" in any fair sense of the words. No. Custer's massacre of the Indians was murder and Orvino-Sorcic relates it almost in a chant, repeating phrases and changing them with precision—pain from cell to nerve to brain to voice: 'a hundred hunted birds', 'a hundred hunted suns', 'a hundred hunted days', 'a hundred hunted songs', 'a hundred falling rocks', 'a hundred screaming birds'. The chant intensifies, culminating finally in the child's powerful song/prayer/vision:

& LIGHT
bright
as a hundred
morning stars
cuts warm the hurt of my face   my
face   faceless   falling
& falling
& falling
into a light
filled with sky .

Orvino-Sorcic's 'history' is not that of some relic as McNamara's seems, but of bone and blood out of our past. Dillinger may be 'higher than death' but it is Custer, finally, who moves among us, within us.

ROUMAIN: EBONY WOOD/what we have to learn

Jacques Roumain was a Haitian poet, novelist and radical activist. He died in 1944, 38 years of age. His novel, *Masters of the Dew*, translated by Langston Hughes and Mercer Cook, was published in 1947. *Ebony Wood* (Interworld Press; translated by Sidney Shapiro) is his first volume of poetry to appear in America; this is a bilingual edition.

As we might rightly expect from a third world poet, *Ebony Wood* works from a strong ideological stance: Roumain is a poet of the oppressed man,

> of dirty negroes
> of dirty indians
> of dirty hindus
> of dirty indo-chinese
> of dirty arabs
> of dirty malays
> of dirty jews
> of dirty workers.

It is necessary, Roumain says,

> that we teach you
> exactly what it costs
> to preach to us with horsewhips and cats-o-nine-tails
> of humility
> of resignation
> to the miserable lot
> of negroes
> of niggers
> of dirty negroes.

Roumain sees injustice, he wants justice, he is tired of hearing 'us' "holler/jesusjoseph&mary/like an uncorked old goat-skin bottle gushing out lies".

Much of the power of *Ebony Wood* lies in the repetition of lines and phrases; in "Sales Negres", "the negroes/the niggers/the dirty negroes" appears again and again, pounding us like hammer-strokes. What is unusual for an ideologically-firm poetry is Roumain's ability to add new meaning with each hammered repetition; by the end of the poem, the phrase "the dirty negroes" glints with flashes of so many injustices, so much oppression, that the very meaning of the words has changed, the language itself becomes fully charged with the struggle.

But, even more striking, for all the ideology and all the repetition, the poetry in *Ebony Wood* achieves a vibrant lyricism that comes through in the turn of a phrase, the striking of a metaphor. "Ebony Wood", for instance, opens:

> If the summer is heavy with rain and dreary
> if the sky veils the pond with an eyelid of cloud
> if the palmtree unravels into tatters

if the trees are arrogant and dark in the wind and the haze. . .
Later the poem continues:
    Africa I have kept your memory Africa
    you are in me
    Like a splinter in a wound
    Like a guardian fetish in the center of the village
    make me the stone of your sling shot
    of my mouth your sore's lips
    of my knees the broken columns of your abasement.
There is power in the way Roumain's lines move, in the carefully chosen, effective metaphors, in the flow of language coming at us like a fist.

We need Roumain's poetry, and that of others like him. In an age when so much of our poetry has become little more than literary exercise, Roumain's poems are part of the struggle going on in the world, they are in touch with man's viscera and his aching back, with the heel of the boot coming down hard. And in an age when our lives are a lot like our poetry, when we merely go through the motions of living, when we ignore the aged, our ghettos, the cries of our children, oppression all around, *Ebony Wood* requires that we take stock of what we are about. In its own right, as poetry, *Ebony Wood* demands our attention; and as a proclamation out of the third world, it teaches us—and we have much to learn.

A SENSE OF PLACE

A sense of place is often tied to a sense of the land. We might say the midwest poet, his roots in the land, is a poet of *place*: but this is not large enough a statement. Place is more than the earth we walk on, it is also something in the mind. Three poets, Martin J. Rosenblum in *Home* (Membrane Press), John Jacob in *Parfleche for Captain Jack* (X an' Z Press), and Philip Levine in *5 Detroits* (Unicorn Press), set down the sense of place as it exists in the mind, at best only suggested by objects which are external.

Rosenblum's *Home,* for instance, records a number of places/states of mind, moving from an almost metaphysical poetic in his first poem, through a number of tight, intricately-worked shorter poems and a long poem of his hometown, to an exacted but more open final poem.

The imagery, almost the symbolism, of Rosenblum's first poem, "The Assumption", is worked hard enough that it "echoes down the marble halls". The lines are stiff enough for a man who "has had to survive himself". Not until near the end, when the man's wife "wants to have his/ child" do the lines begin to loosen and do we know "there is nothing/echoing through the marble halls". The poet's distance from his material here is both as close and as removed as John Donne was

from some of his material. Yet in the title poem Rosenblum moves
closer to the place he lives and would seem more comfortable with; he
says it straight-forwardly:

> there are shadows
> in the corners
> of this house.
> she woke up
>
> when it was
> about light
>
> and the room was hot.

Likewise in the long poem, "The Logs", Rosenblum seems comfortable with materials always volatile for any poet, his hometown. He
moves from "when i/had not/grown//yet//in appleton, wisconsin", to
"i wonder what children we pick for our name" in evenly modulated
tones. A sense of Appleton, Wisconsin, pervades the poem, but it is the
Appleton of Rosenblum's mind—it is switch engines and piles of logs;
the Fox River and carp he caught; Armless Arnie's shack and train rides
to Chicago. It is an Appleton fashioned out of the realization that
"crayfish have a disease and everyone in Appleton knew it" and upon
this central analogy: "the fox river valley//stretches//in appleton, wisconsin./in//my//wife's belly ova//crawl".

In the final poem, the place is put squarely on the map: "the
cracked/soil,/placitas, new/mexico", but again, and especially here,
place is internal, and Rosenblum has "got to be angry at something".

In his short collection, Jacob's sense of place is nearly like that of
the air we breathe: it drifts across the poems like a rich odor. We
breathe it in here, there. It comes like "the old winds/thru dry bones".

"Once the mountains/bent to the smoke & our cries were heard",
Jacob says. And in another poem, "today it was like/the ghost of animal bones". Place is more atmosphere here than landmark; more something rubbing against our nerve endings than clear description:

> these actions,
> movements before waking:
> slow, coming toward
> awareness,
> conception of pain,
> actualization of
> nerves.

It is not any roots in the land that Jacob is setting down. It is roots in
the past which move to define the present existence: "the Cree mouth-
bow/is plucked;/this is ritual;/the time is going/& has gone". Jacob
leaves us finally with some sense of the place he draws his strength
from, the place he rests in sleep.

Levine's *5 Detroits,* though more than a catalog of sights and sounds, does have some of the catalog's qualities—observation upon observation piled up to give some sense of the place. Levine sets down a winter day,

> A winter Tuesday, the city pouring fire,
> Ford Rogue sulfurs the sun, Cadillac, Lincoln,
> Chevy grey. The fat stacks
> of breweries hold their tongues. Rags,
> papers, hands, the stems of birches
> dirtied with words.

But he goes beyond that, into

> ... the cry
> of wet smoke hanging in your throat,
> the twisted river stopped at the color of iron.
> We burn this city every day.

The poems become something of a record of the people of a place, of the kid, for instance, who "Never did nothing right/except to tell the cops to suck/and wave them off like flies".

5 Detroits, whatever the nature of the cataloging, remains Levine's record of observations: filtered through his particular way of seeing, placed in the recesses of his mind. He says:

> I'm my keeper,
> the only thing
> I've got,
> sweeping out
> my one-room life
> while the sun's
> still up.

Like Rosenblum and Jacob, Levine's sense of place transcends the merely local or regional: is shaped by internal necessities. All three poets, for all their concern with where they are, stand above the confines of the strictly local; each puts down his roots not in the land but in the terrain of his own consciousness.

MOVING BEYOND THE BORDERS/some notes

For the man working the land, nature is partner and friend, but enemy as well: nature is something he can control in its details while it exercises over-all control by the cycle of its seasons, the texture of its soil, the shape of its landscape. Whether or not rural areas are "dying" today, or whether or not we can chemically or mechanically change the face of the land, these are irrelevant to an accurate defintion of essential relationships between man and the land: for I doubt if any man, standing out in the middle of a long stretch of flat land that he has to work, will lose the sense that the land may rise up and tower over him—

not in the oppressive sense that skyscrapers tower over us: rather, with an awe that is more mysterious.

The Midwest poet who knows the land feels such awe and is able to incorporate a sense of it into his vision and into his poetry: it is a special sense of place, but it extends beyond the merely regional—and is certainly more than 'local color'. Shakespeare, for instance, could use the idea of the Great Chain of Being to give structure and meaning to a work of art; the Midwest poet uses his sense of the land. But for the Midwest poet, it is more than a matter of literary convention: it is a matter of how his guts move. Like Shakespeare, the successful Midwest poet transcends the particulars of his materials. And though awe of the land seems to be increasingly archaic in today's urbanized society, we cannot grant that it is as foreign to us as the idea of the Great Chain of Being. In terms of urban reality the Midwest poet may seem out of place, but in terms of man's essential dependence on the earth he has important things to say and his material is fresher and more vital than we may be led to believe. The good Midwest poet, like others, moves from the particulars of his daily existence into a coherent vision and a world that has significant meaning for others.

Midwest poetry, as all poetry, must be judged on the basis of its honesty, consistency, and relevance to the experience of other men. The content and technique of the Midwest poet's work will differ from the lower East Side New York poet's, or the black poet's—still, as with theirs, the important elements of Midwest poetry are its art and craft, its honesty towards experience, its meaning extending beyond the merely specific.

It might seem reactionary on my part, in all of this, to talk of Midwest poetry as if it is something apart from the rest of American poetry; there are, in fact, some Midwest poets, and young ones at that, for whom any discussion of Midwest poetry is useless: that it doesn't really matter what the material of our poetry is if it speaks with some universality. But as long as there are, in the Midwest, people, incidents, moods which moves us to poetry, as long as the flat stretches of land seem to tower over us, as long as our special roots here "tug and pull" at us, there will be a distinct Midwest poetry with values its own. As long as our poetry can redeem what we are, where we are, now: then discussion of Midwest poetry is not useless; then such discussion serves to help define the borders within which we move, beyond which we travel easily.

We have in the past few years had more opportunity for such discussion. A number of anthologies of Midwest poetry have appeared, the most notable recent one being, perhaps, *Heartland* (1967), edited by Lucien Stryk. In 1971 the Center for Contemporary Poetry at the University of Wisconsin-La Crosse published the first volume of its *Voyages to the Inland Sea;* the second volume appeared recently. John Judson, editor of *Northeast,* is editor of what looks to be a promising Midwest series, one that "attempts to record what happens when a contemporary Midwestern poet is given the chance to write an essay on any topic concerning poetry, to compile a bibliography of his own poetic work, and to select a group of his poems. . . for book publication." (Introduction to *Voyages, II.*)

As a Midwest poet myself, often complaining that Midwest poetry goes largely unrecognized, I can only applaud the idea of such a project: for its nature and for its possibilities. That the series is being published at all is evidence of a growing concern with Midwest poetry; and the continuation of the series may mean more critical recognition for a kind of poetry that should not be slighted. If the series does realize its possibilities, if it presents Midwest poets' ideas, the essays, and their work, the poems, always with an eye to achievement and excellence rather than with an eye to reputation, age or the like, then it will be a most valuable contribution to contemporary American literature. With but one notable exception, the selection of poets in the first two volumes indicates that the series has at least succeeded in finding the direction in which the possibilities lie.

Lisel Mueller is the first poet of the first volume. Her essay on Midwest poetry is a solid, coherent attempt to come to terms with its essential nature and direction; the prospects, to her, seem dim: "The idea of regional poetry seems an oddly old-fashioned one in this age. . .."; "Admittedly, when we speak of Midwestern poetry, we speak of something that is passing out of existence." Mueller sees the "present generation of Midwestern poets" as perhaps the last to represent "a particular tradition, a special focus, a recognizable community of feeling, which has nothing to do with a 'school', since the poets are scattered and do not adhere to any common literary credo."

When she sets out to define Midwest poetry, Mueller excludes, as I have, the clearly urban: "What I am left with by way of definition is a body of poetry that owes its life to the heart of the heartland: the vast stretches of farmland, the rolling hills with their many shades of green, the great rivers and thousands of small lakes, the forests of Michigan, Minnesota, and Wisconsin, the towns with their rectangular layouts, their elm-shaded porches, their Elks' Clubs, and their dreary Main Streets." Ultimately, she says, Midwest poetry "owes its life to a population of 19th century settlers. . . whose society was founded on such principles as egalitarianism, individualism, and self-sufficiency."

She adds, however, that it is "no secret that poets have no place in American society, and, in the rugged Midwest especially, the folksy, home-spun versifier may be able to feel at home, but the real poet must put up with the status of village idiot. Still, poets have roots no less than other people and, being poets, they are acutely aware of how these roots tug and pull at them."

Mueller presents solid arguments for the judgments she makes, but she is to my mind mistaken on some counts. I won't admit that region-

al poetry is old-fashioned, or that Midwest poetry is passing out of existence. All poetry continues to be regional in some sense or other: it
comes, if from no other place, out of a particular region of the mind—
and these vary from poet to poet, place to place, time to time: the
New York experience being different from the San Francisco experience being different from the Midwest experience. Midwest poetry may
be changing radically, but it is not passing out of existence. Mueller
says that "a poet as young as James Tate. . . can only remember the
breakup; the roots that are still attached to him have lost their purpose,
like outworn evolutionary appendages." To carry her metaphor where
I think it belongs: we might say that the appendages are not really outworn, rather our fins have become legs; it appears that we are only beginning to learn how to use them.

Of Midwest poetry Mueller says, "Nature is not usually presented in
such minuteness." And when nature appears as landscape, "it is never
a poetic foil. . . nor something to be contemplated. It is an existential
force, the land which was the benign or disastrous reality of every set-
tler's life." Midwest poets still "grant it the respect of close observation." While "there is no compromise with physical reality", she says,
the Midwest poet "keeps coming back to the affinity between man and
nature." William Stafford's Kansas poems, for example, "are bound to
endure as testaments of the landscape and its people. . . . Stafford's
landscape seems to be so inhabited by human presences even when no
one is named and a poem seems to deal exclusively with nature. Most
of the time, however, his poems are specifically concerned with people-
and-landscape, or rather, people *in* the landscape." Such a "deeply ingrained humanism, this attention and respect accorded the individual
person, may well be the special contribution of Midwestern poets to
American poetry."

In no sense, I think, can we say that these concerns are passing out
of existence; a substantial number of young Midwest poets are dealing
with them and their books are beginning to appear in print.

I agree when Mueller says ". . . simplicity of diction has remained
the rule", though I might argue her claim that "Verbal innovation has
never made real headway here". It is true enough that "Midwestern
poets believe that the exposed grain of experience is far more beautiful than any glossy finish", but it is also clear that the young poets are
combining, in fresh and exciting ways, language and technique with the
perennial concerns of the older Midwest poets.

Even if we are willing to admit that "The old order is gone: where
there was a center, there is a vacuum; where there was stability, there is
flux; consumer conformity has taken the place of shared beliefs", we
do not necessarily deny the existence of a new order that leans heavily
upon and transforms the best of the old order's values, concerns and
sensibilities. There is a new generation of Midwest poets arising, I believe, that will renew the deeply ingrained concerns for the affinity be-

tween man and nature and the paramount value of the individual. There is something of the phoenix at work here—the new will rise out of the ashes of the old.

Lisel Mueller, as poet, is her own good example. In "The Island" she writes "Stepping on land,/we feel our skins change/to fit us at last." Concluding the poem, she says, "We know we'll flag/a boatload of home-grown saviors,/who speak our fallible language/and fly in the mind only:/our kind, our kind who care." Whether stepping onto an island or out onto the open field, something happens, we do "feel our skins change".

In her "Small Poem About the Hounds and the Hares", Mueller sets down feelings that are clearly Midwestern:

> After the kill, there is the feast.
> And towards the end, when the dancing subsides
> and the young have sneaked off somewhere,
> the hounds, drunk on the blood of the hares,
> begin to talk of how soft
> were their pelts, how graceful their leaps,
> how lovely their scared, gentle eyes.

These richly suggestive lines open up manifold possibilities. I think they show Mueller at her best, though hounds "talking" is a way of speaking that bothers.

In her "The Autobiography of Malcom X", Mueller tries to touch on the clearly social, but she speaks uncharacteristically. Her lines in this poem unwind but, for all her good intentions, fail to open up. She ends the poem ". . . he peels out/always more human, until someone/from a lower order of life/stops his ascent forever." There are few poets who, attempting to be socially relevant, do not border dangerously on propaganda; Mueller's poem indicates, at least, the breadth of her concern— here she simply lacks the art of it.

Mueller's other poems vary in quality, from the strong, tightly moving "Messages" which ends "Holes ask for rain; the stunted corpse of an elm/is revealed as a sign. We keep breaking/the code of the dead, we reply" to her complete catalog of the moon's names and roles, "A Farewell, A Welcome", a poem which remains finally little more than a litany.

Still, Mueller is a fine poet who succeeds to the extent that she is willing to fail. Both her essay and her poems show her to be an accomplished enough writer to open the first volume of a series such as this. John Knoepfle, the second poet, is perhaps the best poet in the volume. Though his essay is concerned with a personal view of poetry in the fifties, both the essay and his poetry indicate his ultimate concern with the land and the people and with what it means to write about them.

Like Mueller, Knoepfle values William Stafford as one who "sets a high value on the places he has come from and come to and he has a tender regard for those people who have lived and died in them without a spokesman. His poems, it seems to me, represent a sustained attempt to confer some small immortality upon the companions and friends of his childhood, a determination that no one will be lost". Stafford is, says Knoepfle, "as aware as Gary Snyder that once a man sets foot in a country, that land lives in him and by him, and that its meaning must be expressed through him, or not at all."

Even while discussing the poetry of the fifties, Knoepfle's concern for the land-and-people shows through; and discussing Yeats, Knoepfle adds clarification to what much of Midwest poetry attempts: ". . . I have been put off by his attentiveness to decorum and ceremony because I have learned that these when ritualized serve to perpetuate injustice." If we do indeed, as Knoepfle suggests, "make poems out of our secrets", then his secrets are found not in his ego, but in that special juncture where ego is in fair balance with the otherness in people, places, and events. And though his essay serves to put him securely among the numbers of those who opened up possibilities for American poetry in the fifties, it reveals also a Midwestern sensitivity which transcends the merely regional and speaks clearly to other Americans, to other human beings generally.

Knoepfle's poetry is able to move beyond the purely descriptive, factual color of time, place and name; his "battlefield at lexington" is a fine example of Midwest experience used in such a way. It concludes: "the river in the sun is a fishhook/that would catch the world//and christopher cries out/you are walking on dead people/there are dead people buried here/his shrill voice darts in the afternoon/like a swallow."

His "poem for a child" is able to achieve a similar universality:

two pieces of bread
on a blue plate
elderberry jelly
purple in a jar
a tablecloth
printed with deep red roses
elderberry bread and red roses
what will you trade for these

Knoepfle is at his weakest when he is attempting clear message: "we halloween/the real dead with candy/for the sake of the children"; but these lapses are tolerable when we can set them against poems like "staring at the wall":

his clenched fist
should have held grain
anger is eternal
we have to be afraid

In Knoepfle's work, this kind of poem comes often enough for us to forgive a multitude of sins.

Dave Etter is the final poet in the first volume. His essay is not one on Midwest poetry or on poetics, but is, rather, 'an autobiographical fragment'. Etter sets down his past, but not his roots; he tells of his first good encounter with poetry, Frost's *The Road Not Taken,* of his menial jobs, his travel around the country: he realized that he "had better get back to the Middle West where I always felt I truly belonged." He can go no further than that: "I cannot adequately explain my deep attachment to the 'heartland' of America. . . . [E]very time I returned it was like coming home again. Now, this time I was going to remain and put down some strong roots."

Etter's poetry curiously resembles his autobiographical statement: it is strong in its record of details, but weak in revealing the sweep of a broader vision; he is seldom able to move beyond the catalogs he sets down, a weakness that makes him the least satisfying poet in the first volume. His poems unwind like broken springs, do not pull themselves back together with a jolt—"and then I count/my library cards/Omaha/ Louisville/Sioux Falls/Kansas City/Dayton/Minneapolis/Pittsburg/New Orleans/Des Moines/. . . . . ./. . . . . ."

"A Dirty Old Man" waits around the drugstore for 15 lines just to "grab a good glimpse/of the biggest pair of knockers/this side of the Cumberland Gap." Where does that leave *us* waiting around? With "The Gospel Singer" on whose car floor "beside a half-empty bottle/of Southern Comfort,/is a flattened condom/that some wag threw inside/ when he stopped at a red light/in Zelienople"? I hope not; rather, I would like to see Etter as sensitive in other poems as he is in "Two Days Out of Three Churches", where he manages a strange combination of humor and pathos that seems genuine; or as tight as he is in these lines from "After Seeing a Photograph of My Great Grandmother": "Your face cracks/in a china sun"; or as suggestive as he is in "Blake's Porch":

> The boy with cerebral palsy
> has a mop of sandy hair
> and round, childlike eyes.
>
> . . .
>
> the old lady has hung
> JESUS SAVES on every wall.
>
> . . .
>
> Now the screen door bangs
> and she's off again
> to cure him with holy words.
>
> . . .
>
> They meet once a day.
> He knows it's inevitable,
> like the next jerk of his head.

It is a disappointment that Etter's poems in this volume do not sustain such sensitivity, tightness and suggestivity.

It is an even greater disappointment to see Felix Pollak open, and appear in, the second volume of *Voyages to the Inland Sea.* What Pollak grasps, even what he reaches for, in both his 'aphoristic mosaic' and his poetry, is finally insubstantial; his 'essay' "Of Wording & Poeting" seems marked by an acute but limited self-consciousness—Pollak is an artist setting forth principles he works by, well in control of them, too well in control, there is no struggle left; his poetry too seems to be wrestling to shape neither a vision nor a language.

Pollak says, "Some poets are born, some are made, and all are on the make" and "A motto earnestly recommended for the mastheads of little magazines: 'Look, Mom—No Friends!' " I find both statements too-easy ways of viewing the difficult process of making literature: there is more to the process than this, and we know it. Not all Pollak's aphorisms are so glib. For he also says, "Poems are not necessarily dreams, but poetry means as dreams do" and "Poetry is the art of conveying in words what words cannot convey"; yet even here there is much more that can be said, that needs to be said, or at least suggested. These are serious statements, but have profound implications that need to be explored if they are to remain serious; what I find lacking is concern for the struggle that brings the insight, for the chaos from which order arose: Pollak might say that this is enough: "To write well means to discard everything but one's after-thoughts." An after-thought is *not* enough if it doesn't shine a light farther into the darkness than we can already see.

Pollak sometimes does follow his insights: "The artificial dichotomy between content and form becomes meaningless when applied to the work of the sculptor. . . . form and content are inevitably, indistinguishably one. This is a metaphor for all true art." Here he is searching for roots and for substance and is discussing essentials; but such discussion loses its force when placed against other of his statements about true art: "Art: the struggle for survival after death" and "The hammer of fate falls on everyone, but only the artist gives sparks under the blows." We might agree with each and every of Pollak's aphorisms, but it is a qualified agreement: the mouth of a river holds little of the excitement of its winding course and its white-waters. Mueller and Knoepfle, in the first volume, make detailed and sensitive explorations of their art, as Etter does his biography. Pollak leaves us mostly the jewels of his thought: the lack of details, of nuance and sensitivity, and of struggle make his aphorisms seem out of place in this series.

Pollak's poetry, likewise, suffers from lack of concern for nuance and detail as well as lack of a larger vision. His poems in this collection seem flat and thin statement for the most part. "Speaking: The Hero", for instance, sounds curiously naive as an attempt at social relevance:

> I did not want to go.
> They inducted me.
>   . . .

I did not shoot.
They said I had no guts.
. . .
A shrapnel tore my guts..

I cried in pain.
. . .
In safety I died.
. . .
They made a speech in my hometown.
I was unable to call them liars.

. . .
I died a coward.
They call me a hero.

If there is no more to this kind of tragedy than Pollak makes evident,
then we indeed live in a black and white world in which good and evil
can be separated by rhetoric. But even if we stand unalterably opposed
to an immoral war, we must recognize the degrees of complexity of
the situation, we must see the shades of our own feelings.

"Of Love" also fails to mark off more than one feeling.

Hurts like hell and doesn't
turn to poetry either.
Dumb as a sophomore
I stare into my you-shaped void
and try to comprehend the phrase
'thinking of you'.

But even when Pollak is not setting down a 'message', his lines are un-
satisfying, as:

The paper boy brings in evening
and leaves it in front of the door.

Pollak is perhaps most successful in these lines from "Excerpts from
the Diary of a Light Sleeper":

He kept on writing poems,
knowing full well
his words were footprints
in the snow.

But this wistful, sensitive mood is mostly destroyed in the next section
of the poem: Pollak spends fourteen lines on the 'light sleeper's' attempt to write down a dream-poem at night in the dark, only to awaken
in the morning to find that the poem was lost, that all along the ball-
point "was dry,/with only a tiny red coagulation/around its tip."

It seems that Pollak's poetry attempts to grapple either with the
"big" questions of the world, "War" or "Love", or with the little questions, the paper boy or the dry ball-point pen: in both cases, Pollak
fails to infuse into his work a sense of the world around us—I'm not

asking that it be a sense of the Midwest, only the recognition of shadows and textures where they exist. Pollak's poetry seems out of place among that of the other poets in the series, both because theirs embody some of the best of the "Midwest", and, more fundamentally, because Pollak's poetry lacks that sensitivity to the complexities of the experience which is characteristic of good poetry, Midwest or otherwise.

Unlike Pollak, James Hearst belongs clearly in a Midwest poets' series. Hearst, more than any other poet here, writes from the viewpoint of the farmer: he says "I decided that America had never had a genuine farmer poet. There were poets a-plenty who touched on nature, there was even Robert Frost struggling to express his New England farm experiences." But Frost wasn't Hearst's kind of farmer; Frost ". . . said when he saw our mile-long corn rows, 'You've got too much land, it's all too big.' " Hearst "decided to try to tell the truth about farming and about life as it is lived on a farm. I wanted to look at it squarely, honestly, to keep the balance between cleaning manure out of the barn and running the cornpicker on a warm October day with the corn going one hundred and twenty-five bushels to the acre."

When Hearst was beginning to write, he was fortunate enough to have this good piece of advice: "Leave Beauty, Truth and Duty to people who don't know an abstraction from a horse turd." He came to the realization that "there is no poetry that does not have strong roots among the worms and clay."

But, Hearst realized also, horse turds, worms, clay, while the stuff of the kind of poetry he wanted to write, were by themselves not enough: the poem, he says, "does not blow the last trump for squash vines as frost does, nor open the first crocus with the spring sun, but it does for the moment fix in its imperishable amber some truth, insight, revelation, or prophetic recognition of human experience."

Like Lisel Mueller, Hearst is his own good example. His poetry does use life as it is lived on a farm as the starting point for his poetry, and he is generally able to go beyond that:

> The barn stood for shelter
> on squared corners with a tight roof
> until wind sucked it up
> and spit it out in a shambles
> of splintered boards. I tried
> to salvage the ruins. . . .

Unlike Mueller, Hearst is able to deal successfully with social problems in his poetry:

> how can I endure the tears
> of a woman whose husband died
> in a jungle?
> . . . .
> . . . who can tell me

what to say when my own anger
calls me to account.

Hearst does fail, sometimes, by being too 'literary' with his material
—"citizens of the barnyard", "The barn humped its back", "Aloft,
deep/in the sky's vault a silver dot/wakes in the sun as it jets north"; or
by pushing his language harder than necessary: "Hard words married to
/burnt toast scar the morning", "Now the appointed place/comes to me
clear,/and your beloved face."

But at his best, Hearst is superb; "The Farmer's Bride" is one of the
most moving poems in Hearst's collection here, and one of the finest
poems in either volume of *Voyages:*

Dry weeds wait for snow,
trees creak, the road's skin
turns gray, a pale sun throws
pale shadows, cold air wraps the day.
I see a bundled man in work clothes
walk across the yard, head bowed
to mark icy spots where a man
might fall, his mittened hands
hang like boards. The dog leaps
to lick his face, cats arch and
weave between his legs, the cows
moo softly at his approach, even
sparrows follow behind his back.
He does the chores before dark,
and locks the barn doors, warm in a
faith he shoulders with all he owns
that a spring sun will sometime
break the winter's back. I stand
and wait where a wound of light
bleeds through the window.

This is Midwest experience and more—it "gives inkling of the meaning
and mystery of existence" for the farm bride, and for others as well.

John Woods, the final poet in the second volume, is one Midwest
poet who is not afraid to talk about the regionalism of his poetry. He
says:

I like a poem which has one foot firmly planted on the earth,
one foot so heavily put down that it doesn't matter where the
other foot has wings for. So heavily put down that the
farthest reach of the poem, inward or outward, will resonate,
ponderable, rooted, inertial. The whole strain of the body.

I want a poem which toils so close to its region, it becomes
that region.

He is insistent about it: "I want my poems to be thick with mold, fila-
ments, amniotic fluid, gibberings, split ends, toolmarks, dog nose knowledge. *Regional.*"

But Woods, like Hearst, realizes poetry needs "more than catalogues of place names and local histories. Strong particulars can carry a poem, even a career quite far, but not out of the minors." He says that "[t]he crumbs are important as the artifact. The insight, yes, the judgment, the celebration; but also the strata of emotion and incident they occurred in."

Woods' poetry does what he claims he wants it to do—toils close to the region—yet does more. It does "draw great energy from some arching universal." His poem of adolescent awakening, "Barney's Sister", touches on a common experience. It opens:

> There's something wrong with Barney's sister
> Under the apple limb. That day
> The door blew wide and stood her, white
> And washing, in my naked eye,
> I knew a sickness had her.

Likewise, Woods' searching for roots, in "Grandfather", is one we all make. The poem opens:

> I don't even know where we came from.
> So many graves stay open too long,
> so many girls lie back tonight,
> trying to be secret rivers in the limestone.
> I want those days when nothing happens.

It concludes:

> Here, on this hill, I see you
> letting out the kite like a far eye
> over the scatter of smokehouses,
> at the field's edge where the town
> thins out into corncribs and fishing shacks,
> old Fords driving a wood saw,
> out past the cannery whistle.
> Then, hand over hand, pulling it close,
> struggling with the wind in it,
> hugging it like the frail ribcage of a young girl;
> and on this morning you made us all,
> holding it to your face until the trees
> stood up red through tearing tissue.

For all his insistence on regionalism, Woods succeeds in recording far more than the specific emotions and incidents that moved him initially. His is the kind of Midwest poetry that rises off the plain, crosses the Rockies, the Alleghenies, touches San Francisco, New York, heads across oceans. His Midwest poetry is among the best.

These first two volumes of *Voyages to the Inland Sea* are clearly solid evidence that Midwest poetry can and does move beyond its borders. Woods and Knoepfle, certainly, and Hearst and Mueller at their best, are poets whose work rises out of the land they walk on; and theirs is, more importantly, poetry which usually transcends any of the limitations commonly attributed to a regional poetry. Whether or not we agree with Mueller's judgment that Midwest poetry is passing out of existence, we must agree, I think, that the best of this kind of regional poetry is more than mere catalog of local color, that it does touch on universals of human experience.

If the two volumes, as the first two of a Midwest poets' series, have a flaw, it may be the absence of the *young* Midwest poets—as evidence that traditions continue. Despite the unfortunate inclusion of Pollak, I will continue to trust Judson's editorial judgment; and I look forward to seeing in *Voyages* the best Midwest poets, young or old, the ones who are building the new order, who are setting down the new vision, who are talking about and handling the stuff of a land their own, who are moving beyond the borders while speaking of the boundaries, as Steven Lewis does in *boundaries, wisconsin:*

> there's something solemn, finally
> about the flat and rolling land,
> the ease with which it moves,
> where the lakes and rivers
> don't begin or end it like the ocean,
> but move into it and become
> boundaries. . .

LITTLE MAGS/SMALL PRESSES: to shape our literature

Without our little magazines & small presses, the making-of-literature in this country might virtually come to a stand-still: for by their nature, they encourage, nourish & make available (to at least a limited audience) the strange, experimental, bold writing that is essential to any continued vitality in our literature. Small press exists for the sake of literature, is not bound by the necessity to produce a saleable commodity or make a profit, is free to disregard current standards of taste and excellence; it can set its own standards & can change them as they become worn. Because the small press has no board of directors to answer to, no profit-loss columns to balance out, no "popular" tastes to fret over, it can be open to, can actively seek out the literature that is fresh, that is making break-throughs in language, form & tones-of-being. Because the small publisher has nothing to answer to but his own sense of excellence, he is free to assume responsibility for the literature-of-to-morrow.

Commercial publishing houses, though they often do valuable service to our literature & culture, exist to make at least a marginal profit; making a profit means publishing best-sellers & best-sellers are generally cliches even before they are published: what most of us buy is what we have been taught to buy or what the current arbiters of taste recommend we buy, what has been tried & found acceptable. In some cases, I admit, best-sellers can be fresh, vital & important; but think of those best-sellers you've read or read about: how many of them seem important now; how many were mere entertainment, inconsequential ways to spend summer afternoons, ice-cubes tinkling in gin-&-tonics. How many *Love Storys* must a house publish before it can risk an avant garde novel, before it can afford to lose money on a book of poems. I ask this, realizing full well that it was Random House that took *Ulysses* before the Supreme Court & the American public: but knowing also that Ezra Pound, T.S. Eliot, William Carlos Williams, & others now considered important, & found as a matter of course in textbook anthologies, made their first appearances in & established their reputations through little magazines & small presses—*Poetry* (when it was still a little & still had some spirit), *Others, The Criterion, The Little Review,* The Objectivist Press & more.

Would we be reading Williams today if the arbiters of taste of his day had had the final word on the worth of his work: even Harriet Monroe was not above capitalizing the small letters at the beginning of Williams' lines without his knowledge or consent; nor was she hesitant about suggesting a deletion of certain lines to Pound, as a matter of taste: all this, while she was publishing some of the best literature of the generation.

It was the little magazine that nourished the development of writers in those years, that gave Pound his influence, that made possible "modern" literature as we know it. Some editors & publishers saw excellence & pursued it with few backward glances at "popular" taste or the accountant's ledger. The same is possible today: it *is* happening. Little magazines & small presses are publishing some of the best (& yes, some of the worst) contemporary literature around.

This is not to say that our small press is pure as the driven snow or that all little mag editors have assumed responsibility for the literature-of-tomorrow. Some 'littles' deserve their oblivion; some publishers have little sense of excellence about literature or publishing; some mediocre writing, rightly turned away by the trade houses, still finds its way into the little magazines and the small presses.

However, despite these & other short-comings, small press does function currently as an alternative to the demands of economic necessity, "popular" taste & reigning standards of excellence. It remains central to the shaping of, & in turn is shaped by, the literature of our generation.

SMALL PRESS: accepting our role

Small press, we might like to think, is on the forefront of the new consciousness emerging in our culture and around the world. We can cite books & magazines that give evidence of the developing awareness, on the part of small press editors & publishers, of Third World writing, women's writing, social problems & concerns of all sorts: I am thinking of such magazines as *The Greenfield Review* (Joseph Bruchac III, ed.), *Matrix* (Idell, ed.), even *Pembroke Magazine*'s (Norman McLeod, ed.) emphasis on Amerindian writing, and such books as Jacques Roumain's *Ebony Wood* (trans. by Sidney Shapiro, Interworld), & D. Colt Denfield's *But Morning Refused to Answer* (Times Change Press).

However, despite these signs that small press is becoming aware of the struggle around us, aware of significantly important writing that is different from our own, we are still finding old prejudices, old ways of thinking, an out-dated consciousness at work: the white-male-supremacy ethos. If small press people are to have any significant role in the development of the new consciousness—one which values women & minorities & gays, all of the Third World, for their true worth & their contributions to human consciousness & human progress—then a lot of current small press attitudes have to change.

We have to stop thinking of ourselves as an elite, for elitism is at root the source of all prejudice. We have to stop being impressed by the name of a writer, and start being impressed by the quality of writing that may be new or strange to us. We have to value literature that comes out of the human condition, rather than out of baroque game-playing. If small press editors & publishers are sensitive to the value of new writing from all the oppressed peoples in our culture, then small press will be truly innovative in what it does. We have not yet, however, become aware of most of our prejudices & the many ways they manifest themselves; we are often content to publish the white, male writers we always have, without asking whether maybe there is writing around that may be far more important.

The answer is not to play the numbers game—such & such a percentage Indians or blacks, such & such a percentage gay & so on: numbers & ratios & percentages do a disservice to both literature & those intended to benefit, both readers & writers. The consideration then becomes sex, or color, or age, or some such—when what we should be concerned with is the quality of the writing & what it achieves.

Nor is the answer rhetoric for its own sake; rhetoric has its place as a tool for educating all of us to our ignorances & insensitivities & stupidities. As such a tool, however, its usefulness is limited—if we want to get at truth, we can't finally, do it with propaganda.

What is needed is a vital openness to important writing, whatever its source; & equally as important, we need to encourage the development of a substantial body of criticism that is applicable to the new writing that is appearing. Both tasks are difficult: we must break down our usual & comfortable ways of looking at things, we must take the new & unusual on its own terms, we must allow the new writers to voice the critical principles which form the ground-rules within which they work.

And, yes, we have to evaluate both the writing & the criticism as fairly & fully as possible & to stand by our judgments—but we can hope that they are sensitive, informed, honest judgments.

The scars across our "old consciousness" are deep & wide. But if we expect small press to command any respect among the oppressed of the world, if we intend to fill our self-defined roles, we have to begin now, eyes wide open.

JOURNALISM: Looking for the Crusader

On October 3, 1972, this item appeared in the Milwaukee *Sentinel:*
2 MINERS KILLED
    Cardiff, Wales—UPI—Two miners were killed Monday when a tunnel ceiling collapsed at the Blaensychan coal mine near Pontypool.
The following day, the *Sentinel* published a similar brief piece of information:
FIVE WORKERS
ELECTROCUTED
    Madrid, Spain—AP—A crane hit a high tension cable Tuesday outside Arganda, near Madrid, and five workers were electrocuted, authorities reported.
Both items, though terse, are exemplary bits of traditional journalistic writing: both report tragedies, answering the tough editor's questions, who, what, when, where, and how.

* * *

When Hanoi first announced possible release of three American prisoners of war to an American anti-war group recently, national television newsmen were quickly on the scene: *on the scene,* that is, in the livingrooms of the prisoners' wives and mothers, questioning them about their personal reactions. Said one probing journalist, "How do you feel about the possible release of your husband?"; the woman managed to mumble an answer to the effect that, of course, she would be very happy to have her husband home again.

* * *

In the September 13, 1973, issue of *Bugle American* (a paper which claims to be Wisconsin's largest alternative publication), Mike Jacobi, an editor, outlined briefly a history of recent underground/alternative press in America. He said it "started out in the mid-sixties with a distinctly cultural flavor. . . . and when the national mood turned political in the late sixties, some of the early papers changed with it." He added that "Most of the papers that turned to politics also turned to rhetoric." But, at present, Jacobi noted:

> . . . most of the alternative papers in the country have abandoned the rhetoric and exist on a third level of change. . . . the strongest of these papers seem to be trying to become somewhat permanent alternatives to the over-monopolized daily press. And some are going to make it.

Jacobi seems confident that the best of the alternative press will survive to serve what I might call an alternative audience, one which lives, today, between worlds.

This alternative audience is living between what-is and what-can-be; between the insanities and stupidities of so much of the world around us, and the possibilities we face. It accepts the good it finds in the world as valuable stones for the foundation of a new society; it accepts its responsibilities towards elderly German immigrant neighbors, foundry workers, unwed mothers, those locked in ghettos of one sort or another, students, heroin addicts. It sees flaws and weaknesses in current plans and programs aimed at alleviating the problems, and yet realizes that it has not found the complex answers needed to build a new order. Poking holes is easy; tearing down a rotten structure is easy. Bringing forth a new world is traumatic as birth; shaping new and viable patterns of living and responding to one another is hard as growth. Those attempting to shape an alternative culture realize this, build on the good that we already have, on the good to be found in our experiments, on the possibilities we can imagine.

* * *

Almost as evidence of Jacobi's claim that the alternative press today exists on a 'third level of change', the *Bugle American,* a few pages following Jacobi's article in the September 13th issue, ran a paid advertisement for a porno film, *The Pigkeeper's Daughter,* with a 400-word note outlining the *Bugle's* dilemma:

> The ad at right is obviously a sexist ad.
>
> But, frankly, we don't know what to do about it. The *Bugle* staff is having a lot of hassles with these things, and we need your help in deciding whether to run them or not.
>
> The basic points in the Great Debate are:
>
> We shouldn't run the ad or ads like them because: It is obviously sexist tripe that treats women like meat.
>
> . . . there are matters of freedom of speech, expression, censorship, and the survival of the *Bugle* to deal with. . . .
>
> The reality of survival forces us to do some things we don't particularly want to do. . . .

We don't want to descend to the level of the [Milwaukee] *Journal,* air brushing out "offensive" parts of an ad and changing copy. We don't want to be censors. . . .

We need your help. Send any correspondence on this matter to the *Bugle.*

The alternative press has, evidently, come of age: "the reality of survival".

* * *

The December 16th, 1972, *New Republic* quotes Peter Bridges (of the Newark, N.J. "Beatty case") as saying that his "responsibility as a reporter consists solely in reporting accurately what is said, and not whether the statement was accurate".

* * *

If a reporter's responsibility is only to report what is said, if he does not feel obliged to investigate its accuracy or its worth, what results is at best a mindless recital of details, as evidenced by the items quoted from the *Sentinel* earlier. Such isolated bits of information, even though tragic, are of little significance in a world already over-burdened with information. The deaths of miners in Wales and of workers in Spain are of importance chiefly to the next of kin, secondarily perhaps to safety-inspection boards; but to readers in Milwaukee, Wisconsin, on a drizzly fall morning, such items are only slightly less insulting as reading material than are the backs of cereal boxes. Such information serves no useful purpose to the businessman, the factory worker, the student, the housewife; it does not affect their patterns of living, their work, or their bowling scores. It only serves to further jam a consciousness already clogged by the innumerable details that are part of twentieth century civilized existence.

Likewise, on the question of the 'human interest' stories, for instance POW's wives' reactions to the possible release of their husbands, and on prying into personal anguish and private joy generally: only very rarely can we afford to push our way into the personal lives of our fellow citizens—only Nazi Gestapo, and perhaps seasoned television journalists, would want to. Such reports do not provide us with significant information nor reveal the broader sweep of the human condition. They only add to the innumerable details and feed bored, hungry minds.

The alternative press, if it is to be a 'somewhat permanent alternative' to the mindlessness of conventional journalism, will reject the reporting of "facts" and "statistics" alone as irrelevant to what it is about; it will not see private emotions but the direction of our development as total human beings as suitable material for news columns; it will present vital information, fair analysis, and important opinion, whether fit to print or not, regardless of advertisers.

Still, if a weekly alternative publication with a free distribution of 15,000 is to survive for long as such an alternative, it needs financial support of some kind. Usually, this means advertisers. The daily press realized this long ago, and accordingly prints all the news that's fit to print around the advertisements. The *Bugle,* and other alternative papers which wish to survive for any length of time, may not be willing to walk blindly down this tried and true path; and yet, 'the reality'. What is remarkable in the *Bugle's* handling of its problem with objectionable, sexist advertising are—its openness; its attempt to establish dialog with its readers; its admission that *objectivity* in advertising policy (and by implication in news and editorial policy as well) is not a fine-tooth comb handed down from the gods; its obvious, though implicit, statement of a belief that readers are best served by a publication which faces reality and forges policy, not in a vacuum at the hands of a few editors, but by editors in response to the good sense of the public they are meant to serve.

Such qualities, of course, are not entirely new to journalism: the *Bugle* is not breaking much new ground here. Numerous other publications have faced similar problems; crusading and avant garde editors generally operate at a deficit, however briefly. William Schanen of Port Publications in Port Washington, Wisconsin, who only *printed* the now-defunct Milwaukee *Kaleidoscope,* suffered loss of much of his advertising revenue for his own weeklies, lost two of his papers, and perhaps died as a result of his conviction that freedom of the press means *freedom of the press, Kaleidoscope* included.

Still, what perhaps is new with the *Bugle's* statement of its dilemma is the conjunction of many elements vital to the shaping of a new (or renewed) honest, responsible and responsive journalism—a conjunction which *Bugle* editors bring about in the open, without condescending to, or grovelling in front of, their audience.

An honest, responsible and responsive journalism is an integral part of the process of building a new world order: it exists to act as both mirror and mold of an emerging consciousness, to shape it and to be shaped by it. But whether this kind of journalism can survive 'the reality' of the economy is another matter.

The Responsibility of the Press (Gerald Gross, ed.; Fleet Publishing Corporation), *Politics & the Press* (Richard W. Lee, ed.; Acropolis Books), *Don't Blame the People* (Robert Cirino; Random House), and *The Paper Revolutionaries* (Laurence Leamer; Simon and Schuster) examine contemporary American journalism from a variety of angles. Except for *The Paper Revolutionaries,* these books are not concerned with the shape of alternative journalism. Still, in any attempt to formulate tentative conclusions about the theory of alternative publishing, such books should perhaps be considered.

Of the four books, *The Responsibility of the Press* has the broadest scope. In his introduction, Gerald Gross states that he has "attempted to encompass the widest possible range of ethical and moral issues relating to the Press' struggle to attain and adhere to higher standards of responsibility." A noble, if difficult, endeavor.

Gross does manage to gather quite a swatch of material, from the Warren Commission Report on the role of the press in the assassination of John Kennedy, to Hy Steirman's admission that he owes "no responsibility to the people who purchase my publications", to Francis Brown's remarks on the responsibilities of the book review editor and Russell Kirk's comments on the freedom, responsibility and power of the student press. Gross also includes, in appendix, such documents as the "Advertising Acceptibility Standards of the *Detroit News*", "The Motion Picture Production Code" and the "Code of Ethics or Canons of Journalism".

The Responsibility of the Press might best be viewed, however, as something of a historical document itself: as source-material for a comprehensive historical study of journalists' beliefs about the responsibility of the free press. The book is certainly that; generally the pieces are solid and lucid expositions, but all are from the viewpoint of persons competent in one or other area of journalism. It includes no statements by day-laborers, welfare mothers, or construction workers. As a result, the collection suffers from professional inbreeding, as evidenced for instance by Gross' claim:

> That there are so many questions unanswered, methods debated and problems examined indicates the strength of the American Press today. It is no complacent fat cat, arrogant of its power, condescending to the creator of that power—the public.

A hungry ghetto kid might be inclined to debate what does and what does not constitute a 'fat cat', what is and what is not arrogance and condescension. A turret lathe operator might see 'questions unanswered, methods debated and problems examined' not as a strength, but as confusion or incompetence.

Even granting that the book operates, then, on only one of a number of possible premises, it still remains bound to the eternal law, "There is nothing new under the sun". Few of us can lay claim to fresh insight—most of our discussions on any subject are at best re-hashings of what someone else has said better; the best we can offer is more interesting illustrative material or more recent statistics.

In 1947, for instance, the Commission on Freedom of the Press said in its Report (included as the first piece of this volume) that there are "five ideal demands of society for the communication of news and ideas":

> (1) a truthful, comprehensive, and intelligent account of the day's events in a context which gives them meaning; (2) a forum for the exchange of comment and criticism; (3) the projection

of a representative picture of the constituent groups in the society; (4) the presentation and clarification of the goals and values of the society; (5) full access to the day's intelligence. Most of the writers included in this book accept these ideals; most of the articles explore familiar pathways between those ideals and the reality; no one takes up at length discussion of the same Commission's recommendation that "the agencies of mass communication assume the responsibility of financing new, experimental activities in their fields." Though Everett T. Rattray asserts that "Newspapers are newspapers, and their responsibility is to print the news and raise hell" and that "Most of them, weekly and daily, are not performing this function very well", he is talking primarily about a crusader-rabbit we already know and he offers more or less traditional suggestions for improvement. Though Thomas C. Wallace argues solidly that trade book editors "are arbiters of culture and taste, and theirs is a crucial, creative and exhilarating responsibility", he does not indicate how avant garde writers can get that first book into public print, nor how, beyond the personal good taste of the editor himself, a trade book editor can avoid manipulating and abusing the public. Though Nick B. Williams notes that "newspapers traditionally have felt a compulsion to act as the independent watchdogs of the public: to search out scoundrels in government, those who cheat and steal, but also those who abuse their powers in pursuit of their own ideologies, or what they believe are the ideologies of those who elected him", he does not point any vital directions for journalists to take in this age of highly partisan politics, nor does he venture suggestions as to how experimental political journalism could be supported.

Perhaps, given the premise *The Responsibility of the Press* operates on, it is unrealistic to expect more than clear statement of what the press' role is traditionally thought to be; if, however, we are concerned with the emergence of a new level of human consciousness, and with journalism's place in shaping it, and being shaped by it, then *The Responsibility of the Press* disappoints. Much the same can be said of another, though narrower, study of the press edited by Richard W. Lee, *Politics & the Press,* a book which "is the result of the 'Distinguished Journalism Lecture Series'" of the Department of Journalism at the University of Maryland.

In his introduction, Lee says that both Humphrey and Agnew, "frustrated by the forms their attempts at publicity had been given, questioned the role of the press." He adds:

> It is equally well to question the role of the politician in this relationship that is so essential to a democratic process where decisions are made by informed voters. And, it is to the questions raised by this relationship that ten scholars and practitioners addressed themselves in the lecture series. . . .

We can assume that the principle underlying these discussions is: in a democratic society, the public is best served by a free press which presents balanced, "objective" information in the best interests of what it considers to be the public's best interest. This principle has become almost a truism, for few journalists today question it, or explore possible alternatives. What role, for instance, do propaganda sheets have in the shaping of contemporary political consciousness; might they not be as valuable in some instances as a free and fair press; aren't they sometimes as powerful; don't lies and distortions and rhetoric call up as useful political emotions as hard facts do? These questions, when explored in *Politics & the Press,* are handled chiefly with reference to traditional journalistic principles, not as questions valuable in their own right.

Some writers here see the relationship between journalist and politician as that of adversaries in struggle. David S. Broder, for instance, admits that he is "personally much more concerned about the failings and the distortions of the press than. . . about the bias of politicians"; he directs his remarks, however, to "the way in which politicians influence the flow of news and information" and exposes two myths: 1) "the myth. . . that argues that something we can honestly call objective news coverage can be obtained through a sort of universality of reporting"; and 2) "the myth that there can somehow be a neutral relationship between a politician or a public official and the reporter or the press." This relationship, he says,

> can be good or bad, it can be tense or relaxed, it can be smooth and workable or angry and contentious. . . . but whatever it is, it can never be a neutral relationship. And the reason I would suggest to you why it cannot is that the process of news dissemination, as the politician would view it, is inextricably involved with the whole process and the competition for power that is at the very essence of the governing process.

Broder acknowledges that what is important to him as a political reporter "is being able to have access to men who are knowledgeable about a situation at a time when the situation is in the public eye." With his sources, the fact remains: "it is. . . essentially a manipulative relationship on both sides in which each party is attempting to use the other for his own purposes."

Broder explores various aspects of such manipulation, but his conclusions about the whole business of political reporting sound remarkably familiar:

> I am convinced that the beginning of an approach, the beginning of wisdom in this area has to be the recognition, by us in journalism and by the politician on his side, that there is a common responsibility to the public which these institutions share and which is far more important, far more significant, than the kind of parochial antagonisms that have grown up between us and which divide us so much today.

Lacking here is insight into what all this means when the political re-

porter sits down in front of his aging typewriter to analyze the significance and broader implications of some new bit of information from a
'usually reliable source'. At this point, Broder leaves the political reporter, and us, to fend pretty much for ourselves.

But, in my discussion, Broder is a scape-goat: other writers here likewise merely clear underbrush off familiar journalistic trails. What is
most interesting in *Politics & the Press* are not such pieces, but the *inclusion* of remarks by Herbert Klein, White House Director of Communications. Though Klein has been a journalist, we may see him here as
the adversary of Broder's type of political journalist. And we may assume, I think, that he is equally as partisan. Many of Klein's statements
are, as expected, somewhat self-serving from the viewpoint of the Nixon
administration, and many of his ideas and arguments are neither new
nor interesting. What is important, however, is the evident recognition
that balanced discussion of politics and the press requires that both the
journalists and the politicians be heard. But, in this same vein, we must
admit that there are numerous other viewpoints which should also be
heard—those of Americans left, right and dead-on-center, who make
the American political process appear to work, for instance.

I do not mean to imply, in saying that there are other voices to be
heard in discussions of the responsibility of the press today, that truth
lies in consensus opinion, or even that the intelligent layman is able to
see the issues any more clearly than journalists. But I do wish to point
out that communication, even mass-communication, has two parts: in-
former and informed. We often enough hear about the responsibility
of the press from those who are dispensing information; for the full picture, however, we ought to hear also from those who receive it. We
must admit that editors can easily get smug enough to think that theirs
is the only significant, valid, and valuable viewpoint—when this leaves
other factors unconsidered. This is what I think ought to be guarded
against.

I certainly do not intend to suggest that anyone can walk in off the
street and tell an editor how to manage his journal, or what to publish
and what not to; nor do I mean to suggest that a majority of readers, or
even all of them, *en masse,* ought to be able to do this. Rather, I am
looking for a sense, on the part of editors and publishers, that they realize the American public is more intelligent than it is usually given
credit for; a sense that the concerns—however mundane—of fairly ordinary people are important concerns; a sense that there is an awareness of the ordinary man with his ordinary job in the ordinary world
he has to live and work and play in; a sense that what the editors and
publishers are doing is significant to that world and those people.

Concern for the average man does not mean abandonment of philosophical inquiry; crediting readers with intelligence does not discredit
the editors' own. But an awareness of these factors makes a fuller picture of the state of things possible. Editors are, finally, left with their

own judgments, their own conscious, solitary thinking-through of values, their own belief in the worth of what they are about. Whether we are talking about political reporting, or other types of journalism, there are unheard voices which offer not final answers but at least co-tangent considerations.

And, throughout *Politics & the Press,* we are aware that a new kind of political reporting is yet to emerge. Perhaps its delay is not so much the result of failure on the part of the traditional journalists as I have indicated; perhaps it has not developed yet because the 'new politics' has yet to emerge.

Robert Cirino, however, in his *Don't Blame the People,* would make few such allowances for the news media today. Cirino's book is sub-titled "How the News Media Use Bias, Distortion and Censorship to Manipulate Public Opinion"; he nails down his charges fact by hard fact, culled from the pages of the best newspapers and from the news broadcasts of the largest networks in the country. On nearly every major issue that has been in the news in the last ten years, Cirino finds ample evidence of manipulation and censorship on the part of journalists.

In Chapter 13, for instance, Cirino presents a forty-four page "Catalog of Hidden Bias" in the media. His argument opens this way:

Man's mind is daily the target that receives the shot-gun-like blasts from the news barrels of mass media. On August 7, 1969, Chet Huntley fired off 7 different news stories at his audience in 58 seconds. On October 16, 1969, Edward P. Morgan assailed his radio listeners with 9 news items in 63 seconds. A reader of the first two pages of the *Los Angeles Times* has more than 50 news stories pass through his mind each morning. A thorough reader of the *New York Times* has to make room in his mind for over 300 stories daily.

Man is capable of absorbing all these news items—events disassociated in time, space, and subject matter—but it is impossible for him to make any meaningful order out of the never-ending kaleidoscope of world events that make up the day's news. . . . This explosion is a threat to man's sanity. . . .

This situation enables the clever newsman to slip his bias into the news, unnoticed by the news fan whose attention is focused on the event itself. The reader or listener is lucky if he can understand the news item and fit it into some kind of pattern; he can hardly be expected to analyze carefully the bias inserted by the communicator.

Through the rest of Chapter 13, Cirino exposes and analyzes the types and causes of biases; a look at sub-headings in the chapter may indicate his scope: bias that results from the source of news, the selection of news; bias in headlines, words, news images, photographic selection, and captions; the use of editorials to distort facts; hidden editorials. He is not merely haranguing journalists, but is presenting fairly

careful studies of their methods of reporting the news. On the bias in
the selection of news, for instance, Ciriono says:

> In another study, ten daily newspapers together covered 69
> different stories of national significance. A majority of the ten
> papers ran stories on only 7 of the 69 items. Only 3 of the 69
> items were covered by all ten newspapers.

But there is a difficulty in arguing, on the one hand, that the news
media are daily bombarding us with more information than we can assimilate, and on the other, that a majority of ten newspapers ran only
7 of 69 possible stories. The more stories that newspapers print, the
more the readers are flooded with information, useful and otherwise.
Shot-gun coverage is not the most suitable way to combat distortion
and prejudice in news media; the blast of information may only serve
to confuse futher. The act of editing must necessarily be selective;
there is little value, for instance, in including all 69 stories Cirino talks
about if they do not add anything significant to what we already know
or need to know. The day of the reporter whose "responsibility consists solely in reporting accurately what is said", and not whether the
statement was accurate, and more importantly, whether it was valuable,
is over. The good reporter, more especially the good editor must make
careful selections, he must weigh values, rank stories and ideas according to their importance, publish material according to some standard
which is his own.

Some publications have very strong biases which come through clearly. Yet these publications are certainly valuable and we can feel comfortable with them, trusting the judgment of the editor, knowing that
we are not being coerced and manipulated. The fact is, there are some
biases which are better than others, just as there are some human personalities which are more pleasing than others. What makes some publications' biases useful and valuable is that they are sincere, they are
well-intentioned (in the best sense), they are set forth honestly and
openly—and they do not coerce, but rather present the possibilities and
alternatives that are open before us.

These publications, and their writers, are in touch with, are responsive to, yet are not slave to the man we might meet on the street, the
world we actually live in, the problems we face. The editors of such
publications have their strongly-held set of values yet are not slave to
them, are open to new and unsafe ideas from others. It may sound as
if I'm saying that the end justifies the means; to some extent, I am: the
end may justify the means when the end is well-intentioned and set
forth as openly and honestly as is humanly possible, when it holds promise for the improvement of the human condition, and when the means
for achieving the end are not coercive or back-handed manipulations of
the reader, and the reader's intelligence, emotions, hopes and dreams.
An editor who can be trusted to be honest and open about what he is
attempting, who is not manipulating for personal gain, has a publication

which is able to rise above the information explosion, to cut through a mass of unimportant details, to stand above charges of distortion. It is this type of publication which has value for today—however appalled Cirino would be to hear me say it.

The research in *Don't Blame the People* is impressive; the evidence Cirino presents is voluminous and almost irrefutable—he includes, for instance, twenty tables summarizing information. The chief flaw of the book, however, is Cirino's highly partisan theoretical structure: a book such as this takes, perhaps, a dogged and heavy-handed writer to dig up all the evidence Cirino has; it takes, perhaps, a man from outside journalism (as Cirino is) to believe such an exhaustive study is necessary; and it takes, perhaps, a practical sort of man rather than a theoretician or philosopher. Nonetheless, though Cirino has martialed the facts, and though he has stated and argued important theses, he has not done it entirely successfully; where at times delicate, pen-knife dissection is called for, Cirino uses a meat-cleaver; which, though it may well serve to present the issues at hand, does not finally allow the whole picture, and especially its theoretical ramifications, to be seen clearly. But Cirino does sketch out an important picture here and this much must be said: *Don't Blame the People* is a book essential to any comprehensive study of the role of news media in contemporary American society—when the next philosopher of journalism starts testing his ideas, he will have Cirino's hard facts to deal with.

Unlike Gross, Lee, and Cirino, Laurence Leamer's chief concerns in *The Paper Revolutionaries* are not the responsibilities of established news media or their failings. Rather, Leamer's study is a history of the "rise of the underground press".

Looking for its roots, he sees such publications as the *Masses, The New Masses,* the *Daily Worker,* the *Village Voice,* and Paul Krassner's the *Realist* as precursors, if not true ancestors, of the underground publications of the sixties.

It was on May 1, 1964, that what we have known as the underground press in the United States started moving, according to Leamer. On that day, Arthur Kunkin handed out copies of what was to become the *Los Angeles Free Press;* and soon thereafter underground papers began appearing across the country, to serve the needs of the new hip communities that were forming, or in some cases to function as catalysts in the creation of the new community. John Kois, founding editor of Milwaukee *Kaleidoscope,* stated in a *Bugle American* interview (December 1971) that at least in the case of *Kaleidoscope,* the paper preceded the community:

> . . . the community that *Kaleidoscope* represented initially was an illusion. It was a myth. But at the same time there was a direct correlation between a certain fantasy or myth presented in *Kaleidoscope* and its manifestation some months later. So the community, in fact, followed the myth. When the myth becomes

fact, because of a weird relationship, a lot of people who identified themselves with that community felt a spiritual ownership of
Kaleidoscope.

The formation of the community, as well as the formation of the underground press, were achieved only with trials and hardships; both
the people and their papers were harassed, in Milwaukee, in New Orleans, in Texas. Leamer is aware of the difficulties of the struggle and
he chronicles the changes that the alternative culture and press have
come through with a fairly careful eye to detail and nuance. Like Jacobi of the *Bugle,* he sees three stages in the development of the underground papers, stages which reflect the alternative vision—the cultural,
the political, and finally the third generation papers to which, says Lea-
mar, "will go the task of proving how noble that spirit is, how rich that
vision, how attainable that dream. There is nothing inevitable in the
outcome—but for the underground press there is no looking back."

Leamer's book has a few minor errors of fact, e.g. confusion of Milwaukee's and Madison's *Kaleidoscopes;* but still he handles admirably a
difficult, tenuous and sometimes impossible subject. *The Paper Revolutionaries* seems an accurate account of the events, personalities, and
struggles that initially shaped, and continue to shape, the alternative
press. It is not a study of the theory of alternative press, but a history.
As history, it succeeds.

What comes through Leamer's book, and what should be clear to
those who have watched alternative publications over the last eight
years or so, is that the underground press in this country started not as
an economic venture, rather as a philosophic or sociologic one. Milwaukee *Kaleidoscope* did not publish, as the Milwaukee *Journal* does,
to make money, but as Kois points out, to shape a community. And
despite the honorable talk of the journalists in *The Responsibility of
the Press* and *Politics & the Press,* we are aware that today conventional
journalism and the business of publishing function on two interrelated
levels. On the economic level, a newspaper like the New York *Times* is
intended to be a money-making venture. Newspapers have a readership;
businesses need to reach a large audience; newspapers sell advertising
space to business: ideally in this arrangement both parties benefit—the
businessman with an increase in sales and the newspaper publisher with
a profit after expenses. The recent demise of *Life* magazine demon-
strates that, on the economic level, when the publishing business is no
longer a profitable one, it is time to get out.

Commercial publishing houses today work on a similar principle,
though theirs is a more tangible product: books. To put it in meat-
cleaver terms, books are marketed the way clothes or soaps or perfumes
are marketed. If a particular item doesn't sell well, that item is no
longer produced; if another item is selling like the oft-noted hotdogs at
a baseball game, then various companies compete in the market place.
Whether it is soap or books, the operating principle is necessarily the

same: what we are selling is what people are buying.

As I have said, however, publishing today operates on another level also; this second level is more complex and more closely related to the idea of publishing as a philosophic or sociologic venture: publishers for whom publishing is an economic venture, whether it is the newspaper business or the book business, are almost of necessity stalwart defenders of the status quo. There is some dark principle which links publishing-as-a-business with the way-things-are. Newscasters, editors, newspaper and book publishers by and large support the present structure of of things, politically, culturally, economically. They may well suggest some minor tinkering with this or that part, but they do not call for a complete overhaul of the structure. Cirino's book deals at length with the various journalistic manifestations of such thinking, with the news media's use of bias and distortion to re-enforce its own views of the world. We might argue that the publication of the Pentagon Papers by the New York *Times* and others is evidence to the contrary, that it indicates journalists' efforts to function as catalysts of change in our time. We might be inclined to say that here was a truly radical act on the part of the established press. However, there was nothing uncovered in the Pentagon Papers that has not been known from other sources; anyone who has watched the development of the Vietnam war was not surprised by any of the *Times'* revelations. The fact that the *Times* published the Pentagon Papers perhaps added credence to what had already been said in the underground papers around the country; it also enhanced the *Times'* prestige and made American newspapers once again look as if they were truly the public's indispensable and invaluable watchdogs. But I am sure, also, that the Pentagon Papers helped the *Times'* circulation. All this, without ever risking a radical transformation of our values: rather, only an intensification of the power-struggle between big press and big government, neither of which give many tinker's dams about the man on the street.

The worst, and sometimes even the best, of the book publishers do no better. Because a book is a product to be marketed, it must be a product that will sell. The staples are the westerns, the detective stories, the Harold Robbins' novels, light summer reading. These are innocuous enough and certainly do not encourage the public to demand radical change. Those books which may encourage such change are either 1) not published, 2) are so naive, adolescent and impracticable that nothing will come of them (I am thinking of Reich's *The Greening of America*) or 3) end up, for various reasons, largely in the hands of those who already see the need for change and are already calling for it.

If an important book is not published, we need never know about it and the declining publisher need never lose prestige because of it. With such books as *The Greening of America,* the simple-mindedness of the thinking acts to ensure that the status quo publisher, while looking "relevant" and gaining prestige, goes on making money without risking any kind of revolution.

There are, on the other hand, a number of publishers who are bringing out truly important books; though often enough these publishers are content with the way-things-are, and though they too must balance their ledgers, their editorial vision is broader and they are willing to risk changing the world by sending out important ideas. These publishers, out of economic necessity, have to have their share of best-sellers: still, they make the important books available. Sadly, however, such books generally reach those who have already been unsuccessful in mobilizing the public for change, all they might try. Such books are generally ineffectual in everday living.

The shape of our culture today suggests various reasons. There is, clearly, a dichotomy in this country between ideas and things. Ideas are something confined to universities and research laboratories and magazines, not something that find themselves worked into the everyday scheme of things. Though this has not always been the case, it is very seldom that the scholar and the foundry worker meet each other, and very seldom that they wish to. In addition, our education system has gone to great lengths to separate and keep separate the two types: shop and home economics for the "technical" student, literature and sociology for the college-bound. The dichotomy is deepended by short-sighted men who are out for the easy dollar: the audience that *True Confessions* claims, for instance, is more a creation of that magazine than it is an actual class of people in the world; but, told long enough what their characteristics are and how to behave, *True Confessions'* audience begins believing what is said about it and begins behaving as it is said to. It is another class entirely which subscribes to magazines such as *Harper's* or *Atlantic,* but this class too has been similarly created: you become what you believe you are. In an earlier time, fraternities served to take the rough edges off the country bumpkin and to invest him with a "civilized" image. Today, the press functions to serve up a whole menagerie of possible self-images.

"Best-sellers" likewise are made when they create an audience for themselves: when people come to believe that *Love Story* is their story and holds something special for what they think they are. It is *Love Story* and such poetry as Rod McKuen's which attract readers: the human animal, in these visions, is not a complex one, not a difficult one; the self-images offered are easy ones to assume. It is the easy course of action that the most of us pursue, being human and not being asked for our best.

But, perhaps because we are lazy or because we are not asked for our best, difficult, important ideas cannot create a mass audience: few of us are willing to take the hard course; few important ideas, when "popularized", i.e., when watered down to what is considered the ordinary reader's level, keep their value and substance. The problem is not that the man on the street is incapable of understanding the complex; it is that he is not asked to, either by himself or by the demands of our culture; it is that he has deeply ingrained in him the belief that he is incapable of such understanding.

Thus, when important books do appear from "commercial" houses, they are passed over by the mass audience who have been fed pap and taught to like it. In one sense, publishers are to blame—for flooding us with the easy visions, so that it becomes difficult to find the really important ones. In another sense, however, it is not entirely the publishers' fault: they alone did not create the dichotomy between ideas and things in our culture.

Part of the blame, I think, lies specifically with our book reviewing mechanisms. Reviewers should be sifting books and ideas, selecting the important ones for consideration and emphasis; but most reviewers tend to take the same easy course we would—a juicy biography or collection of memoirs, it seems, holds the most interest. When important ideas are discussed, too often they are pushed around on the page neatly and cleanly so as not to infect the reading public.

Yet in all this the central problem remains: though some publishers are bringing out important books, for various reasons these seldom touch the man on the street. As long as publishers, even good publishers, continue to handle books as products, as long as publishing is an industry instead of a service, the problem will remain. What is needed is not a better method of "marketing", rather a fresh view of the publisher—of books, and of newspapers and magazines. For, in the present scheme of things, important ideas stay caught in the world of ideas and on the printed page; they do not reach out into the lives of "common men". Partly, as I have said, it is a matter of marketing; partly a matter of the way our culture moves. But as long as we conceive publishing primarily as an economic venture, we shall remain trapped in the status quo. Ideas will not move out and penetrate any farther than they have in the past or than they do now. But we can no longer be content with the "popular" and the watered down; we can no longer be content with seeing important ideas touching only those who are already "believers".

What I am proposing is another view of publishing—of books and periodicals—which sees it not at all as an economic venture, but entirely as a philosophic one, as a service to people, to ideas and things and our culture generally.

In such a view, the 'reality of survival' is not a factor entering in: money is not the object; restructuring the world is. Each act of publishing is, therefore, economically detached from all past and possible future acts. The prime consideration is only: how, at this time, can a publisher best serve ideas and things, and our culture, for the sake of the people; this means that the human condition and the direction of human development and consciousness are the primary objects of study, that "news columns" are not given over to trivia, but to substantial information about the important movements of man in the world;

it also means that conventional, radical chic, and even alternativist ideas and prejudices are examined and shaken apart and re-examined, that the good in all of them is sought out and made note of and underlined, that experiments of value are looked at thoroughly and explored for all possible ramifications. The concerns are not so much polished writing or entertainment or "personalities", but fertile ideas which still have the dirt hanging on them, our directions and our possibilities. The intent is not financial success, but the improvement of the human condition: with one issue of a magazine or paper, or with a hundred; with one important book, or ten or twenty. What I am talking about is a new generation of an old type of publisher—the crusader who says what must be said and sees to it that he is heard, despite the personal and financial costs.

In practical terms, such a view of publishing is, I admit, highly unrealistic: because in practical terms we come back to the logic of economic necessity. However, it is not on the practical level that our considerations should begin: rather, if we are publishers, we ought to define what the goals of our publishing are, then explore the various ways of achieving them. For if we are interested in the possibilities of man, as publishers our aim is to affect and effect those possibilities, in spite of the overwhelming demands of "practical terms".

※

1973

DECEMBER

We stand around with our hands in our pockets.
december vol. xv, nos. 1 & 2. 280pp. A double issue—280pp. And more material here than Carter's: if *december* is not among the most important little journals being published today—it's only because we're using out-dated measuring sticks.
50 contributors; poetry, film criticism, literary criticism, fiction. R. Crumb drawings.
Who wants to read interesting or solid or important writing anyway?
Richard Kostelanetz contributes "The New York Literary Mob" from his *The End of Intelligent Writing;* Lee Wallek alternates between tickling us and knifing us in his "Readers Right—or The US Lit-Sit To-day. . . and just Yesterday (Part One)" [Part On—Put On]. A mini-anthology, "The Washington—Baltimore Corridor" edited by James Haining. 54 pages on "The Movies" edited by Robert Wilson. 280pp.
& The Beat Goes On.
We stand around with our hands in our pockets & only God can make a tree.
What is your defense.
"A Magazine of the Arts and Opinion." A lot of the arts, some of the opinions. More, perhaps, than we're ready for because we're content standing around with our hands in our pockets.
It's fall & there's a chill in the air/ blue under our nails & our lips are chapped.
America—scratch that: AMERICA, where will we say we were when it went right past us? standing around, hands in our pockets, popping our little liver pills: **DECEMBER**, *read it, relish it or condemn it.* But for god's sake, don't ignore it!

WHEN MORNING REFUSES

But Morning Refused to Answer, edited by D. "Colt" Denfield (Times Change Press), records the 'lives and words of people who live in prisons, reformatories, & mental institutions'; the title comes from prisoner Milton Collins' poem which opens: "And in the early morning/ he shouted from the window,/hoping for an echo/to assure himself that /he had not vanished in the night.//But morning refused to answer".
This is not so much an anthology of "prison writings" as a document describing what it means to be confined—from the confined person's point of view. The list of demands from Attica is here, a number of letters by prisoners detailing what their days and their lives are like, a

list of "Patient Demands: Requests for Survival", as well as excerpts from the prisoners' handbook of the Connecticut State Prison and illustrations of "drawer arrangement", i.e., in which drawer and where in the drawer to put bras, panties, stockings, etc., in a women's institution. The book certainly achieves its purpose, certainly shows why "Morning refused to answer', and why, as is noted incidentally in an anonymous piece, "Ink and paper are cheap in prison almost as cheap as people." What comes through clearly is: "The faces change, the appearance and ceremonies remain the same. The result is also constant—a horrible waste of everything."

It is truly a powerful book: for those who have been looking at prisons and other such institutions through rose-colored glasses, *But Morning Refused to Answer* will shatter those lenses; for those who already see what such institutions are and what they do to people, the book might well reveal a metaphor for our whole society, on all levels. The book is meant to be read; but, more, it is meant as a weapon—a 12-guage shot-gun blasting holes in our comfortable beliefs.

A GALLERY

In *Gallery* (Poet & Printer), John Wade is attempting, as he says, "to recall a specific time and place", New England in the late 1930s and early 1940s. What Wade is doing, actually, is drawing character-sketches of persons, personalities, as he knew them then: the charm of these poems lies in Wade's brushing careful, evocative portraits with a minimum of strokes, with a tightness of image and language that leaves no word, no line unnecessary.

Wade largely succeeds. In "Greatuncle Crowell", for instance, he shows us his greatuncle, but he shows us more than that—his mother and himself, living in difficult times. Wade employs situation and suggestion for his purposes, giving us perhaps the 'essence' of a larger drama that we can flesh out from our own experience and the secret reserve of our moods. The poem opens:

> Great-uncle Crowell slapped my face
> when my marble of spittle
> rolled down his vest.

The greatuncle reacts; the poem continues:

> When one is five, one is surprised
> that grown-ups are capable of storms:
> the mountainous thunder of Crowell's voice,
> and lightning splintering the knotted
> pupils of my mother's eyes. And then
> my uncle, who had no place to go,
> took cot and bowl and a soiled vest,

and fled.
He went to the barn to live.
'The final insult,' my mother said.
But I thought of the drooling cows; thought
of the wind slapping the faceless trees.
In but seventeen lines, Wade reveals the full picture and we carry it
away, expanding it in our minds.

In some few of these poems, however, Wade fails to create such an
"expansive" portrait, and leaves us only a static snap-shot. "Alex" is
one such: "I knew Alex Goldsmith/ when he was old. Laughter/ didn't
crease the leather/ of his face. . . ./ . . . The smell of snow/ was in the
air when I/ knew him. And often, we laughed/ together because he
liked me." The movement in this poem is linear, too straightforward
to leave any corners for us to explore ourselves; it is too brittle to stand
our handling the mood. We are fortunate, though, that such portraits
are rare in this gallery.

For the most part, because Wade is a solid technician, because he
does have an eye for the important detail, he is able to evoke another
time and place with surprising immediacy and power. Most of the portraits will not fade nor yellow with age.

LEGENDS

In terms of handling their materials, Eugene Warren, in *Christographia* (ktaadn molehill) and Bill Butler, in *A Cheyenne Legend* (Turret Books), stand in marked contrast. In a short note on his book, Warren explains, "these poems attempt to express personal views of, & per-
spectives on, Christ." Butler notes that his work "is an adaptation of
the translation of this legend." In terms of impact & immediacy, Butler's is the superior book.

The central problem with *Christographia* is this: Warren is attempting to set down his views of Christ, yes, but he uses as means a formal
poetry and formal (& too common) symbols. His personal perspective
is couched in cold language & cold formula that have, at this late date,
lost the power to move anyone but a believer. From Section II:

In the center, the Bread, enthron'd
in a silver dish
(a shallow boat gliding to the breaking
& the Wine, casting blood-shadows
as the light sings thru it)
calls me. . .

We know, of course, that Warren is speaking of the Eucharist & of what
it means to him:

this Bread carries our wounds,
& this Wine's wet with pain

we own'd. . .
the Voice dances from throat to throat, granting us
song in our measure,
& joy without measure or reserve.

I don't doubt that the Eucharist can bring Warren "joy without measure"; I do contend that "Bread", "Wine", & "Voice" in such a context have become staid symbols, in terms of poetics (whether or not in
terms of faith, I am not judging here), and that their use in expressions
of personal sentiment make more distant rather than more intimate
what Warren intends.

Warren's irritatingly facile techniques, at some points, add further
distance: he says in Section IV, "The Castle Joyous":

joy, us; we're the cast
all walled with light.

This is a light moment, perhaps, in serious personal reflections: but
these easy lines distract from what Warren is attempting; elsewhere,
syntax inversion, out-dated language & archaic symbol not only distract
but deter the reader.

Only in Section VI, where the influence of such poets as Donne &
Herbert is clearly in evidence, does Warren achieve some success:

Discomfort me,
Lord, with Thy comfort:
most sweet
& difficult:
only those who
consent to the universe may have it. . .

and further, concluding the section:

Things are what they are:
unwise Hell insists they be otherwise.

I find this to be an out-moded way of speaking, but there is one re-
deeming characteristic: Warren's own voice, at least, is carrying the burden here, not ineffacacious symbols.

In matters of Christ, Warren's poems are a source 'secondary' to the
Gospels & related texts; Bill Butler's *A Cheyenne Legend* is more nearly
a primary source; in an entirely different context, it may be equivalent
to a Gospel. The text of the *Legend* is largely narrative (though it does
move occasionally into lyricism):

Barely
more than a kid she said
                              young
she said tend to the dark
come down beautiful star
& I'll marry you. . .

This is the story of Falling Star, of how he came into the world & of
the six things he did for 'the people'.

Because this is 'primary' rather than 'secondary' text, we look for narrative rather than personal immediacy; as narrative, the Legend succeeds precisely because throughout it we can visualize one of the Cheyenne elders at the fire, telling the story again. The narrative is well-honed & tight, as if from frequent retelling; the lines are the speaker's breath-lines, are his inflections. There are cuts & turns in narrative direction, for emphasis & tension; there is also, and this is important, a preciseness of image & metaphor—they are integral to the narrative development.

The first part of the poem tells of the woman who begat Falling Star, climbing higher & higher in a pine, chasing a porcupine, "dinner ahead", until

> the air got so thin
> that the last
> birds swam below her like blackfish

and not a wasted word in this description of how high she had climbed. The story of Falling Star's birth, fruit of the union of a woman & a star, when his mother fell from the tree,

> all the way home
> bones broken
> dead from the fall
> > not her kid
> born from the shock
> half-star
> he was hard like stone
>
> Meadowlark flying by
> heard the bawling
> took him up to her nest
> stuffed him with grubs
> > > all spring
> > > summer

is as fantastical as any story of virgin birth. And yet, because the narrator here is removed from his material, because this legend needs no personal logic and demands no personal commitment from us, & because the language, the imagery, & what symbolism there is, are fresh, we can accept this telling.

The balance of Butler's poem concerns the six feats Falling Star performs, to save the People; these are as fantastical as his birth. Falling Star destroys the 'great hairy lizard', the 'white ghost owl', 'a great white crow', 'Winter Man', 'old Double-Eyes', and finally "some old witch in the village/ [who] had snatched them [the People] all bald/ for a robe/ she needed a couple of scalps/ only to fill it". The separate, unrelated feats of heroism are held together by the bold voice of the narrator speaking of Falling Star between incidents: "I will tie another one [great deed] to it."

What Butler leaves us with may well be a Cheyenne legend; but the retelling here is powerful & immediate. Butler succeeds in making his mythic material come alive for us, where Warren, concerned with personal perspective, largely fails. Butler has both a well-honed narrative & a finely modulated voice at work. Warren has personal reflection, couched in & unbolstered by worn symbols & weary language. Butler's handling of his material suits his purposes; Warren's does not.

THE CALENDAR

I have complained elsewhere that the imposition of an externally defined structure on a group of poems can result in a weak collection: the necessity to fill it out, to flesh in the skeleton, complete the parts, can lead a poet to include bad poems for the sake of the entity. Happily, in his *Calendar: A Cycle of Poems* (The Baleen Press), Richard Shelton does not work with bad bones: his description of the months of the years, the moods of the months & his own moods, the changing temper and shape of the landscape and its details, is fresh and vibrant and vital. Each poem belongs in its place in the cycle and none detract from the whole.

Shelton's collection opens with something of a prologue called "Cholla Woman". Its first section begins: "We came to the disheveled desert/ and built our house on greasewood/ and old fans." and closes: "We develop pain. We teach it nothing/ but it learns anyway. We let echoes follow us around touching on our silences."

The second section opens: "At night I look out and see/ the holy Cholla Woman/ standing in the ruins of her long/ blond hair. She lifts/ gray arms to the sky, and rabbits avoid her."; it closes, describing loneliness: "There is no/ loneliness like her loneliness,/ without sisters, needing no friends./ All her children were born far away." In the third section, which opens, "We are learning to translate what the stones/ say" and closes, "Each year a huge re-arrangement of time approaches./ Holding up our empty calendars/ we run to meet it.", Shelton again becomes more personal. "Cholla Woman", as prologue to the actual calendar, serves to map Shelton's concerns, to define the boundaries of the desert and the coyote "whose song was the absence of music", of the loneliness, of "what the stones say".

The first month is "January": "his gloves were meant/ for better hands/ his hands for better gloves/ the story of his life/ gets smaller and disappears". Further, concluding the poem: "but poor winter has looked/ into so many houses/ he knows that when you are poor/ nothing is ever enough/ and when you are rich it is the same."

In "March": "it is almost spring/ and nights come toward me/ like words on the page of a book/ fallen open at random". "April": "returns like an expatriate, a defector/ from the frost. Her feet are wrap-

ped in old rose petals, her eyes/ are the color of wet sand under moss".
In "September": "the wind goes by flapping its arms/ in a coat with
ragged lining".

What Shelton achieves throughout his calendar is a delicate balance
of precise image and fully suggested mood; what is remarkable, in these
poems, is Shelton's ability to make image and mood work together. His
images are not intended as symbols, but are meant to be more than pictures—what they hold beyond mere description is shade and nuance of
mood. In turn, Shelton's moods infect his images. The result is a fruitful interplay, image suggesting mood, mood holding further ramifications for the original and subsequent images, again suggesting further
nuances. It is not often we see such an apparently stark yet wholly rich
poetry.

The poem, "Requiem for Sonora", closes the collection; it serves to
show us clearly where the calendar has brought the poet, and where it
has brought us: "I am older and uglier/ and full of the knowledge/ that
I do not belong to beauty/ and beauty does not belong to me/ I have
learned to accept/ whatever men choose to give me/ or whatever they
choose to withhold/ but oh my desert/ yours is the only death I cannot
bear." Having been through the cycle, through the calendar with Shelton month by month, we know why.

THE HEADLANDS & BEYOND

The poetry of Mary Shumway's *Headlands* (Sono Nis Press) evidences a remarkably rich and intricate interplay of language, image and insight. Her language is foremost a language we *hear*: the lines move and
turn and echo and turn back on themselves, sounds piling up like bright
fall leaves against a wall. A poem stands as well-tailored as Joseph's
coat.

Shumway is able to gather her materials like so many straws and
weave them together into a coherent whole. "Surface Hunt at Indian
Springs", for instance, opens showing us at once the roots of language
(all language is metaphorical in some sense: words standing for something else, a link between them in the mind), and how much farther a
poet is able to take language (giving the common metaphors of language
another dimension): "Turning out of time. . ." is both *like* turning off
a road, and is *actually* turning off the road, as the poem continues:

Turning out of time
I drive the black road down the river

    holing out trunks
    and sudden eyes

and leaps
hooved out of marsh. Leaves climb
the slow wind.

In other poems Shumway achieves a similar effect; for instance, "Vers
le nord" opens: "I weather north across a land of low relief"; from
"Passage": "light rides the wings of heron" and "you remember only/
storms of apple blossoms in the starting land. . ."; from "The Sanil":
"Silence skims the Plover". The poet is like the candle-maker or the
blacksmith, a craftsman who knows her materials: words; like other
craftsmen, the poet is especially sensitive to her materials, aware of the
secrets and the possibilities within. A poet as fine as Ms. Shumway is
able to crack open such secrets for us, hearing her, reading her.

But the good poet cannot be content with one secret only, and
Shumway is not: in "Surface Hunt" she sets to exploring further both
the experience which elicited the poem, and the language itself:

Behind
night closes on the Chev, a red mist

   runs the window.
   I park and slam the door
to warn the darkness in. Still,
the deep ravine slams back.

The stanza is description and narration, and is more: the car does get
parked, the door slammed, yes; but 'warning the darkness in, the ravine
slamming back' works to suggest a mood, the mood of the poem as a
whole. When the details of the event have been finally set down completely, it is the mood of the poem which must be resolved or brought
to conclusion. In another poem, "The Burrow", the poet shows us
clearly how such a resolution can come: the poem opens,

fall
when foxes game in musical trees
and snakes in winter rye trip
      on the tilting sun
I stir to think to chance
and chance on nothing

the mood set, and develops through the next two and a half stanzas; the
poem is concluded and the mood resolved in these lines:

with what I know I keep the season
      in my way
I take the last of nothing

with what sun
and sleep

In "Surface Hunt", the experience and the telling of the experience re-
verberate with whispered, quietly revealed suggestions; the final lines of
the poem indicate the source:

I listen for the passage while the rain
unearths new traces of the ancient site

but only hear
the rye grow, the river moss, the slow sleep
    of bears
    in a deep ravine.
Then I remember why we stopped here
by the water once and drove in the dark
and sang the slow earth light.

The poem comes to an end, but our appreciation of it does not. Its
mood envelopes us; we hear its sounds echo and re-echo, the rhythm as
gentle as rain. We exhale, satisfied.

If Shumway's poetry has a weakness, it rises out of her strength: a
very few poems here, attempting what the poet achieved in "Surface
Hunt at Indian Springs" and most other poems, indicate how the thread
of metaphor can be stretched too thinly, revealing little. From "Mister
Patches":

Sun's alley empty
when I rise, over morning's ledge
lean far enough, and, yes, the gentle mender
climbs with his load of light.

Happily, there are few such lapses in *Headlands*; we are aware of them
as unsuccessful experiments, and appreciate that. Most of the thirty
poems are successful: creating their moods, revealing their secrets, suggesting the possibilities in our language and of images. The insights are
the poet's; the caliber of her craftsmanship makes them ours as well.

THE FARMER'S VOICE

"There is always the rock:
That, first and last, to remember."

William Kloefkorn's *Alvin Turner as Farmer* (Road Runner Press) is

one of the most powerful pieces of writing, of any kind, that I have read
to date. This is Midwest poetry at its best and it stands well against
other schools, other styles, other regions. *Alvin Turner* has a structure
something like your grandmother's treasured album of photographs:
all the important pictures, randomly arranged, telling the family's story.
In this collection, each of Kloefkorn's poems is independent of the
others, but each adds depth and power to the next: you have seen your
grandfather as a young man, at the birth of his first child; you have seen
him five and ten years later, the toil beginning to show; you have seen
him stooping into late middle-age; you have seen the old man, having
seen him coming through the changes.

    Alvin Turner as Farmer has such a quality about it. This is not a nar-
rative poem in the usual sense: rather, as the vignettes are etched, a lyricism rises out of the revelations, rises out of the struggle against the
rock-marked land, against the illness and death of a wife, against the
loss of a daughter.

    The hidden rock blunts the plowshare: "Yet somehow I expected
yesterday's blunted share/ To be the last. That part which I cannot see/
I said, cannot reduce me." The hogs are loose again, Turner's wife helps
to herd them, "hip-deep in muck", "*Manure*, she calls it, and I don't argue":

> At such a time
> The lifting of a single thread
> Unhems the world.
> The price of corn is up.
> Hogs are down.
> The next thing you know
> The government will place a tax
> On prayer. All this, and more,
> As we change our socks
> And put on new faces for supper.

Turner stands, gentle and sensitive, a man for all seasons while
thoroughly a part of his own, a man strong enough to say:

> After a difference
> We go together as
> We fell apart: with words.
> They are clear and clipped and
> Gently strange,
> And after hearing them I think
> Their sound is like the little noise
> Of needles, knitting.

I am one of the first to demand that 20th century poetry rise out of

20th century experience, that our poetry reflect the shape of the places we have been, the things we have touched, the dreams we have had, that what goes down on paper or into breath and sound be true to the world we inhabit; and I would be one of the first to admit that Kloefkorn probably has not lived *Alvin Turner*, nor even "stood there in the furrow/ With the rock raised above my head,/ Powerless to reduce it/ Or even to lose it to sight." And yet, for all this, reading and re-reading *Alvin Turner as Farmer*, I see life and truth for our own age suggested by another time and place, I see the figures of my own grandfather and great uncles silhouetted against the rolling horizon, I see half-dreams and memories of my own: if Kloefkorn has not lived as Alvin Turner, his grandfather did, and my grandfather, and countless other men who have struggled against "the rock", who have juggled the price of hogs and the cost of corn, who have buried a wife and daughter in the land they loved, and who have been buried there themselves. The world that comes through *Alvin Turner as Farmer* may not be Kloefkorn's personally, but it is still somehow his, and mine, and our fathers' and uncles' and brothers': a world that is part of our experience because it is roots of a tree we are part of.

ANTHOLOGIES: FOCUS & PURPOSE

Good anthologies are like good magazines: edited with focus & purpose. We might say, in fact, that an anthology is a one-shot magazine, published at a particular time, out of a particular need. But many magazines, & likewise many anthologies, are at best fuzzy collections because their editors did not have a special focus in mind at the time of editing, did not edit out of a need or with a purpose. The best magazines & anthologies, however, manage to achieve an intensity, a clarity, a sharpness of purpose: what they especially intend becomes the cutting edge separating each from the other.

Puposes & focuses & aims, for anthologies, can be as various as the editors themselves. One editor, for instance, may be so frank as to call his anthology simply *My Favorite Poets*; another may be attempting to anthologize a "school" of poets or type of poetry; still another may be interested in cross-sectioning a city or region. Whatever the editor's intent, his anthology can be judged on what he seems to intend & how close he comes to realizing it.

An examination of a number of anthologies of various purposes & various types of production may reveal some of the possibilities inherent in the nature of "anthology"; it may also indicate the broad sweep, in terms of physical forms, that anthologies can take—from the very "small press" to the slick commercial—& show the advantages & disadvantages of each.

Are You Ready For The New Ultra Violence? (Cat's Pajamas Press),
edited by John Jacob, is clearly small press, & intends to be: this is mimeo production at its cheapest; the poetry is diverse, most of it from
small press poets who have received some recognition. Included here
are Bertolino, Stokes, Woodward, Gitin, Montgomery, Lifshin, Carande,
& others: familiar names with two poems each.

If this anthology is meant as a fairly representative cross-section of
what happened, at least in one part of small press last year, it succeeds
admirably. While we could wish for better quality on some of the poetry, perhaps, we can accept *Are You Ready* as a news bulletin sent out
in haste, revealing the state of affairs around it. When the shape of
things changes, as it must, there will be another news-flash anthology
sent out, defining the change. An anthology such as this can succeed
precisely because it can be fresh—it can give a glimpse at the current
state of the art; it is meant to be distributed in the traditional underground manner—mailed out free, passed hand-to-hand; it is not meant to
sit in some basement waiting for orders to come in.

The argument can be raised that if what is anthologized is worth an-
thologizing, it is worth spending the time, effort, & money to make the
physical product solidly crafted & attractive; that if the work is good,
it will still be fresh after six or eight or ten months "in press".
There is substance to the argument & small press publishers should consider it fully; still, the idea of a minimal time-lag between the writing &
the publishing remains appealing. *Are You Ready* has that appeal. As
an editor & publisher, John Jacob is one of the best proponents of
"guerrilla" publishing, and *Are You Ready For The New Ultra Violence?*
underlines the merits of that position.

Jukebox Poems (The Alternative University Poetry Collective) is
meant not so much to be a news bulletin as to present an alternative
to what-seems-to-be. Included here are poems by Richard Friedman,
Peter Kostakis, Donald Nisondorff, Darlene Pearlstein, Bob Rosenthall,
& Barry Schechter.

Physically, *Jukebox Poems* might seem superior to *Are You Ready*;
it too is not the kind of anthology that is meant to be kept in the basement waiting. The book must be passed around now because a good
deal of the poetry here is that easy kind of surrealism which makes more
than passing reference to all manner of fads & short-lived incidents—to
things in the world which will be forgotten in four or five years. Because so much of this poetry is built so solidly into the soon-forgotten,
much of its intelligibility will be lost in, say, five years. There is, undoubtedly, a place for foot-notes in the understanding of literature—but
I have the feeling that when many of these poems have lost their meaning, their impact, their context, we will feel that their recovery just
wouldn't be worth the effort. This does not, of course, deny the impact
these poems may have today, in context; & I will readily agree that our
poetry has to be written out of today's world & for it: but our poetry

must also transcend our own time & place & our own petty concerns;
it must move beyond the smallest moments of our lives. *Jukebox
Poems,* by & large, manages no such transcendence—& will sound, five
years from now, much like pop-hits from five years ago sound today:
we wonder what moved us.

Freek Poetry, in three volumes, might be said to have more or less
edited themselves. I usually decry this kind of editorial policy as slop-
py & flabby editing, for it seems to go clearly contrary to the idea of
focus & purpose. However, in the case of Jim Spencer & Karl Young's
Freek, an almost boundless energy & vitality result: we see revealed
some of the mystery, some of the kinkiness, even the voracious appetite
for all kinds of experience that mark grass-roots poetry. This vitality
seems to define *Freek*'s reason-for-being, seems to focus the reader's attention on kinds of poetry, on ways of seeing & speaking, that are fresh
& unusual, that are the products of a broad range of experience & value. The focus *Freek* has lies in its democratic ethic: the rigid frame-
works, within which we as readers so often work, are knocked down,
blow by blow; we are set investigating further, in many directions.

Most of the material in *Freek* comes from Milwaukee & Wisconsin,
though some of it comes from other parts of the country & Canada.
But *Freek* is less a Milwaukee than a grass-roots anthology. There are
poets whose work appears here & nowhere else; & yet many of these
poems are solidly crafted & should be widely read. If nothing else,
Freek tells us that a city or region may have more ways of seeing &
speaking than can be adequately handled by conventional publishing.
There is, necessarily, a flaw inherent in such editing, such publishing;
dull poems do stand beside the interesting. Given the way an anthology
moves, we come to expect that; considering the overall diversity & vitality of *Freek,* it seems well-compensated for. Here, more than in any
other anthology I've seen, the rule seems to be: "one man's meat is another man's poison": it is the key to such democracy.

Freek, as a physical product, is a surprising piece of small press
craftsmanship: when we realize that most of the printing here was done
from paper off-set plates, rather than plastic or metal plates, we must be
surprised at the quality. The care taken in handling the physical details
of production is a tribute to the ingenuity, patience & sheer doggedness
of the typists/printers/publishers. Studying the pages themselves is a
lesson in production-technique, one perhaps both the small press publisher & the general reader can learn from.

The Musician Plays For Richard (Spring Rain Press), edited by Karen
Sollid & John Sollid, might well be called a cousin of *Freek.* The editorial policy, though not the same, is similar: the editors seem intent
not so much on grass-roots or region or school as on presenting in fairly well-crafted letter-press work by eight highly competent poets who—
like the poets in *Freek*—evidence a wide range of vision & technique.
As an anthology, *The Musician Plays For Richard* is an alternative for

eight separate & very thin chapbooks, perhaps. What holds the collection together is not so much the mystery & kinkiness we find in *Freek* as the consistent quality of the writing. And though *Freek* came off paper-plates & *The Musician* off letter-press, we see a link between the two in terms of the care & pain taken in production.

If *The Musician Plays For Richard* has anything to teach us, in terms of focus & purpose, it is this: an anthology need not serve only a city or region or school of poetry; it can also serve as a fine vehicle for presenting a number of poets linked not by image or concern or technique but by their striving for excellence & their striving for possibilities: concern for craft in all of it. As in *Freek*, there are poems here which should be widely read; this is a pleasing format in which to present them.

Two anthologies which take "city" as their chief focus are: *Raleigh Poetry: The Seventies*, a special issue of *Southern Poetry Review* with the work of 33 Raleigh poets edited by Guy Owen; and *This Book Has No Title* (Third Coast/Amalgamated Holding Company), edited by Roger Mitchell, Roger Skrentny, & Kathleen Wiegner, presenting 30 Milwaukee poets. Though *This Book Has No Title* is the more visually exciting, the two books share much in common: both are interested in the breadth rather than the depth of the poetry being written in the respective cities. Each allots space for one-to-four poems per poet; what results is a broad over-view of the work going on in each city. Side by side, the two books reveal the two cities' differences of concern; yet together they show also the common concern for craft & its possibilities, experimentation with technique & image, with thing & idea & language. And, not surprisingly, the two books show us each city has its very good poets, as well as its poor ones. What holds each anthology together is the accident of place, but it is more than that as well: for whether we admit is or not, our work is shaped by the work around us, unless we live in a vacuum; yet, in touch with more than our own city we are not bounded or confined by it.

The editing in these anthologies is not so democratic as in *Freek*, not so tight as in *The Musician Plays For Richard*; if *Are You Ready For The New Ultra Violence?* is a news flash sent out in haste, *This Book* & *Raleigh Poetry* are feature stories, filling in the past, projecting into the possibilities of the future. Both books are best seen, perhaps, as records, but not in any stultifying sense: records of the shape of the poetry of a particular city over a certain period of time. In this they are valuable.

The Giligia Press's *Down At The Santa Fe Depot: 20 Fresno Poets* (edited by David Kherdian & James Baloian) & *Brewing: 20 Milwaukee Poets* (edited by Martin J. Rosenblum) look at the city in a way different from *This Book* & *Raleigh Poetry*; the perspective is equally as valuable. Neither *Santa Fe Depot* nor *Brewing* is concerned with breadth so much as depth. Each volume presents the work of twenty poets &, including photograph and biographical statement, allows each poet generally six to eight pages. As with *This Book* & *Raleigh Poetry*, these volumes evidence both differences & similarities between the poets of Fresno & those of Milwaukee. The poets in the Fresno anthology are linked less by common vision than by similarities of techniques; the poets in *Brewing*, on the other hand, share more their concerns than techniques. But what comes through each volume is a fairly clear picture of the shape of poetry in each city.

Both types of editing—that for breadth we find in *This Book* & *Raleigh Poetry*, that for depth in *Santa Fe Depot* & *Brewing*—are valuable. Ideally, perhaps, we might find, as we do in Milwaukee, an anthology of each type: one to complement & fill out the other, to allow us to see the broad sweep & to plumb the depths.

The two Giligia anthologies also serve to indicate another side of what is, in one sense, small press publishing: highly professional looking uniform editions. Both books meet, I'm sure, most of the production standards of commercial presses; but neither is confined by the standards—the intent may be a saleable product, but we do not find the slick flash & glitter common to many commercial books. However Giligia might be defined, it retains some of the best qualities of the small press.

Books from New Rivers Press are generally as well produced as those from Giligia, and *Towards Winter*, edited by Robert Bonazzi, is no exception. We might complain about the illustrations in some other New Rivers' books, but in this anthology of largely quiet protest poetry, the drawings by Lucas Johnson fit the mood & temper of the work. The focus in *Towards Winter* seems to be American poets' quiet & continuing anger against both the large & the little atrocities we perpetuate upon each other—the Vietnam war, for instance, or our own petty in-fighting.

We might consider *Towards Winter* a highly selective "national" anthology, bringing together poets not of city or region as do others I've discussed, bringing together not the "New American Poets" of *Contemporaries* & a hundred other anthologies, rather bringing together poets from across the country, poets such as Bly, Wright, Simic, Knoepfle, Lipsitz, Mitchell, Truesdale, Mark Van Doren, Merton & others whose poems here are linked by mood & concern &, in some cases, the use of image. What is intended in the anthology seems to have been clear from the beginning, in 1968 when the first edition was produced; this second enlarged edition explores the ground more fully, finding fresh nuances in the quiet anger.

Towards Winter is clearly an anthology of theme. In the anthologies already discussed, theme was an incidental concern; though the critic may discover common links of concern, image & idea in an anthology out of a city or region, the intent in such cases is less theme than a fair reflection of the shape of an area's poetry. Indeed, an anthology such as *Jukebox Poems* reveals six Chicago poets' affinities—the concerns, the moods, even the techniques so common to all; but, I think it may be fair to say, this is a social rather than a purely literary phenomenon.

Likewise, whatever common themes & concerns are seen in the work of the poets in *Contemporaries: 28 New American Poets* (Viking Press), edited by Jean Malley & Hale Tokay, the purpose is to present a broad range of work by young poets, "mostly in their twenties". Some of the poets are black, half are women, & most have published books with small presses or have appeared in little magazines. For the most part, this is fresh poetry; the poets are in touch with the Seventies; the twenty-eight idioms, the twenty-eight visions reflect this decade. The editors are also in touch with the mood of the times, and not only represent women fairly, but also reflect the trend to include "songs" with poetry —we find here lyrics of three songs by the Chicago Women's Liberation Rock Band.

Though at the opposite end of the spectrum, *Contemporaries* might best be compared to *Are You Ready For The New Ultra Violence?* because what each intends, what each achieves is a message, at a certain time, out of a certain awareness, about the current shape of things—in small press, or the 'new poetry' or whatever. It is difficult to call a 228-page book a news-flash, but *Contemporaries* has that feel—more so, for instance, than Spring Rain Press's *The Musician Plays For Richard*.

If *Contemporaries* has a weakness, it is its cover & the kind of thinking the cover represents. We find a pop drawing incorporating the style, the images, the color of 'chic' awareness; that the Statue of Liberty on the back cover is flipping-the-bird rather than holding the torch can only be intended, I would think, to help sell the book: yes, boys & girls, be the first on your block to have this book of poetry by men & women not afraid to tell it like it is. What I object to is not the almost quaint (nowadays) obscene gesture; I object to the crass commercial incorporation of the hip "new awareness" by a big house publisher intent not upon further development of awareness nor even radical "chic" imitation but upon commercial appeal. The cover is, in effect, a sellout of the concerns, sensitivities, visions of the poetry within. I recognize Viking's need to have a marketable product, but I can more easily excuse a messy small press production job which, while it may detract from the poetry in a given book, does not, at least, run essentially counter to the grain of the poetry's intent.

I am making the cover of *Contemporaries* a scape-goat, of course; I do not mean to detract from the poetry in the book itself; I do mean to emphasize what can be seen here as one of the significant differences between straight & small presses. Small presses might bungle the production of a book of poetry, but there are few which would sell the poetry out. The fact that *Contemporaries* is intended to put a large number of people in touch with good, solid writing by young, 'contemporary' poets—a worthwhile endeavor, to be sure—does not excuse the cover.

It is difficult, ultimately, to make any final & definitive statements about the nature of 'anthology' from an examination of so few anthologies. However, I think we can see that, as I indicated earlier, a good anthology has to have its special concern—be it the city, the mood, or the shape of things; it is as if a 'situation' prompts an anthology, the situation being revealed as we read, the editorial hand showing through. And I think we can also see that if an anthology, as a physical entity, serves the purpose of the editing—whether it is mimeo-produced as a small press news-flash or produced professionally as an enduring record of poets' common anger—then the physical document itself serves a useful & vital function interrelated with the editorial vision.

There are, undoubtedly, more editorial visions & more technical methods of production than we can ever adequately discuss. But the ten anthologies I've examined might hint at least at directions & possibilities we can explore at our leisure.

FIRST ISSUES: FIVE NEW LITTLES

We are born. We live. We die. Hopefully, when we go, we leave something of value. Our children are born, they live; they die; and their children. Process: generation/decay. There is a metaphor here. New little magazines commence publication; old ones cease; some run for one issue, some for five or six, some for longer than we care to read them.

In the first issue of a new little, *Openspaces* (Los Angeles), the editors call the magazine "a field of poems. Play the field. . . An open space, windowless." This too can be a metaphor: new little magazines springing up, unbounded by windows or traditional ways of doing things or traditional prejudices. No hard rules, no set laws: variety, limited only by the limitations of the editor/publisher's vision, energy, and talents. Such variety can be healthy; we do not need, yet, to publish as underground Russian writers publish, in *samizdat*, typed copies of manuscripts passed on and re-typed, passed on and typed again. We are not strapped so tightly, yet; and perhaps the ongoing process of little magazine birth-death-rebirth, generation/decay, may help prevent such a state of affairs in our culture. The act of publishing separate from all economic necessity: the little magazine can be a hand pulling cultural strappings loose, owing nothing to anyone, standing only by the editor/publisher's integrity. If we appreciate our writing and *Esquire* doesn't, if our friends value it and *Poetry* doesn't, if we have something of value to pass on to a larger audience than our manuscripts can reach: then the little magazine, then the small press book. Publishing as a philosophic necessity: the object is not to move from the little magazine to *Esquire, Playboy, Atlantic;* the object is to say what is to be said, in a forum available and to the purpose. If present cultural conditions demand that a sizeable amount of new writing appear only in little magazines and the small press, then each new magazine to appear can be another hand at the strap, promising a kind of publishing that is directed at a fresher culture. The first issue of each new little magazine becomes a sign of health.

It is perhaps especially first issues that can interest us: holding the promise, pointing directions, displaying perhaps rough yet radiant vitality. In later issues, we may find ourselves measuring a magazine against what it had promised, and judging it as we ought to; and later still, sometimes, we see the old-timers begin to ossify, energy dissipated or vision constricted or original purpose outlived and out-moded. With first issues, though, we can imagine what there is to be imagined: tell ourselves, for all the setbacks around us, all is not lost.

Openspaces 1 is handset and handprinted in an edition of 450 copies; contributors include Jarold Ramsey, John Leax, Larry Levis, Dudley Laufman, Bob Brown, Carl Selkin, Geoffrey Greene, and Elizabeth Brown. The production job is clean and clear; the editing is not constricted, shows the poet "as the complete editorial farmer".

Jarold Ramsey presents both a visual poem and three linear, verbal poems. Ramsey is comfortable with both the more formally stated poem, (e.g. "Ergo Propter Hoc": "When we stood in the swelling moon/ knowing our old powers renewed/ in the gleam of an eye or tooth/ and three times you found a star and cried/ *Look how it moves!* and it did. . . " etc) and the more conversational ("The Courier, A Gratuitous Myth": "After endlessly hemming and hawing/ God decided to cancel death./ Anyway he had made his point./ Anyway the quick/dead distinction/ had grown more degree-wise than kind-wise. . . . If you know someone with a foot in the grave/ say to him *Friend, sit tight!*).

And the editors, likewise, are comfortable with a variety of poetries. We find John Leax's taut, worked poetry in his "Three Poems for Linda"; from "1":

a year
has only

if anything

nourished
that
shiver
i felt
when you first
blossomed
pink
in my eyes. . .

We find a strange, loose sort of surrealism in Levis' "Into the Late
Show", the surrealism inherent in the material itself, descriptively recounted. And Levis writes the rich, quiet lyric also, as in "nights" which
which reads in full:

On nights
when the snow threatens to keep
falling until misery is extinct
we could pass by and nod
and say only
how cold it is,
how quiet. I will think of how
the timber wolf's back turns white
as he goes on trotting

*

On Hollywood Boulevard, they leave
the lights burning in upholstery shops
all night

*

This morning the bare elm is full of crows again.

Verbal and syntactical elements are explored in *Openspaces 1*, nota-
bly in Dudley Laufman's "If Only", which reads:

If Only
it were
Friday
were
Christmas

were not
Monday

were me
or her

instead
of letters

were such
that she

were always
I wouldn't

have to even
think of

sitting &
saying

The kinds of poetry in *Openspaces* shows the editors essentially correct in saying the magazine is "a field of poems". There are few straight rows in the field; rather, a rich variety of materials, set down according to need.

Pot-Hooks & Hangers (New York), like *Openspaces*, presents a variety of poetries: but instead of hand-worked letterpress, production is clean, clear offset; instead of eight contributors in 40 pp., we find twenty-six contributors filling forty-eight pages. And the writers fill the pages well; I confess many of the poets included in this first issue are unknown to me—and the contributors' notes, though interesting, do not help me place them; but these poets are good evidence there is considerably more good writing around than can be adequately published by conventional means, or even unconventional means for that matter.

There is, here, the striking clarity of Barry Wallenstein's "Light in Her Window", which reads:

It was the season of her dryness.
Above the wax of candles
the flame itself failed:
after the wax the candle failed.

Electricity drew the moths.
Changed, they flew out of their bodies.
Soon they forgot they were once not dry.
Hitting her window they shed their powder.

All light gathers living things.
But this time, by lamp light,
this girl reads alone.
Her memory omits the striking of wings.

A pack of insects, dry as dust,
pile at the window.

The precision of the imagery, the cohesion of parts in the poem, the fresh turns of language ('her memory omits'), and the whole metaphor/

mood set by the poet around 'this girl reads alone', make the poem as
an expression/relation of an experience, and as a linguistic contrivance,
a remarkably tight & rich creation.

Wallenstein's is not the only poetry here: we find also Kathleen Cho-
dor's almost sardonic linear musings in "Thought Before the Saline In-
jection":

> you wanted me to be
> and I expected to be
> the tragic heroine. crying,
> wringing my hands, unnerved, guilty;
> thinking in terms of a life and a murder,
> souls and sin. instead,
> I find myself more annoyed
> at having to lay out my winter coat money
> because you were too selfish
> to put on the bag.

Not especially remarkable as a poem (the white/male critic speaking),
yet poignant, an awareness that may be new to some of us, for which
we are inadequately prepared to criticize. Similarly, we are faced with
Deborah Keenan's less linear yet equally sharp perceptions in "Jane and
the Theory of Relativity":

> Jane told me today
> in the midst of sunlight
> flashing through B-kin
> that we are particles
> of light
> reflecting to a degree
> unheard of before
> in my literary life-style
> Jane told me today
> that we are waves of the
> cosmos   glinting
> lavender   purple   green
> my first thought
> was
> Jane is too intelligent
> to be my best friend
> my second thought
> was perhaps, jesus
> had a halo
> because his light particles
> were not in tune with
> the universe

my third thought
was i am probably a very
chunky particle
of light
and i might be of scientific
interest
in a laboratory
my last thought
was the sunshine
came through her hair
and made it glow
with autumn colors
through the dark
and that she was
beautiful

If there is a weakness in this issue of *Pot-Hooks & Hangers,* it is the few easy poems: the cliched image or word, the prefabricated emotion. In the main, however, the magazine has that vitality characteristic of first issues, and has something more: solid writing, crisp editing—and if not the newest of breakthrough poetry, at least it is highly competent, and of several kinds.

Old Friends (Washington, D.C.), in its first issue, seems to have a purpose different from either *Openspaces* or *Pot-Hooks*: "*Old Friends* is a literary magazine published quarterly by a group of writers and artists in and around Washington, DC. . . " We find work here by four of *Old Friends'* six editors, and by one other contributor: not an intrinsically evil or insidious way to publish, but the result in this case seems to be a lack of editorial rein. Poets are not always the best judges of their work, and editor/poets likewise: I am not criticizing self-publishing as a way of publishing; rather, if you want to publish yourself, have someone more distanced do the editing. *Old Friends* is by no means the only little magazine that suffers from such closeness, but it is fairly clear evidence that a writer and an editor and a publisher do not always successfully function in one person, especially when the editor is editing himself. *Samizdat*, the Russian form of self-publishing, seems to have inherent editorial standards: manuscript re-typing is both tedious and dangerous, and works so reproduced would be, I would think, closely judged by those doing the work as to whether they are worth the time and the risk. Self-publishing in America is easier and less dangerous, and lacks the standards inherent in the Russian method.

All of which is not to say that there isn't good work in *Old Friends*: Kelp Homburger (the non-editor contributor to this issue) has a number of good pieces, e.g., "For Rent":

We live together on a month to month basis
    Renting our space in each other's lives.

Subletting our love.
Using it as a temporary refuge.
And prepare to move out before the first of next month.

Or co-editor William Mayville's "Latticework Time":

Latticework time has come,
when porchfronts need covering.
Saplings ooze life and prepare the earth
for the trunks of aged trees.
A firebird is among us with blossoms
in its beak to pass as a magnolia tree
in bloom. I have seen some
that would pass as love.

Or a few other scattered pieces in the issue.

The problem, with too large a share of the poems, is sentiment: language, imagery, line, the bag of tricks we use as discipline in poetry are not enough in evidence here, cannot in such sparing amounts, keep sentiment from slipping into sentimentality; David Allen's "Old Friends" is one example:

Poems are old friends that i used to know
and the new ones yet waiting to be met.
sometimes they're so complex
i can't remember their names,
sometimes they're so simple i can't forget.
stranger companions
could never be found
they bring you down when up
and up when down.
but in the lonely night
they provide a lamp of light
and my heart smiles with contentment
to their sound.

We cannot condemn *Old Friends* as a publishing venture: 'If we appreciate our writing and *Margins* doesn't, if our friends value it and *Margins* doesn't. . . " We can hope, though, that the editors are successful, in future issues, in widening the circle of friends and friendly contributors.

Star-Web Paper (Laurinburg, NC), unlike the other four first issues examined here, is crowded; it is also set on typewriter rather than compositer. Yet in many ways both these physical realities add interest to the magazine: we find 'little' in little—38 contributors in 30 pages, plus artwork, photographs, contributors' notes, etc. Some of the writers

here are 'known' among small pressmen—Randall Ackley, Ronald H.
Bayes, Peter Wild, Ben L. Hiatt, F.A. Nettelbeck, Lyn Lifshin, John Ja-
cob, Stephen Morse, Emilie Glen, A.D. Winans, etc. Others are local
(Chatham, NJ) or just less well-known writers.

As with *Openspaces* and *Pot-Hooks & Hangers*, there is a variety of
materials; there is also a good deal of variation in the quality of the material here. Ben L. Hiatt contributes a highly evocative, tightly worked
"Mountain Dream" which ends:

> these seemingly ageless
> hills
> age with
> a different measurement
> of time
> than any
> man could recognize
>
> who knows what
> spirits
> walk
> the mountains
> when the moon goes bad
> & another barren year
> half gone.

Brother Dimitrios sets down the "Birth of the Avenging Gods" in the
strange way he sees it. The poem opens:

> w/ my first kicks rhinos reached for their rainbows,
> albinos bowled bronze bricks into bronco busting beauticians
> peacocks & peasants jittered in the jasmine
> & Tooshboombaloomba, Me Kusmik Mum,
> sucked lakes Tanganyika & Titicaca dry . . .

Larry Robert Zirlin's "Storm" winds itself down, finds silence:

> The air
> snaps
> apart
>
> sound
> of leather
> on leather
>
> a knife
>   slits

```
        the middle
of    a    taut
sheet

a floodlight
behind it
flares
burns
out
```

Unfortunately, however, some of the poems in this issue are marked by roughness of, & insensitivity to, language, lack of opened inherent form, lack of awareness of what makes a good poem: some such poems may be said to be competent, in an academic sense, but good poetry requires more than what we are able to find in Amy Chalif's poem, for instance:

```
    I clench my fists
            and cry
            a little.
    I cannot comprehend
        the worthlessness
                of living
    and think it unfair
that death
    should be the only one
            who knows
                what he's doing.
```

Or in S. Peterson Fisher's:

```
Let's go together down to the sunrise
See the mountains, stars, screaming out,
Past it all further out and then. . .
```

Still, the magazine is physically intriguing, and there is, yes, a good deal of solid material here. What we find on one page may not be to our taste, but there is enough poetry that, by the end, we find more than a little to appreciate.

Isthmus: the first crossing (Berkeley) is the largest and, in one sense, the most professional of the first issues I am examining. Thirty-three contributors present 104 pages of poetry, criticism and artwork. Several poets contribute three or more poems; Andrei Codrescu gives us eleven, including "For Phoebe, Nancy, Alice, Lewis, Bill and myself":

```
There has been a shower of babies around here
as if the sky needed the clarity,
```

the clean clarity of our bodies
emptying themselves and
continuing.
There has been an anxiety here before these babies,
a question from the beyond.
Since we have answered in the affirmative
and since we are part of each other
we can now look at a flower
and not think of something else.
It's been good coming clear through.

Later, editor J. Rutherford Willems evaluates three of Codrescu's books
in a lengthy essay.

Other contributors include David Meltzer, David Gitin, Lewis Mac-
Adams, Diane de Prima, Paul Mariah, Theodore Enslin, etc. And Julie
Vose, with "Unmoney My Love":

our fleece changed hands
so many times
we thought it was money
Blood we had is holy
Bread & honey
let itself without leeches
disappear into our rooms
How our windows of tight water
slip down
old walls full of face fish
Everything we or the land
stick up
MELT
Intelligent cell make the way
to carry itself
fruit
If there must be tools
HAMMER!
nail our eyes shut
in the beginning

Isthmus has much to recommend it as an ambitious magazine. Yet,
I have an uncomfortable feeling, like an ache behind my eyes, dully:
the editorial vision, perhaps, is not quite clear, or some of the contributors blend into the next, or something equally difficult to get at; I am
hoping to see a second issue soon, to ease the small discomfort, to show
a sharpness equal to the breadth of the ambition evident here.

Five new magazines aren't going to shake the traditional literary establishment apart, much less make any changes in our culture; change is

a far slower process: generation/decay, in a time-space continuum. Yet: each new perception, each fresh awareness, presented in these five magazines, or in older magazines for that matter, alter to some extent subsequent perceptions of the readers they touch. We cannot hope for cultural revolution in a broad-ranging and immediate sense. Rather, we work for the small changes, finding something useful today, leaving something useful tomorrow.

OPENING SOME DOORS

William J. Robson's *Holy Doors* is a big (136 pp.) one-shot anthology of poetry (mostly Southern Californian), prose (some interesting stories), & criticism. Included here are an inside look at Marvin Malone's *Wormwood Review* (as well as two letters by James Laughlin responding to Malone's charge that New Directions has collapsed inwards) and an interview (by Robson) with Deena Metzger, a Los Angeles poet. Both pieces are interesting & valuable in themselves, as information—& are particularly so for those who enjoy reading about writing and publishing.

Included here also are pieces by Hugh Fox on the business of publishing in America, Rich Mangelsdorff on the current state of reviewing & criticism, & Felix Pollak on "What Happened to the 'Little' in Little Magazine?"

In his piece, Fox grinds what seems to be an old & dull ax—the difficulty of getting his manuscripts into print; the burden of the blame seems placed on the publishers rather than on the manuscripts themselves, something that John Martin of Black Sparrow Press, points out in response to Fox's criticism of his publishing. Fox's piece, & another by Steve Richmond, prompt other infighting: a letter from Charles Bukowski on writing & getting paid for it, on being "known & unknown", etc. Ashbel Green, managing editor of Alfred A. Knopf also answers charges by Fox; though disagreeing with him on most points, Green concludes his letter: ". . . but I'm glad that alternative publishers exist to show us up when we go wrong." At least, Fox's piece, & the responses to it, air some dirty laundry.

For his part, Mangelsdorff notes that "criticism gets more 'micro' all the while; it is, for the time being, perhaps, being 'microed' right out of any meaningful existence at all." He makes a fairly good point, if you can get past Mangelsdorff's tone & way of talking.

Felix Pollak, in his piece, overstates the case for 'elitism' in little magazines. Though it may well be true that the history of little magazines has been one of elitism, it is a mistake to patently project such elitism into the future: Pollak, I think, is more interested in talking about what little magazines have been, rather than about what they can become.

He says that "A true littlemag is one that would not be big if it could; that is, not kept little by need, by tight purse strings, but that would shun book-keeping hassles, invoice-in-triplicate, a distribution apparatus and all attendant bureaucracy and red tape. . ." But aren't book-keeping hassles as much "need" in Pollak's sense as "tight purse strings"; certainly, this is no way to define little magazine.

Pollak says further: "A true little mag would rather address itself to a selected (elitist) group of kindred spirits than to an inchoate faceless void of anonyms." The choice Pollak offers, apparently, is only between the 'elite' and 'the faceless void'; however, there are more alternatives than that: the fact that small press people have in the past talked pretty much to themselves is no argument for their continuing to do so. What is needed are not further calls for elitism, but solid explorations of possible ways little magazines & literature-in-the-making can reach out into the community to affect the contemporary sensibility & the shaping of our culture. I realize that little mag editors feel isolated and alienated, & that there is comfort in kindred spirits: but are we isolated because others shun us, or because we shun them? Too often, I think, our dogmatic elitism requires that we *not* give the intelligent reader the opportunity to see & understand the processes that go into making & publishing literature. I am not asking that we accept the evil in the world around us, the shallow values or beliefs, the requirements of 'economic necessity'; I am not asking that little magazines publish & distribute 2,000 or 5,000 or 10,000 copies of an issue. Rather, I am asking that we change our stance toward the American reading public: not lower our standards, not publish 'popular' trash, but to change the popular taste where it must be changed, educate where education is necessary, & at all times have the decency to allow the intelligent reader to use his intelligence. If we don't, if we continue to lay bricks on the wall already between small press & the American reading public, I'm afraid we shall one day find that for all our good intentions we are no longer in touch with any real world, that we are locked in ivory towers as remote as any ivy-clad scholar's.

Still, Pollak's piece, & *Holy Doors* generally, might serve to encourage the reader to look at other little mags & small press publications; & this too is useful.

REVIEWING THE REVIEW

There is an incredible amount of energy flowing through small press today: no doubt about it. The number of little magazines & small press books that appear here daily is clear evidence, something important is going on. This is not to say sheer numbers, quantity, guarantees quality; on the contrary, we have to pick through little magazines & small press books as carefully as we do through publications from university & commercial presses. We have to admit that, for all its energy and vitality, small press does suffer too often from inbreeding & snobbery.

Inbreeding is perhaps a natural consequence of the state of small press today: much of the energy that flows, flows in a circle. Editors & publishers encourage & support each other (as well as attack & criticize): ideas & plans & theories are worked out in bull-sessions, or more often, in letters. We modify each other.

Snobbery, too, is perhaps a natural result of the present condition. Shunted to second or third place (or farther down the line) by the "professional" critics—or even worse, ignored by them—small press folks take refuge in elitism: in the belief that the disdain for or the slighting of the small press occurs because we are ahead of the times, because the critics & public are not keeping step. Often enough, perhaps, this is true; but it does not excuse snobbish isolationism.

The problem is this: if small press is to exist as a workable alternative to the commercial & university presses, it must break out of its closed circle & begin to direct its energy outward. There is material of value in small press, but inbreeding & elitism keep it here. The task is to get small press materials before the reading public: I am still so naive as to believe that once the public has access to it, they will appreciate its value &, we hope, lend it support.

Small Press Review has been the trade magazine of small press since 1967. Len Fulton seems, to a large extent, to have seen the need to turn our energies outward. *Small Press Review* is one result. Fulton's *Directory of Little Magazines, Small Presses & Underground Newspapers* is another. Both publications go some way towards making the small press more visible & more accessible. *Small Press Review*'s circulation is listed at around 2,000; so it is out "there" &, we hope, making some impressions.

But even in *Small Press Review*, what we read too often sounds as if we are talking (again) to ourselves. The writing is sometimes too familiar (Jack's mag, Bill's poem); sometimes clipped references allow only the 'initiated' to know what is being said. I admit to this fault myself: there is some consolation in having knowledge that others lack, & in flaunting it. But if we want to avoid ending up with our noses stuck in the air or in each others' ears, we have to be clear, critical, complete, and maybe, interesting; we have to be facing outwards when we are speaking.

I do not mean to sound as if I'm attacking a Chevrolet for not being a Ford: I mean to underscore the fact that we have to remember who our audience is, or should be: what literature is & whom it is for.

Needless to say, as the primary trade journal small press has had, *Small Press Review* to date has done the small press scene any number of good turns. It has probably reviewed more little magazines & small press books than any other magazine around; has pointed out impor-

tant work we might otherwise have missed; has, in effect, been recording the pulse of the small press scene when there were no others to do
it.

There have been errors of judgment, of course. There is much more
to be said for women's literature, for instance, than was said in the special women's issue edited by Alta. Again: some of the reviewers are beginning to bore me, chopping at old corpses with dull axes.

But in the main—& this is its strength—*Small Press Review* has af-
firmed the belief that there is much of value in the small presses; that it
should not pass unnoticed; that, for all the kinks & quirks in it, this is
where the literature is in-the-making. In the face of the continual frustration & discouragement that seem to mark small press, *Small Press
Review*'s first six years & 13 issues are no small achievement.

NOTES ON WOMEN'S PUBLICATIONS

There is little doubt we need, and need very badly, such women's
publications as *Amazon, Marin Women's News Journal, Aphra, The Ladder, Libera* and *Moving Out*: in these days, our culture has become cultures, and such journals can and do provide ongoing records of new perceptions and fresh ways of being. It is not only women's publications I
am thinking of in this regard, of course, but publications of several sorts:
black, Amerindian, Chicano, and gay, to name some. We can hope that
such a variety of publications serves to inform, educate, guide, arouse
American readers as is necessary if America is not to go, in the long run,
the way of the Roman and the British and various other empires.

When we exclude, when we belittle and denigrate, when we deny an
effective voice to any sector of our population, we are signing our own
death warrants. If this society and its culture is to be healthy, to become healthy, new viewpoints, and old viewpoints too long ignored
and pressing once again, must be heard. We cannot afford to close our
doors, close ourselves in: especially at this juncture, when so many human possibilities can be realized if we open ourselves to them, women's
publications and others can make fertile what is sterile and constricted
in our male-dominated literature.

Fresh consciousness, and fresh perceptions about ways of being and
behaving in the world, new treatment of old "classical" materials and
attempts to form literature out of new and hitherto untouched areas of
human experience and concern can innervate and invigorate our literature and our society: *if* such consciousness and such perceptions are given voice and space and audience.

There are several forces working against just such a turn of events,
and these have to be overcome: and overcome with conscious, careful,
deliberate work. The most immediate contravening force is, perhaps,

the power and the prejudice of editors and publishers in America. Few want to be the first to send up the balloon, to test the untested and give approval, to stick the first neck out; the power of the American publisher lies wasted, in safety. It is, however, a continual problem, one faced when William Blake was around, faced again by Wordsworth and Coleridge, faced admirably in the early part of this century with the first modern littles. Today, however, the new idea is even less safe—perhaps partly because of vast increases in the cost of publishing, but otherwise chiefly because we do hesitate gravely to alienate those we already have on our side (i.e., subscribers, patrons, regular contributors, and their esteem) and go against the weight of literary tradition; and we do, for all our proclaimed openness, cherish our pet values and theories to the point that they often blind us to values inherent in other viewpoints.

But publishing, if it is to remain vital and become more significant a force in our daily lives than it has been in the past, is going to have to cease being the industry it is and begin functioning as a service to ideas and people. And today, effective service to people and ideas demands that editors and publishers have an "effective" openness to new kinds of writing and thinking and living—not the tokenism of popular publishing on popular topics of the day, but substantial work that innovates, risks, and yes perhaps fails.

We can no longer expect commercial publishers to make significant breakthroughs in this regard. The trade houses made their contribution in the twenties and thirties, publishing the writers we now come to read and revere. Since then, however, their surest course has been generally the safe course, though of course we can cite exceptions.

We who consider ourselves alternative publishers might like to think that the "underground papers", as an example, have made significant progress in the area, for instance, of giving women equal participation and equal voice. However, a recent study published in *Underground Press Revue* indicates that it just ain't so: in most of the radical-underground journals, women still serve in traditional capacities.

And, more to the point here, editors and publishers of little magazines and likewise small presses have either not seen their responsibilities toward vast sections of the population, or have seen and ignored them.

Little magazines are seldom more "integrated" (in all senses of the term) than are the larger more prestigious journals, and seldom more sympathetic, aware, or interested in many instances. Women writers, for instance, can and do complain about white-male editorial judgment and values: partly the problem is one of isolation and exclusiveness, in terms of what the little mag is attempting. But partly the problem consists of lack of interest: failure to remain open to what has not received the approval of fellow-travelers; or failure to consider the larger responsibilities of publishing in our culture as responsibilities for which the little magger has to answer. The white-male editor's problem (and it is his problem) is compounded by the traditionally defined male identity and role.

What courses are open to the "new" writers whose viewpoints are being excluded space in small journals and elsewhere? They can and must, first, establish and publish their own journals. The condition of women today requires feminist publications of several types. But, secondly, if women and others have regard for the larger ramifications of what they are about, they may see the need, as I do, for cross-fertilization: for informing and educating and raising the consciousness of the white-male editors they can often rightly despise; if what we are aiming at is a human and humane civilization, then at some point, now or 20 years from now or 100 years from now, each of us is going to have to be aware of, sensitive to, affected by the other.

Women will lose, I think, if the "official" culture continues to be male-defined and male-dominated. For, like it or not, it is the "official" culture which has the most significant effect on the largest number of Americans, that touches the daily lives of the citizens as our publications do not.

White-male editors will not have met their responsibilities until American women have freed themselves. Women writers will not have achieved any final and lasting breakthroughs until they have been able to affect and change the male-dominated literary hierarchy: women's journals alone are not enough—what is also required is cooperation with sympathetic male editors and publishers, not subservience or yes-saying, but solid work by equal partners, significant and substantive discussion of differing viewpoints; and, as few of us change easily, badgering and harassment when it is called for, and sometimes when it's not called for. Sometimes even literary saturation bombing.

The goal, the desired outcome, is responsible and responsive little magazines and small press publishing. Feminist publications, yes, and little magazines that are sensitive to a far broader range of materials than is presently the case. Ultimately we need a working definition of publishing that goes beyond concern for merely the traditionally acceptable literature, or the traditionally 'unacceptable' literature of the little magazine: hard goals to achieve, for new writers now excluded, and hard goals for smallpresspeople. But they are goals worth striving for.

The second force working against new consciousness and new perceptions receiving voice and space and audience is, I fear, the traditional structure of idea/information dissemination in our culture. These include: the review journals which call attention to publications, magazine and book distributors, and libraries: all three are of concern here because all three have vast powers to promote or soft-pedal or to halt the advancement of new ideas. And it is here that there may well be mutual interest between new writers and current smallpresspeople, for both have grave difficulties in these areas.

I am doubtful that the current mass-circulation book review journals can be changed much: their areas of concern seem rigidly defined and adhered to.

I am doubtful that the more usual magazine and book distributors will prove significantly useful to the purposes either of the new writers or of smallpresspeople.

In both these areas, the record of the past is pretty clear. What seems required are viable alternative structures, i.e., review journals and distributors of our own which are able to reach into the community, pass on information and ideas, call attention where attention is deserved, set critical standards, deliver the goods where traditional structures have been unable and unwilling.

Small Press Review (Paradise, CA), *Shocks* (San Francisco) and *Margins* itself are, I think, valuable alternative review journals which are beginning to call attention, however limited, to significant ideas and resources that are otherwise ignored, and are beginning to help set the necessary critical standards. Likewise, there are a number of small distributors such as RPM and Serendipity, and mail-order houses such as Asphodel, which are making serious efforts and some progress in getting small press and other ignored materials before the reading public. Beyond these attempts, successful or unsuccessful as they may be at this point or in the future, the whole question of reviewing and distributing procedures deserves serious and extended study by interested organizations and individuals.

Libraries, in contrast to mass-circulation review journals and traditional distributing structures, because they can and do reach a large readership and because librarians do by and large feel a serious responsibility to their patrons, and beyond the patrons to Culture and cultures, hold a good deal of promise, in my view, as effective agents for the dissemination of new and unusual work. In the past, smallpress has had difficulty in this regard, to be sure, and I expect new writers looking for an effective forum will have similar difficulties. Although there are and will be difficulties, we should not abandon our efforts with respect to libraries and librarians, for libraries will, earlier than the reviews and distributors, see and accept their responsibility toward significant new publications, out of the small press and elsewhere.

We need a good deal of concentrated effort on the part of smallpresspeople and feminists and others: searching out librarians, talking to them, educating them. Budgets, with librarians, like budgets elsewhere, are probably a primary factor inhibiting progress in this area. The new and the strange and the small press usually end up receiving the crumbs of the budget, while the more usual publications, the prestige journals, commercial and university publishers' books, get the lion's share.

This is a natural consequence of traditional structures in our lives, but not one which cannot be surmounted with diligent work and long patience. Efforts to inform librarians to the value of little magazines, small press books, feminist, black, gay journals and publications, without putting that value out of true focus, will ultimately, I believe, be a

fruitful undertaking.

The final force I wish to discuss, one which both the above contravening forces may well be part of, is what we might call the slow-reaction-of-the-dinosaur syndrome: "official culture" has become monolithic in many respects, has become the dinosaur of our age: new ideas, new perceptions are incorporated into the system of cultural values slowly, often painfully so. When what is new is incorporated quickly, it is usually only in a chic or hip way, often for the purpose of selling something, i.e., Peter Max's drawings for one product or another product's use of "the female is the weaker of the sexes" as a truism that isn't always true.

Substantive change, however, reaching out into the lives of citizens, is far longer in coming than that: and when the change does come, it does so usually in ways far removed from what we might like to expect. Polemicists and fiery propagandists serve to raise issues, get them public attention, but it is usually the moderate, middle-of-the-roaders who finally lead the greatest numbers a little way along the road of progress. The next bit of progress comes similarly, and so on, as what at first seems radical and impossible infiltrates the thinking of a larger and larger number of people. But it is slow-paced change, and in the long run, we best serve what we value if we accept its reality and use its structures to our benefit, at the same time creating our own structures.

This is the practical approach, which may well stand in contrast to our ideals. But we must remember that we have many actual and potential audiences: those who are aware of, and agree with what we may be saying; those who are uninformed about our goals; and those large numbers for whom any change is frightening, and who are, therefore, perhaps hostile to our way of thinking. We can speak clearly to the first audience. We can inform and educate and argue with the second. But the third audience, those whom change frightens, we must leave, finally, to the moderating voice of those who can be reassuring.

I do not mean to say that we ought to temper our views for the sake of one or other audience. Rather we ought to be fiery as we need to be, for the compromise proposal seems all the more modest in comparison. And it is most often by compromise that change occurs.

Changing our culture's stance toward women, and women writers, seems an especially difficult task. Women have not lived separated from men by ghetto walls, however invisible; men and women have rubbed shoulders, though seldom on an equal basis, and such familiarity leads to stereotypes that are perhaps more difficult to overcome than stereotypical views of those who have lived apart from the dominating culture. The traditional role of women, deeply locked into our consciousness, our legal structure, our culture generally, so patently an unfair and oppressive role, has centuries of precedent and tradition and mythology: because cultural dynamics so heavily press women into that role, without their deliberated consent, measures to correct the situation need to be drastic: consciousnesses must be raised, those of women in the first place, as has been and is being done; but further those who wield power in this culture must be made aware of the grave injustices, editors and publishers, in this instance, and librarians, book reviewers and professors and booksellers.

The task of redefining the role of woman belongs largely to the women. In the past, the task has gone almost entirely to men. At this late date, the boot still pressing heavy, breaking the shackles that bind women requires that women act strongly, vehemently, violently, (violent, Webster's: 'marked by extreme force or sudden intense activity'); requires that they make their voices heard, and heard clearly, despite the opposition inherent in traditional structures.

In the case of women writers, this means seeking out and creating appropriate vehicles for their work: feminist journals and feminist presses can and do provide a forum in which the voices can be heard without distortion and misrepresentation and without being incorporated and neutralized by the larger culture. Feminist journals are the truly appropriate places to speak to the rest of the culture.

Unfortunately, however, with but few exceptions, feminist publications (like most alternative/small press publications) presently reach only a limited audience. The "women's pages" of large metropolitan newspapers reach a far larger audience, and though they sometimes do present information of value and insight into the women's movement, the whole question is one of the "women's problem": until traditional categories are broken down, until fair treatment of women is seen not as the "women's problem", but as a problem central to all our cultural structures and norms, progress will be nearly impossible. Television talk show interviews with leading feminists serve, as far as I have been able to discern, curiosity to a far larger degree than they serve the cause of women: feminists are viewed as aberrations to be put on display, poked at, parried with, for the sake of entertaining bored minds. The reality is, however, "women's pages" and talk shows reach the American public as feminist publications have not been able.

The answer is, it would seem, that feminist journals continue at all costs their vital work, but that extended efforts be made to influence the citadels of power: the temptation might be to moderate, but moderation and compromise are not for those at the front, not for those pulling the brand from the fire.

Women's publications, which in the context I use the term is synonymous with feminist publications, can and do serve various needs within the women's movement; some provide chiefly information for local needs, others are intended for a larger audience and present far ranging ideas and proposals, still others are interested in defining and publishing feminist writing. Each such goal is valuable—and perhaps there are other areas being covered, or needing to be covered, which I haven't mentioned.

Two journals, *Marin Women's News Journal*, published in Marin

County, San Rafael, California, and *Amazon*, published in Milwaukee, Wisconsin, serve primarily local needs. Both provide information about local events, resources, and services of interest to women. Both are vehicles for local poets, writers and artists. And both do, certainly, handle ideas, but often in the context of local circumstances, i.e., an article in the July 1973 issue of *Marin Women's News Journal* opens, "Several political events have occurred in Marin in recent days all of which have made a profound impression on me." The author, Barbara Boxer, goes on to analyze the events, theorizing as she goes, but also indicating practical directions that can be taken and giving phone numbers to call if the reader is interested in taking action. Similarly, in *Amazon,* June 1973, Andi McKenna, in her "$ and Medicine" discusses a local health services' situation. But certainly the context of her concern comes through clearly. Additionally, both journals do provide local writers space to discuss questions not necessarily related to local conditions, "think" pieces which often drive to the heart of problems women face; and sometimes, testimony (i.e., women's accounts of their oppression and their moves to overcome it, narration of events leading to personal liberation, etc.) plays a large and important role, first as witness to others embroiled in the struggle, and secondarily as a record of the struggle itself. Now may not seem the time to speak of the long range value of such records, "historical" value, but truly such documents may one day help plot other liberations as well.

Women's Studies Newsletter, subtitled "Clearinghouse on Women's Studies" and published by The Feminist Press, is comparable to the above two journals chiefly in the sense that it too is a vehicle for information: not so much on a local level as on a national; not so much on gut issues as those more institutional. The newsletter is academically oriented (i.e., "Closeup: Portland State University's Program", and "News from College Programs and Courses"), though "Tillie Olsen's Reading List" and "Books, etc." and information on women's conferences do serve wider needs.

But clearly *Marin Women's News Journal* and *Amazon* move from a source different from that of *Women's Studies Newsletter*: the former are gut-issue, grassroots publications and the concerns are highly charged and personal; the latter is more distanced, more reserved, more concerned with the academic side of the women's movement. Both types of concern are valuable, and both, I think, serve needs in their respective communities. Meeting personal and meeting institutional needs are complementary roles.

Because of the nature of the women's struggle—recognition and opportunity for achievement in an offensive and oppressive structure, the movement is necessarily highly political. And, accordingly, out of need, women's publications are political, both those openly political and those which are more nearly 'literary'. The political and the literary meet in women's writing as it has not in the white-mlae literature since the 30's, notwithstanding poets' involvement in the anti-war movement of the

60's, which while it made poets highly political, did not produce a literature rooted essentially in a new way of seeing and being, so much as
old perceptions re-stated. White-male political poetry, as a result, has
been largely propaganda, in its baldest form, rather than art intricately
and essentially correlated to politics. The politics is hung on an old poetics rather than informing it. The possibilities of a new political art
are still before us, and are achieveable, but not without some new fundamental fusions.

Because feminist art has resources deeper than "craft" and "material", i.e., because the new vision of the woman, and its expression in
poetry, fiction, art, photography, is rooted in and essential to what is
uniquely woman's—her perceptions, her dreams, ambitions and disap-
pointments—and because such vision is necessarily political today, woman's art fuses to itself a 'stance in the world' (that is, a politics). A
good deal of current political art fails, as I have said, because its stance
is separate from its poetic: though increasingly, I admit, to write at all
is a political act, fresh perceptions are becoming, more and more, revo-
lutionary, though the ultimate result of this condition is as yet unclear.
It may mean, by force of circumstances, that any poetry, even the simple nature lyric, is political art; or it may result in a 'clean' poetry that is
acceptable officially, and a 'dirty' poetry that is linked essentially to actual struggles in the world. Or, if worse comes to worst, and artists
aren't up to the challenge of ordering (some kind of order, defined by
the artist and not by Nixon, Mitchell, et al.) new perceptions, the final
outcome may well be the death of poetry with any real significance;
the neobaroque fiction and poetry current today should be a warning
that we are on the brink of such an eventuality. ("We", the white-male
writers in this culture who need more often to move beyond facile technique to substance).

Women's writing, I think, and that of others necessarily thrown into
the struggle for the sake of survival do not face such a dire possibility
so imminently, as is evidenced by the editorial note in *Libera no. 3:*

> On a political level, *Libera* deals with the contemporary woman
> as she joins with others in an effort to effect a change in her
> condition. Emotionally, it explores the root level of our feel-
> ings, those beyond the ambitions and purposes women have tra-
> ditionally been conditioned to embrace. One of our objec-
> tives is to provide a medium for the new woman to present her-
> self without inhibition or affectation. By illuminating not on-
> ly women's political and intellectual achievements, but also her
> fantasies, dreams, art, the dark side of her face, we come to
> know more of her depths, and redefine ourselves.

It is seldom that a more usual little magazine sets for itself such basic
and essential goals: often the goals are purely literary in the palest sense

of the word; but if a magazine does not transcend concern merely for problems of craft and writing as an exercise in self-preening, it will remain pale.

Libera, by its own declaration, sets its concerns deeply in the human condition—in its case, women's condition—than in craft alone: it is a political journal necessarily, not only in its dealing with "Vietnam: a Feminist Analysis" or "Female Heterosexuality: Its Causes and Cures" (in no. 3), but also in its poetry and fiction. Sharon Barba's poems are a case in point. "Little Poems for Sleeping With You" is a love lyric in the usual sense,

> It is where my arms stop
> that yours begin—someone is always
> resting a leg across a leg or
> tangling up in hands. . .
>
> we have lost the boundaries
> but forget to be afraid wondering
> when you lay yourself against me
> whose pulse it is you listen to.

but by the poem's final statement Barba is viewing woman on a fresh level. The poem concludes, ". . . even my sleep contains you". The poem is not polemical yet its message is clear—women are defining themselves, they and their visions and the pulses in their bodies are valuable —for women, for men, lovers or listeners or readers. "At Last" is more openly political, yet it too succeeds: speaking about a marriage apparently come to ruins, speaking to Martha, "No one counted/ your grief, his/ was so big/ we snagged on it." The final realization: "And [we] turn toward you,/ years late, learning,/ after his example,/ how you rise/ from any wreckage,/ fierce and/ unattended." In her "Letter Reaching Out to My Sister, 1600 Miles", her voice becomes more strident—"I cannot think of you/ apart from your men/ all those years/ you were potential for them"—though, speaking to her sister, the poem ends warmly:

> We are sisters
> we are the halves of woman
> Someday we will be healed
> and made whole
> and our daughters will not
> distinguish between us

This range of voices in Sharon Barba's poems are indicative of the range and tone of *Libera* as a whole. Even Joan Hand's "Female Heterosexuality: Its Causes and Cures", with its obvious political points, displays flashes of wit and humor and a keen sensitivity. The essay concludes, in part:

This paper was written in retaliation to the bullshit that's been coming down about all oppressed minorities. Poor people, women, blacks, chicanos, gays and all people who constitute a threat to white middle- and upper-class males are defined, classified and put out of the way.

As a gay woman I refuse to accept their definition of me. Possibly, if the other side is analyzed in the same way it dissects us, other oppressed people will throw away the headchains psychology has placed on them. The arguments they use to make us look sick can be turned around and used against them.

The Ladder, which commenced publication in 1956, was "published by Lesbains and directed to ALL women seeking full human dignity. . ." "Initially", its editorial statement continues, "*The Ladder*'s goal was limited to achieving the rights accorded heterosexual women, that is, full second-class citizenship. In the 1950's women as a whole were as yet unaware of their oppression. The Lesbian knew. . . . *The Ladder*'s purpose today is to raise all women to full human status, with all of the rights and responsibilities this entails; to include *all* women, whether Lesbian or heterosexual." For more than 16 years, a good deal before the concern became more commonly-shared, *The Ladder* was exploring the condition of women, and the more oppressed Lesbian.

It perhaps ought to be noted that, given the condition today, Lesbianism is a political as well as sexual way of being; Lesbians do not have the option open to heterosexual women—accepting traditional structures, fitting themselves unthinkingly into oppressed roles. And from present indications, Lesbians will remain on the forefront of the movement to free women from the structures to which they have been bound. And *The Ladder* for its part has presented substantial information—in terms of hard facts, and in terms of theory and idea; a look at an issue reveals fairly wide concerns, from "Sex and Sexuality" to "Middle Class Rape" to the proper perspective on Willa Cather, to women's stories, poems, plays. Lesbianism serves politically to give impetus—but the area of concern grows and grows.

Moving Out likewise has a broad range of interest; of itself it says, "*Moving Out* is edited by a cooperative of women who recognize the need for a medium through which women can share their experiences and ideas." It continues, "Publications dominated by males rarely provide an outlet for work which goes beyond traditional feminine limits. We need to encourage women to develop their talents as writers, artists, and editors."

The magazine devotes more space to the arts than was the case with

The Ladder. Where *The Ladder* may have some affinities with *Marin Women's News Journal* and *Amazon*, in terms of providing practical, action-directed information and analysis often in context, *Moving Out*, like *Libera* and *Aphra*, is more strictly literary within the context of the 'stance-craft' definition I gave earlier.

Like *Libera*, both *Moving Out* and *Aphra* display a range of voices, from quiet tentative explorations to strident cries of anguish. From *Moving Out*, "no. 2411" by Margaret Kaminski (Bennett):

> Funny how you begin
> to notice these things.
> So Penelope waits twenty years
> while Ulysses fools around
> with Calypso and Circe.
> So there's a token woman
> in the control room
> of the *Enterprise*.
> (She can at the same time
> serve as token black).
> Yes; a very open show.
> As open as the costumes
> the intergalactic cuties wear.
> (Even in other galaxies
> they get their hair done!)
> But with no avail,
> for Kirk is married to his star ship.
> But if he ever did squeeze
> a woman in (or squeeze into one),
> she'd wait for him
> just like Penelope.
>
> funny how you begin
> to notice these things.

And Georgia Kouklis's "Crete":

> Viewing the Minoan artifacts,
> vases of bare-breasted goddesses,
> the daughters of rocky and ancient soil,
> I meditated upon olive-skinned sisters
> and a woman's culture once more.

In *Aphra*, Rachel DuPlessis's "A Poem of Myself":

> Sometimes I cannot move at all and will not either

I imagine myself looking over a group of hills somewhere else, away.
In Italy.
The trees begin swaying as I watch them
Turning inward onto myself.

No. I am sitting on a terrace and no one is bothering me.

Standing in entrances. About to come in.
My shoulders are hunched forward to hide my breasts.
When am I going to come into the room?

Come in, come in, I say to all the fragments

And Barbara Gravelle's "The Fallen Woman":

The fallen woman fell
out of her husband's love
Their arms couldn't support her
any longer
She slid nonmelodiously
down the monochromatic scale
unaccompanied

Sitting on the bar stool
in one of "those bars"
she wondered how
to let the first comer
know that she had a price
tag on her rejection.

Manifestos of various sorts are in evidence in both journals, as they need
be; the focus, however, is explorations of the possibilities of women's
perceptions, and the artistic forms those perceptions can take. *Aphra*,
perhaps more than *Libera* and *Moving Out*, has the spare, clean look of
a professional journal professionally produced; but it retains, with the
two other journals, its links with gut issues of the women's movement.
The range of materials, and of production in these three journals, and
The Ladder too, are necessary for defining the issues, identifying feminist art, for putting women into a perspective that does them full justice.

These journals are not flawless, of course; they and the women writing for them are, however, making extensive and solid explorations of
both woman's condition and her art. Self-definition is a difficult task,
finding proper voice is an artistic struggle for the woman or any other

writer. I don't doubt that there will be mistakes of analysis and mistakes of art—but when the possibilities open before women writers hold so much promise and can bear so much fruit for the improvement of women's condition and concomitantly for expanding and refining the sensitivity of others in the culture, such mistakes in the long view may seem necessary for the sake of exploring all the possibilities, and consequential for the knowledge they can give.

The task before all of us—women, editors, publishers, reviewers, librarians, distributors, and readers—is not an easy one. It is not a responsibility we can afford to ignore, but one that calls us to set ourselves for the long, difficult struggle.

CENTER FOR CONTEMPORARY POETRY
Meeting Its Responsibilities

The following conversation with Ed Hill, curator of the Center for Contemporary Poetry at Murphy Library, Wisconsin State University—La Crosse, La Crosse, Wisconsin, was conducted in the summer of 1973 in a small, comfortable cottage above the Black River north of La Crosse. In a week-end of canoeing, turtle-egg hunting on sand bars, grilling bratwursts on an open fire, and swilling beer from "God's Country", we managed, I think, to discuss cogently matters related to problems of collecting writers' and smallpress materials; the following information and ideas should prove useful both to librarians interested in starting a collection of the kind found at the Center, and to little magazine and small press editors and publishers attempting to fathom the necessities of institutional libraries. I believe the conversation, though relaxed, is cogent and telling.

One matter we did not touch on at any great length, but which perhaps requires some explanation here, is the Center's *Voyages to the Inland Sea* series. The Center for Contemporary Poetry has published, each year, one volume in its Midland authors' poetry-and-essay series. The purpose of the series is to highlight and emphasize Midland authors who too often—because of our perennial pre-occupation with the East and West Coasts—are passed over and slighted. The series is edited by John Judson, editor of *Northeast* and Juniper Books and faculty member of WSU—La Crosse.

Ed Hill, curator of the Center, is a friendly, energetic, wiry man in his thirties. His duties at Murphy Library are time-consuming and exhausting. Yet he has time—rather makes time—to fulfill the several obligations he feels he has to poets and smallpress editors/publishers in his area of concern.

Our conversation, slightly edited for readability, follows:

Montag: What year was the Center founded?

Hill: It would have been 1969. I want to point out here that Bill Birdsall, who was my predecessor here on the library staff, was instrumental in defining this program and the direction it ought to take. It was his judgment that we needed something unique to this region. It was my judgment that the poetry of the younger and lesser known poets from this area was something no one else was covering adequately and that this was an area that we might step into. And this is what we did. That was in 1969.

We started, of course, because we wanted a program to give this library something unique. Every library can order books and process routine subscriptions. But I think the thing that makes a particular institutional library unique is some unique collection.

Montag: Was your purpose to create a unique collection, to have something special; or was it to collect an important body of literature?

Hill: It wasn't simply something to provide laurels for the library. As far as we knew, no one in this portion of the country was doing this kind of collection. Washington University in St. Louis is collecting poetry and poetry manuscripts and important works. They deal mostly with firmly established poets and writers. They have an artist, a poet-in-residence, who acts as an advisor. They feel that the first contact between the library and a potential contributor should be made by another poet rather than a librarian.

We didn't want to go about it this way, for several reasons: first, we didn't have the kind of money they have there; we wanted to feel our way into it. We did send a number of letters around asking for advice and so on, but it was pretty much an amateur and original effort as far as we were concerned.

Montag: Is the focus of the Center for Contemporary Poetry midwestern, or is it broader than that. Are you interested in poets from the areas around here, or are you getting manuscripts from people on the coasts and elsewhere?

Hill: I would say that the focus of it is midwestern, yes. Most of the effort, most of the financial effort, is directed towards the poets of this particular region. And I think again we give particular emphasis to Wisconsin poets. We do collect the published works, broadsides, littles, small press publications and so on, of poets from all over the country that for one reason or another we're particularly interested in. Now that usually means I'm interested in them, that I like their work.

Montag: So that it's a very personal collection.

Hill: Yes. John Judson who is in the English Department here at the University frequently recommends work to me, and whatever he recommends of course we try to get. But aside from his personal influence, and mine, we're very general. That is, if there is personal taste, it is mine and it's John's. And it seems to me any collection like this will probably be directed by this type of personal taste. Poetry is a personal matter and since it seems there are so few people interested in pursuing the matter as we want to do it, these judgments come to me by default, more than anything else.

Montag: I know that you have standing orders with Monday Morning Press and Membrane Press and Harpoon Press and you did have with Albatross; do you have standing orders with most of the small presses and little magazines in Wisconsin or a select number? This is something actually aside from the collection of manuscripts that you're doing, the particular author's works. How do you spread your energies in terms of the publishers?

Hill: We would like, really, to have representative samples and, in most cases, comprehensive collections of all the small press publishing done in the state, and a reasonably thorough coverage of that done in the midwest. Now this is one of the areas where we had great hopes, great aspirations, and have not succeeded. There are a couple of reasons for this, but probably foremost is simply the fact that we underestimated the time and energy and money it would take to do this adequately. It turns out to be a far bigger job than we anticipated; there are many more presses, magazines, and individual poets than I ever expected to see.

Secondly, we are dependent to a great extent upon the cooperation of the editors and poets themselves. Where I have expressed interest in a particular journal or poet and that poet or editor has in return expressed a mutual interest and indicated some degree of mutual cooperation, we have managed to get that particular publication. Some of the editors and poets we are interested in have not followed through. We must depend upon them to alert us when something new is coming out.

Montag: If a press brings out a new publication and doesn't send it to you, you have no way of knowing about it?

Hill: Not usually. We can learn about it later indirectly and try to pick it up, but when you multiply this kind of problem over dozens of times, it's very wearying; if something has to go, in terms of effort or money, those are the ones that will slip first. So we are very dependent upon the cooperation of the editors and poets.

Montag: I know that you, yourself, are very conscientious about keeping after these presses and poets, and giving of your time and energy; is part of the problem, though, the structure of the library itself, and economic necessities of the bursar of the university and that sort of thing, so that presses have to send a minimum order of, say, three or four dollars accumulated, before the business office will look at the invoice. Do structures larger than yourself create some of the problems you're faced with?

Hill: Yes. This is true. You had an article in *Margins* by Felix Pollak several issues back (no. 5, April-May 1973) in which he discussed some of these same problems, the problem simply of dealing with the institution of libraries. We're aware, of course, that to many poets and

editors, the library represents the kind of establishment they really op-
pose, and that they have very little sympathy with it. With those poets
and editors, it's very difficult to come to terms. We may be interested
in them, but just in simple logistics, as you say, of dealing with the library—in our case for example, we need two copies of a signed invoice,
the receipt of the check will take 6—8 weeks, we like a minimum order
of several dollars, and all the problems of correspondence, postage, billing and so on, for what really amounts to small profit margins for the
poet and the editor. These things get very much in the way.

Montag: The question is, though, doesn't a library such as yours provide a readership or an audience that an "easy" sale to an individual
doesn't provide? For instance, a library could provide 20 readers while
a sale to an individual provides maybe three or four. So that in terms of
affecting people beyond the magazine itself a library has, say, at the
least twice the influence of a sale to an individual.

Hill: Well, we would hope so. So far as I know, no one has undertaken any studies to see what the influence or effect of a particular
small press publication might be. We hope that these magazines and
these books are read by students, that they will be assigned at least occasionally by instructors in the various composition or literature or poetry classes. But I don't really know precisely what readership we do
provide. We do provide some, but I am also aware that there are journals, books of poetry, that are seldom, if ever, read.

Montag: Partly, then, the collection that the Center is compiling has
a twofold purpose: first, to make available to what audience there is a
representative collection of midwestern poetry and poets; and secondly,
to preserve for future use a representative collection of small press from
the sixties and seventies.

Hill: Yes, that's correct. One of the reasons why large readership
of some of these individual works is not important to me is that I do
take a long view of this; that is, I feel that there will certainly come a
time when the writing that is coming out of these decades will be the
subject of scholarly research, all the way from the undergraduate classroom to the graduate dissertation. And this is where I feel that we can
contribute most. I'm also aware that this is not precisely the kind of
readership many editors are looking for; they want their readers and
their recognition now. We can hope to assist in that, but in my mind,
what I'm really after is to establish a body of writing coming out of the
midwest in these times that we can preserve.

Montag: You're a librarian, and you say that a good deal of what
you're interested in for the Center for Contemporary Poetry is based
on your personal taste to a large extent, and on the recommendations
of John Judson; do you feel that this is the case for many or most other
libraries around the country, that what small press collecting they do
is to a large degree influenced by the personal taste or biases or quirks
of whomever happens to be curators of special collections?

Hill: I suspect this is true. Some few publication, of course, make it into the journals that review these things and the librarians read them and select according to those sources. As you very well know, this covers only the tip of the iceberg. Where a library sets out to collect in contemporary poetry, let's say, that collection is certainly going to reflect the personal tastes and biases of a very small group of people within that particular school or library, perhaps one or two librarians and one or two faculty members.

Montag: People have said to me, and I've come to believe, librarians are very harried people and therefore they tend to order things that are recommended by the people who do the recommending for them, the people they trust, *Library Journal* or *Choice* and so on, so that if a little magazine gets a good review in *Library Journal*, it'll get orders; if it doesn't get reviewed at all in *Library Journal,* it won't get orders. And if it does get a good review, it'll get orders from those people who are inclined that way in the first place, who have that particular taste. Do you think that this is a flaw in our cultural structure, that a few journals and a few librarians can exercise that sort of influence? Or is it a blessing that at least some books and magazines do get attention?

Hill: I can't really call it a blessing that a few small presses or small magazines get attention, because the number is so small and there is so little spin-off to the lesser known publications. It simply is not enough. It does not cover the field, even a little bit. This is true not only in small press publications; it is true in general trade publication.

If your book, published by one of the big commercial houses, is reviewed in the *New York Times Book Review*, that's wonderful for you —of course you're going to become purchased by libraries, your sales are going to be up, your profits are going to be up. There is a whole hierarchy of reviewing journals in which we'd all like to appear.

This is one of the purposes I know, for *Margins* itself, to come back to this other level that never makes it into the big magazines and to assist the librarians, the editors and publishers in their own choices and in seeing what's going on.

It is true that librarians are harried, they tend to take the easy way out, as I think anyone else would in those circumstances, when you're dealing with a great deal of money and thousands or hundreds of thousands of volumes of books, thousands of periodicals. The whole thing becomes an unfortunate numbers game. Unless some one or two or three people take it upon themselves to expend the extra effort to become knowledgeable in a particular field, then all this 95 or 99% of publications that don't get into library journals will never be seen by anyone.

Montag: Let's go back to the Center for a while and talk about what you do have —in terms of authors, what kind of manuscripts you are getting in, who you're getting them from.

Hill: We don't really have a great number of poets represented in our manuscript collection; we're being very careful there. We have to

be very selective, we don't have very much money and can only make
one or two or sometimes three of what we would consider major purchases in a year. We don't have anywhere near the money it would
take to thoroughly cover the field, and to pay what needs to be paid.
We have some of the manuscripts of Dave Etter who was represented in
the first volume of *Voyages to the Inland Sea.*

Montag: How did you secure his manuscripts? Was that an effort on
your part or on John Judson's part?

Hill: I believe John Judson suggested it first; of course, once we publish a poet that way, it gives us a bit of leverage or at least some justifi-
cation for both collecting that poet's papers and for asking for them.

Montag: Once you publish him in *Voyages.*

Hill: Right. In Dave Etter's case, he had published two books, I believe, with the University of Nebraska Press; and after we published him
in Vol. I of *Voyages to the Inland Sea,* we asked him if we could get
some of his papers dealing with what he had contributed to that particular book and it turned out that he had not done anything with the
papers for his previous two books either. This gave us a natural time
and place to suggest that La Crosse might be the logical repository for
his papers and he agreed. That started that and of course we will continue to collect his papers as we can. Once we begin with a poet we feel
is important to our purposes, we want to try to continue to collect
those papers. Comprehensiveness, we feel, is important to the kind of
research that will eventually be done with this collection.

Montag: What does this require on the poet's part, that he send you
original manuscripts as they pile up, send you copies of publications in
which his poems appear, new books as they appear?

Hill: We have a great deal of flexibility in the way we deal with a
poet. I think that whatever way the poet wants his material to appear
with us will probably be the major determining force in how we collect
and what we collect. Now some poets of course save everything and
others save virtually nothing. In some cases we will only collect the papers dealing with a fairly important published work, the papers in the
background of that particular work, worksheets, drafts, and so on. In
other cases, we'll collect or attempt to collect virtually everything the
poet has done and is doing. Again, we depend a great deal upon the poet and what he wants to do.

Montag: And the way he works, too, I suppose.

Hill: Yes, and the way he works, correct—if he chooses not to send
us everything, that's the way it will be; if, on the other hand, and this
is true of the younger poets more than of the established poets, if they
feel that their poetry is achieving some significance, some recognition,
and they have not yet committed their work to an institution, to a library where it can be collected, we can frequently convince them to
send virtually everything to us—all the papers dealing with any published work, published book that is, either xerox copies or tearsheets

or original copies of publications within magazines, anthologies, small press reviews and so on. And in some cases they send us poetry that has not been published anywhere; they simply have hopes for it.

If these poets then achieve some prominence later, and we gamble of course that some of them will, we then will have a very useful collection for any student or scholar who wants to study that material. We will have excellent background; we will have, in many cases, correspondence with other poets and other editors involving this poet; we will have reviews of his work and reviews written by him, if he does that kind of thing; poems, drafts, finished copies, and so on—we'll have virtually everything he's done.

Montag: You've mentioned Dave Etter. Who are some of the other poets whose papers you're collecting?

Hill: We are getting most of the work of Felix Pollak, who appears in Vol. II of *Voyages*. One young poet who has impressed me favorably is James Bertolino and we're collecting some of his material.

Montag: He was originally from Wisconsin, right?

Hill: Yes, that's right. He was here; now, of course, he has since moved. But in a case like this, the regionalism, if it has been established once simply through residence, is enough for us; that is, if someone moves out of the midwest to the East or West Coast, it doesn't mean that we're going to discontinue our interest in him.

We collect several younger poets to some degree or another. Some of them send us virtually everything they do. Others are sending us only their published work. I'm interested in Greg Kuzma who is in Nebraska. Kathy Wiegner in Milwaukee I think is a fine poet and I'm interested in collecting her work; Roger Mitchell in Milwaukee; these are, most of them, connected with schools, and are teaching and writing poetry. In most cases we're collecting them simply because I like their work, and that's the way it began.

Montag: Once you make a commitment, it's a fairly long-term and comprehensive commitment to collecting that poet?

Hill: Yes. We like to write into whatever contract we have something involving a lack of interest on the part of either party; if we feel that further attention to a particular poet is no longer justified for our purposes, we may stop collecting him. That has not happened yet. It may never happen. On the other hand, if the poet feels he's getting a poor bargain with us, or wants his material collected in another place, he has the right of course to discontinue the arrangement. There is no legal contract that is binding for either one of us, except for fair payment, fair negotiated payment for a block of material, and the implied hope that once started the program can continue.

Montag: As long as the Center is limited in its funds and the amount of energy—you're not a full-time curator for the Center itself, you also have other responsibilities in the library—you're limited in what you can do.

Hill: It really would take a staff of a full-time librarian and a full-time secretary and probably some student assistants to administer this program even partially as it should be administered.

Montag: In many cases, it seems a matter of your personal correspondence with a mutitude of poets that keeps the interest between the Center and the poets alive. You have to contact these poets initially, for instance, and then stay in touch with them. That is also, I would think, the bulk of the burden, keeping track of where the poets are and what they're doing, if they're cooperating, sending according to whatever arrangements you have made.

Hill: Yes, of course. Once this material begins coming to us routinely, that is, we can buy this on something approaching a standing order basis, where everything that the editor or everything that this poet is doing we get, that makes it much easier.

Of course, I still correspond, there is still the billing and invoicing, but once we get on a mailing list, these people route the material to us—that takes the bulk of the paperwork out of it. Now, this does not decrease the obligation, what I feel is the obligation I have to maintain a correspondence with these people.

One of the most useful things about all this is what I learn from the editors and poets about what else is being done. These people have contacts that I couldn't possibly maintain on my own. There's a whole network, a whole grapevine in this area of publishing that is very intricate and without the help of all these people who write to me, I don't see how I could possibly manage at all.

Montag: While in one part you're doing small publishers and poets a favor, they are also doing the Center a favor in turn, feeding information to you, so that the Center can be in touch with and aware of publishing and poetry in the midwest, in the area that is your concern.

Hill: Quite right. These people very often, in fact almost always, will suggest a book that I should know about, or a new poet that I should know about. This is how the collection really grows. This is also part of the mutual backscratching that I don't like, that is, where poets and editors simply route their work back and forth to each other and the whole relationship becomes very incestuous. But where I'm getting suggestions from a good many places, outside of the midwest included, then I think our chances of getting a good mix which avoids bias is very good.

Montag: Do you feel that having John Judson, who is editor of *Northeast* and Juniper Books, in the English Department at the University in La Crosse, is a very valuable asset to the Center, not only in the fact that he is editor of the *Voyages* series, but in the fact that to some extent he can keep you informed and shape some of your decisions—do you feel that he is an important feature of what the Center is doing or an important arm of the Center?

Hill: Yes. This is another case where I'm not really sure how successful we could possibly be without that kind of help. He has contacts, he has rapport with these poets and editors that I don't have in most cases; he can make suggestions, he can initiate negotiations for papers, he can suggest to other poets and editors that they contribute and so on. I don't think that a program like this could long survive without someone who is a working poet or editor.

Montag: How would you define the differences between what the Center for Contemporary Poetry is doing and what, say, the University of Wisconsin-Madison is doing, with its little magazine collection—which is probably the largest in the world. You're not interested so much in having the complete collection of the magazines as having a representative sample of little magazines of the midwest area, a fairly complete collection of Wisconsin publications, and then the midland's author's papers.

Hill: Yes. We want something that is representative, I think that's the best word. It would be foolish for us to try to rival or duplicate what the University of Wisconsin-Madison is doing; it would cost them additional money, it would cost us additional money and when we were all through we still would not have anything near what they have. This is something that I've seen over the years I've been working in this particular project: I must not try to duplicate precisely what another library is doing. Correspondingly I don't want to find myself in a situation where I'm bidding competitively for the works of a particular poet or publisher. This I think does more harm than good; of course, the editor or poet could end up with more money if libraries bid that way.

It is far better once a collection is established for—say—Robert Bly, somewhere, that all of Robert Bly's works, his papers, correspondence, and so on, go to that research source, so that somebody doing work on this poet can find virtually all he needs in that one center. He won't have to go to eight or ten different libraries to find it. If I find that another library has already started collecting a particular poet, or has the bulk of the poet's works, I'm not even going to try to start collecting that poet: it belongs there, and if somebody comes up with papers, I'll suggest that he go to that library with them.

You know we went into this in a rather naive way. We really hoped to accomplish far more than any library could hope to accomplish. There isn't much literature available to the novice collector in libraries—there is such a wide variety in the kinds of material that can be collected, the time period to be collected, and so on, that without establishing some limits, libraries, including this one, can find that they have bit off far more than they can chew. And we have certainly found this to be the case here.

I really hoped at one time to be able to collect virtually everything being done in small press publications in a four or five state area in the midwest. That has turned out to be impossible. It might still be impossible if I had the advantage of a full-time position in it myself and several full-time assistants. The difficulties are tremendous in this.

I would certainly recommend that any libraries undertaking a collection set about, first of all, to discover what is most important—and this is, of course, a matter of constant judgment; it fluctuates; it's not a stable thing; evaluations and judgments must take place almost constantly. Whenever these libraries begin a collection, some sort of perimeter must be drawn around the collection they eventually want to hold. Certainly they should not undertake this except as a long term venture; things move quickly enough and names and titles come into being and pass away often enough that the over-all effort I feel should be toward gradual accumulation of what is being written during a given decade in a certain area.

I believe it would be unrealistic for any library to set about to collect everything being done within these perimeters. There's always a certain amount of ephemera, trivia that should be eliminated—it simply doesn't deserve the time and effort that go into this kind of collection. Again, judgment by either the librarian or perhaps a small informal committee of two or three individuals—librarians and faculty members, some cooperating poet or editor—must constantly evaluate the quality of what is being collected.

This gets into a very sensitive matter, of course; there are poets and editors who want to be collected, and the librarian perhaps feels that the quality is not of the kind that would justify a long-term or permanent collection. If error must be made, however, it probably ought to be made in the direction of too much material than too little. This is one of the situations where every ten years, every five years or perhaps at a longer period, the whole collection might be reevaluated. It will be determined from time to time that some material has not justified collection and does not justify further collection. This material can be discarded. The weeding and evaluation go on constantly, at least a beginning has to be made.

For the Center for Contemporary Poetry, our scope has been narrowed considerably, out of simple necessity. I found that I could not keep up with everything I hoped to do; the correspondence itself could become a full-time job for two people. What we're doing now is concentrating on the poets and publications, and in certain cases, trends or styles of writing that we feel are representative, best representative for this area and this time—the rest of it we will try to get, we'll get as much as we can; we know we're going to miss a great deal of it. It simply will not come to us, for one reason or another. I've learned over the last couple of years to accept this. It's enough now for me to do what I can and admit freely to anyone who inquires that we ought to be doing more.

If other libraries in this general area—state or region—come for advice or with the suggestion that they're going to start their own collection program, a cooperative effort is far better as a way to do it than for libraries to duplicate what another collection is holding. If some group of librarians—and this has happened—comes to me, with the information that they intend to start a program, what I will do is attempt to get them to collect comprehensively in an area I'm not collecting.

It is far better for me to be able to send a scholar or a student to one library where virtually everything he needs is held, than to have to recommend to this researcher that he visit three or four or five different libraries because they're all trying to do the same thing, which means that none of them is doing the job well. If there is no major collection effort, then of course a library new in the business can get in wherever it likes and undertake anything it likes.

Frequently a library will wish to begin some collection in the area of small press publications and find that other libraries nearby are doing roughly the same thing. When this happens, areas of responsibility should be assigned. Duplication is probably one of the most expensive and frivolous aspects of any collection effort. Because the collection of small press publications is considered a luxury in many places, every effort ought to be made to make it economical, to make it a logical kind of collection with every purchase being justified without the burden of duplication.

I have found too that form letters, even on routine matters, are frowned upon by editors. Once the collection effort gets started, a great deal of personal correspondence must be maintained; there is no other good way to do it. There are a great many editors who are not friendly in the first place with establishment institutions and libraries—our establishment—and to put correspondence on a formal, extremely business-like basis is to undercut the collection effort.

For my own part, I have found that the correspondence with editors and poets is one of the most rewarding aspects of my work. The friendships I have gained this way, I think, will outlast—at least personally—all other aspects of my work. For the collection itself, the advice and cooperation from these people represent an invaluable asset. A collection of this nature is to me of obvious mutual benefit: we can provide order and permanence in an area that is chaotic in many ways.

I think I have seen a direct relationship between the degree of cooperation I get from an editor or poet and the quality of the work he's doing. That is an easy judgement to make, of course, to collect only those people who cooperate. But I think I've found that this holds true. That the material most worthy of permanence and study is the material that a library is most likely to successfully collect: after all, if an editor cares about what he is doing, about the quality of it, he cares about what happens to it.

Montag: I know you've done some reviews for *Northeast* magazine, among others I think, and I'm sure you have opinions on the shape of poetry today and the shape of small publishing today. You said earlier that future generations will be studying the sort of things that you're collecting at the Center. Would you amplify on what you think the shape the small press scene is today, particularly in your capacity as curator of the Center for Contemporary Poetry, and as a librarian?

Hill: I hesitate to make any pronouncements on this subject because I haven't been around long enough to have any perspective on it. There is much that is being published today that I admire a great deal. It seems to me as good as anything that's ever been done. I find it vital, lively, significant to everything writing ought to be about. On the other hand, there is what I would consider a fringe area of publishing and poetry for which I have little sympathy. It seems to have very little discipline, and even very little literacy. It bears the stamp of people who don't really like words. Much of it is very political, much is very temporary and spontaneous in interest and five years from now no one will have the vaguest idea of what they were talking about. But poetry and publishing have always been like that. They are fluid, erratic, uneven. Something good always surfaces. The rest will fade. Beyond that, I am unable to define the shape of contemporary poetry.

Montag: It was about 1965-67 that small press publishing started to blossom and various people have said that it has come in waves or one wave has ended and the second wave is beginning. Do you think there is any particular significance to the wealth of activity that has gone on in the past few years and is going on now, and the spark of interest that's occurring in libraries around the country? I've been in touch with several libraries who have said they're very interested in collecting little magazines and small press publications. Do you think this promises something for the future in terms of how librarians are going to be defining their responsibilities toward small publishers?

Hill: I would hope so. I tend to suspect many libraries in their motives; that is, much of this interest may have been caused by a surplus in their budget. Certainly they are told frequently enough that much of what is great in contemporary literature began in the small or alternative publications. What I would really like to see would be for more libraries to go out on a limb and begin collecting on their own—make their own judgments, cover one field well, and hang in there.

Montag: Do you think it would be, for instance, valuable for one or two libraries in a particular state or a particular area to make themselves collectors of that area. for instance, say, the University of Missouri, collecting at least a representative sample of Missouri small press publications, little magazines, and then spread that out through the country, Montana and so on. Do you think that would be a valuable function, in terms of what the responsibilities to whatever audience there is today and to whatever audience there will be a few generations from now.

Hill: Yes, I do. I think ideally every area of the country would be collected by some library; that is, that library would collect representative examples, it would collect comprehensively in certain fields—so that if you were interested in the small press publications of, going back to your example of Missouri, you could go to one library and get a good basic background on what is being done in that state presently and over the past several years—

Montag: At least the most significant journals and a fair sampling of journals of lesser interest.

Hill: That's right. This as far as I know is not being done systematically. There are libraries that are collecting, of course, but as far as I know, there has not been a systematic application of a general collecting policy.

Montag: Librarians seem independent sorts of people, so that to systematize a suggestion, the implementation of a suggestion, would be virtually impossible, wouldn't it? To suggest to a hundred libraries around the country that they become regional centers for such writing.

Hill: No, I don't think librarians are so independent that they would object to that. What it would take would be some national commission or some strong recommendation by the American Library Association or by the Association of College and Research Libraries. It's not likely to come out spontaneously; it's going to have to be done at the urging of a national or regional policy-making organization. Then I think they would probably do it.

Montag: What could an organization like COSMEP (Committee of Small Magazine Editors and Publishers) or what could any motley collection of editors and publishers do in practical terms to perhaps start something like that in motion, to send a spark to the American Library Association? Would letters from various editors be effective, or letters from COSMEP, would that start some wheels turning, would that get some response?

Hill: I don't really know how to answer that. I would hope that it would get some response. I suspect that something like it may have already been tried at some time. There are a good many problems facing this kind of application. One would be, simply, making enough noise to get a policy established at a national organizational level. The next one of course would be assigning what the coverages would be. These things, as I have watched them, tend to get buried in committees, standards committees, membership votes and a number of other things. I don't hold out a great deal of hope until such time as all these libraries recognize the importance of what this project could do. And I'm not convinced that many libraries will ever be convinced that this is worthwhile in terms of assigning personnel and a great deal of money to it.

Montag: It would take, because of the time and energy involved, personnel and money, which in the current state of the economy is becoming a rarer and rarer commodity. Libraries are being cut back just as universities are being cut back, as everyone is being cut back. The whole problem isn't finances only, though; there is a great deal of resistance on the part of librarians as on the part of the American population generally to such publications, and in part, not seeing the significance of such publications because they haven't been stamped with approval.

Hill: This is a difficult area for a library to cover and I think the small press community is very much aware of this. In the area of books and trade publications or mass circulation journals, subscriptions can be handled fairly routinely. But the small press publications are one of several fringe and difficult areas in library acquisitions. It's one that is likely to be dismissed or passed over lightly any time there's a crunch for time or money.

Montag: A good many libraries order from national jobbers, with blanket orders for all books published in America in English except cookbooks and so on—couldn't a national commission or a national committee of librarians, if it did come to pass, set up say fifty regional centers, one in each state—for the collection of the works in that state—couldn't they blanket order from a selected number of presses or whatever representative samples, so that everything would be through one organization, to take some of the pressure off individual libraries?

Hill: This would make it very easy for them and I think they'd love to see it. But do you realize the problems involved in setting up regional jobbers for small press publications? There's a very high attrition rate in small presses, and in journals; issues are missed frequently, and editors change or move, or the price changes and so on. It's a very difficult world to keep up with, and it would be just as difficult if a trade association of some kind—say COSMEP—undertook this project which would be a really formidable thing—I think that past experience in the jobbing of small press publications has shown that it is fraught with difficulty. It's also fraught with failure. I don't really know the best way out of this. One is tempted to recommend a massive shot of federal money to see what could be done, but even then it would take a great deal of devoted effort.

One of the most logical and exciting ideas is the concept of the local or regional distibution outlet such as you are setting up in Milwaukee. You're in an excellent position to know what is going on there, to maintain contact with the poets and presses of the Milwaukee area. And if you can get a few dozen copies of the publications and make them available to subscribers of *Margins* through a simplified price list, you have efficiently eliminated most of a library's red tape for acquiring these things. It's not a new idea, of course, but it's workable, it's logical, it makes eminent good sense. I hope it works, and any similar distribution center in this region can count on my support. I'll help make it work.

Montag: Perhaps the answer is more dogged, determined effort of this kind that you're doing—the personal interest, and the personal taste which is a resultant part of that, on the part of a particular librarian in a particular library, who sees the necessity for collecting the publications and the papers of poets. Perhaps eventually it will be only on that level that we will find success.

Hill: Even without a nationwide and systematic effort, there is something that individual libraries and librarians can do and ought to be doing right away. If the librarians will look around, they will find that in most cases these small press publications are not being collected in their area in anything but a helter-skelter kind of way; they may subscribe to a few of these things, they might buy an occasional one—but it's a hit or miss effort. What needs to be done immediately is for one librarian, or possibly two or three, or hopefully a faculty member if it is a college or university library, to look at what is being done in this particular area and set about to collect these things. They can send, first of all, to the small presses they're already aware of and set up standing orders; they can also ask for suggestions and advice from these people. They should certainly set about to establish as much contact as possible within the area of small press publication, make as many friends as they can. There is an underground at work here; as long as the librarian is outside of that, has no contact with that, any collection is bound for failure. There is simply no way to keep up in this area through the legitimate and mass-circulation press. It is not covered. These librarians, as I say, with the assistance of a faculty member who may be interested or may have some 'in' as an editor or poet, must find out what's being done, see who's publishing what, what the best efforts are, what the new efforts are, what the directions, the trends of publishing and poetry are; then collect them, get it going and start the collection. In most cases, there will be no one else making this kind of collection effort. Through default, this material may never be collected. This is something the libraries can be doing right now.

For my part, I tend to take a very critical attitude towards those libraries that are not collecting in their areas of responsibility. Poetry is one of those responsibilities. For some small but at least locally significant publishing effort to mature, to come into being, to mature, to publish for a number of years and then perhaps to die as many small press publishing efforts do—without ever having been collected by the nearest college or university or public library represents to me a gross dereliction of duty on the part of these libraries.

ITS REACH AND GRASP

The Review Journal in the Literary Situation

If we examine the literary situation as it exists today, we find two things: first, a very substantial amount of good writing is being done; and second, the traditional methods of channeling good writing before the reading audience are now virtually clogged. Richard Kostelanetz, for his part, has gone to some lengths documenting causes of this situation. For myself, I find American readers, and those elsewhere, are today more literate and more sophisticated than any mass audience in the past has been; and, as more and more readers discover that the whole of truth and goodness has not, in fact, been defined and pinned down in established cultural values, the sophisticated audience for good writing will continue to grow. Yet our traditional publishing enterprises seem aimed to please the "mass" audience of a generation or two ago, the great "unwasheds" which may no longer exist, or may never have existed except in the imagination of "thinkers". Publishing which views itself as an industry, as a commercial enterprise, finds itself chasing after that which, on appearance, seems to be the "popular" taste. Such publishing relies heavily on the easily marketable item, the best-seller, the steady seller: that publisher is in business to make money—and must continue to make money in order to stay in business. This is the truism and the axiom which in large part leads us to the current paradox: rather meager offerings among the deluge of books from commercial presses, in the face of massive amounts of high-quality unpublished writing. Additionally, as Kostelanetz points out, there is a good deal of "literary-politicking" involved.

Even so, commercial publishers do not bear the guilt alone. Concurrently, bookselling—which in the past had served writers, publishers and readers well by making literature available—has died. No longer is the ordinary bookstore a workable means of passing literature on to its readers. A trip to nearly any bookstore (except those few, rare exceptions where the bookstore is not intended to be a "money-making" venture in the first place, but rather exists as a personal cultural service on the part of an interested party who can afford the losses or only breaking even, who has means of subsistence from other sources) will indicate the degree to which the bookstore today has become very much like a meat-counter in a butcher shop. The choice cuts become rarer and rarer —hamburger is featured in larger and more colorful displays. Customers pass by, with side glances, sighing. Few venture a purchase, for even the choice cuts are becoming stale, turning slightly green. To meet the costs of light, heat, rent, employee salaries, etc. and still make a profit, the bookstore has opted to stock only best-sellers and steady sellers; its floor and shelf space is taken up with them. It cannot, and does not, give space to more esoteric items which have lower rates of turnover and therefore are less profitable. If an item does not sell briskly, it is taking up, unnecessarily, useable space that might otherwise turn a better profit per-square-inch.

My meat counter analogy is not so far-fetched as it may seem. There is a bookstore in this area which recently sold books *by the pound*. Are we talking about books as pieces of writing which can affect our outlook, our values, our way of seeing and being in the world; or are we talking about books as hunks of meat. More and more, I fear, books are becoming hunks of meat.

We can hope, certainly, that bookstores will not abandon their efforts, however much they seem useless. The audience for good writing exists, widely scattered perhaps, but it nonetheless exists. The personal-type bookstore does serve at least a part of this audience; additional efforts and experiments on the part of other bookstores are in order, if there is any future at all in bookselling. Otherwise even small presses with solid distribution networks, such as Black Sparrow, will find massive returns from bookstores financially crippling; the prohibitive cost of a high number of returns will mandate other, protective measures for such presses—and though we trust they will not turn to the best-seller—the result well be detrimental to publishing and to literature.

Bookstores and publishers need to realize that there is an audience, but it needs to be served in new ways. Bookstores were, once, more central to the literary (writer-publisher-reader) community; but the demands of economic necessity have moved them from responsible functioning in that community to (in many cases) blatant profiteering. The solution to the small publishers'/the booksellers' problems is no longer simply a matter of getting publications of value stocked on the shelves; rather, it becomes the literary-sociological challenge of creating a new community of interests whose needs are served by the bookseller. There was a time when the bookseller was also publisher, was also patron to the writer, was also propagandist of literature. The bookstore has lost these roles, and with that, its usefulness as a "marketing outlet." Booksellers, if they are to be forces in our culture, need to reformulate their roles in terms of their larger responsibilities.

The situation of commercial publishers and booksellers should serve also as some indication of the state our major review journals are in. Review journals, especially the major ones, ought to be channels of information, ideas, and—yes—opinion; they ought to reflect, evaluate, comment on the great wide diversity of literature (literature in its broadest sense—writing of any type) being produced at a given time. They ought to weigh a piece of writing on its merits—not on the merits of its publisher, its publisher's advertising budget, the name-and-reputation of its author, or other extraneous factors. Reviewers ought to approach each new publication freshly, not with tired ideological formulas. However, our most prestigious journals—namely *The New York*

Times Book Review and the *New York Review of Books* fail often, and on many counts.

Partly, of course, the lackluster fare being served up by the large New York houses is to blame; but when the editor of the *Times Book Review* laments the 'fact' that so little poetry is being published today, you know he has not looked nearly far enough—he is, in fact, ignorant of a whole world of literature, and his ignorance is a sign of continued irresponsibility on his part. We could understand such ignorance, perhaps, if small publishers were adverse to publicity, but they generally are not. The fact is: the *Time Books Review* for the most part just is not interested.

Local metropolitan papers do no better and generally far worse. The Milwaukee *Journal's* Sunday book-review page, for instance, is in large part an open insult to the paper's readers. Its editor is content to run off to New York, talk to publishers about the coming season's line up of "big books", chase the tastiest of literary rumors, and present in review as narrow a selection of books as can be found. I wonder, sometimes, if the editor intends to serve his readers, or if he functions entirely as a mouth-piece for publishers' public relations offices.

Such journals as *Library Journal, Choice,* etc. are service journals and they do for their readers exactly what their readers expect and want: they reflect publishing in a fairly standard way, for the needs of their readers are 'standard'. The cultural values of such journals are the accepted ones, and their responsibility does not extend to propagandizing new and innovative writing and publishing, nor can we realistically expect them to assume this function. In fairness, though, it should be pointed out that the "magazine" section of *Library Journal,* as one instance, is making determined effort to notice and comment on small journals of interest, but such notice is hopelessly inadequate. Small presses and little magazines need (and deserve) more.

Even journals in which we might expect and want to find book-reviews of merit, and solid discussion of important literature, disappoint almost completely. Few underground or alternative papers seem very interested in writing or in books.

It has been in small journals that we find attention being given to little-magazine-small-press publications; though there has undoubtedly been a good deal of mutual backscratching, uncritical adulation, and partisan reviewing published in such journals, they have presented also —and importantly—some of the most perceptive and the most responsible critical commentary on new writing today. In spite of the limited circulation of the journals, that commentary has fortunately reached many of those who are in good position to assimilate and appreciate it, other writers; the same commentary, however, ought, in my view, to be read and appreciated by a far larger audience. The answer, of course, is increased circulation for the valuable little magazines, but we know already how successful attempts in the direction have been.

Any small press or little mag editor can tell you that writing is not dead: such an editor reads, in manuscript, an unbelievable amount of contemporary poetry and fiction; there is—it should go without saying —a good deal of out-and-out trash; but there is also a surprising amount of writing which is substantial and fresh and deserving of an audience. Publishing, and even the alternative structures of the little magazine and the small press, are not adequate to accomodate fairly what is being produced. The situation is this: many little magazines and small press books are published at a personal loss to the publisher. Small press people who believe publishing is a service can accept such losses and live with them, and undoubtedly will continue to do so. And though current small publishing is not adequate to the needs of current writers, small press has grown greatly in recent years, and promises to continue growing. But I cannot foresee small publishing, as a way of publishing, increasing nearly fast enough to adequately handle even the best of writing that will be done in the next few years.

The concern, then, even of the small press publisher who is meeting his responsibilities admirably, ought to be twofold: first, since the publishing small presses are doing is not adequate, what are the alternatives; and second, given the fact that small publishers are doing important work, what are the best ways of making their publication accessible to interested readers.

For the first part—what alternatives exist or can be made to exist— there is much which needs to be done. Self-publishing as one alternative is in the noble tradition of Blake, Wordsworth & Coleridge, and others; even William Carlos Williams' first book was self-published. Writers joining together to form cooperative publishing ventures (such as the Writers' Cooperative: Montreal [reported in *Small Press Review no. 14*], The Minnesota Writers' Publishing House [reported by Robert Bly in the Spring 1973 issue of *The Lamp in the Spine*]), are another possibility being explored. As are the possibilities of Richard Kostelanetz and Henry Korn's collaborative *Assembling*, and Albert Drake's experiment with his magazine's sixth issue, *Happiness Holding Tank no. 6* [reported in *Small Press Review no. 18*]. An alternative we have yet to consider more fully is author-subsidized publication by established small presses who are undercapitalized and over-committed (not self-publishing in its usual sense, rather an author's involvement [financial and otherwise] in the production and the publication of material which meets editorial requirements, and afterwards, his involvement in its distribution).

For the second part—how to get literature before its audience—the problems have seemed almost insurmountable. We recognize that we cannot and will not get notice in the influential journals of review. We recognize that, as it exists today, bookselling is dead, and though we can hope, we do not expect miracles in this regard. We recognize that many established distribution organizations are clogged for us. We recognize finally, that as small publishers, we are alone with our visions and our possibilities.

Of what—in terms of getting literature passed around—do those possibilities consist:

1) We must assume, first, that the responsibility of the writer extends farther than merely getting words down on paper in a clear, legible fashion; that the responsibility of the publisher extends beyond merely getting the work into print; and that the responsibility of the reader goes beyond merely enjoyment of the writing. It seems as much the writer's and reader's duty to make good literature known and accessible as it is the publisher's. If the usual channels are clogged, and they are, then the creation of new channels must be assumed by the whole of the literary community—writer, publisher, and reader alike—and extensive cooperative efforts in this community ought to prove worthwhile.

If a group of poems was worth the writing in the first place, they are certainly worth the author's efforts—not merely with holding "autograph parties", but with sustained efforts. And if the writing is worth the reading, the reader's responsibilities are equally clear. Even so, such efforts likely won't be enough.

2) We must, furthermore, create systems of distribution that go beyond merely the writer and the reader meeting their responsibilities: as publishers, we fail grossly if we put a book in print and leave it sit boxed in a basement. What is being done: currently there are several energetic and reliable alternative distributors in the United States. They are having varying degrees of success. The central problem is related to the death of bookstores and the scattered state of the audience. There are, in addition to distributors, mail-order houses such as Asphodel which are assuming a good deal of responsibility for small press material. And the Committee of Small Magazine Editors and Publishers has recently undertaken and will soon be completing its whole-earth type *Whole COSMEP Catalogue.* Further, a few regional organizations are being set up to study member problems, to advertise, publicize, and distribute their publications.

3) Finally, and correlative to both the above, we must create alternative critical and reviewing structures which are adequate to our needs —surveying, reflecting, evaluating, criticizing the whole great diversity of literature from small presses, and literature neglected by the established journals.

Such an alternative reviewing structure will have, necessarily, several thrusts: first, it will examine the entire literary-political situation in which writing, publishing, distribution and reading goes on. We must be aware of our environment, for unless we are cognizant of the nature of the problems we face, unless we are assessing alternatives as solutions, unless we are acting in practical ways to test our alternatives and effect (and continually evaluate) our programs, unless the reviewing-critical structure explores the larger issues, its "reviewing" function is an empty and useless one. We must know how the land lies, the soil conditions, the length of the growing season, expected rainfall, the weather report; otherwise anything we plant will survive only by serendipity: even the most perceptive critical essay will be useless if it cannot be effective; and it cannot be effective so long as it exists without reference to our condition. The same principle applies even more forcefully to the straightforward review.

Secondly, and concomitant with assessing, our reviewing-critical structure needs to establish values not only for "literature", but for the whole process of making literature, from the writer and his writing to the publisher and distributor, to reading, and yes even to reviewing-criticizing itself. It is the duty of the review journal to define such values, but more importantly—in many instances—to create them. The world of small press has been, in the past, marked by a touch-and-go attitude; our music has been played by ear. But today, with the development small press has taken even in the past year or two, we have become more sophisticated and more cognizant of our role in the making of literature. And though I do not mean to imply that the critical-reviewing structure's purpose is to set down hard and fast rules and regulations as if it is all some sort of game, I do want to make clear that the journals ought to be creating possibilities for new premises and procedures by exploring and evaluating new ideas, penetrating to central issues and problems and exposing them, and setting out appropriate courses of action. On this level, establishing standards becomes a serious and necessary venture on the part of these journals. We would be meeting less than our full responsibility if we are content to say—see, this is what is being done. We must say, in addition—see, this is what can be done; and see, this is what ought to be done.

Part of the critical faculty assesses, and part creates. The whole of the critical faculty values. Accurate perception of value, as it exists and as it can exist, is the mark of the good critic, and of the good critical review journal.

By defining the role of the journal in such a way, however, we cannot ignore its several other roles. The review journal must, thirdly, be an important source of information. It must evaluate the literary environment, certainly, and having done so it must place accurate information effectively before its readers. Especially in the area of alternative-small publishing, where so little is known and understood and so little is accessible to the general reading public and the institutions which serve that public—libraries and so on—the informational-educational functions must remain a constant concern. When I place emphasis on one aspect of the review-journal's role, I am not detracting from its other aspects. Achieving the proper balance between various elements is the good editor's dilemma. Thus, while we have our "heads in the clouds" of value and evaluation and creative publishing possibilities, we cannot neglect informational material and plain "reporting", for relevant "hard facts" are useful and necessary as tools for change, as supporting evidence for our arguments.

At the same time—with assessment of idea, creation of possibility, and presentation of information well controlled—the review journal has a fourth, and perhaps overlooked function: it must be, in part, an organ of polemic and propaganda. I wrote a friend recently that as an editor-publisher of *Margins*, I am probably three-quarters propagandist. And there is good reason for this. Small publishing suffers in part, as I have said, from lack of effectively disseminated information; but it also suffers, and to a serious degree, from lack of fiery, brand carrying propagandists. There is a commitment in small press—the best of it— that is kin almost to religious fervor; with that zeal, the good work of the small press needs to be proclaimed. If the review journals do not accept this as part of their function, the proclamations will not be made. Certainly the usual organs of information and review will not take up the task.

My chief reason for valuing the propagandist function of the review journal has to do with what I consider to be an effective dialectic—not *the* dialectic, perhaps—which is significantly a part of the human educational and consciousness-raising process. Someone can relate to us the most amazing of facts with quiet voice—but not until he shouts them, until he hounds us and harasses us with them, are we likely to take notice. When he finally has our attention and our interest, he can go back to his quiet recitation. We may not—to be sure—agree with, or even value, what he has to say; but once we have listened—after he's managed to get our attention with "a stick"—we have something to mull over, consider in light of our own values and perceptions; we have another view to compare with, and perhaps by force of argument, change our own. Such a dialectic is a continual-continuing process, and its implementation ought to be integrated into the work of the review journal.

As I say this, of course, I am well aware that there can be—in this dialectical way of proceeding—outright dishonesty or the appearance of dishonesty. Shout small publishing's work at the top of your lungs, I say, realizing that not all the work small press is doing is valuable and significant. A good editor would not consciously be dishonest with his readers, and I am not asking that; in fact, the good editor of a review journal must adhere to the strictest standards of honesty. He must avoid even the appearance of dishonesty. Whatever is of value in the small press is best served by honest assessment. As for appearance— in several issues of *Margins*, unfortunately, and in many reviews and critical pieces in small magazines, we get the appearance that most everything the small presses publish is valuable. The reason for this is simple enough: most reviewers are interested in talking about work which *moves* them, i.e., solid, significant writing; few enjoy doing the axe-job even when it needs to be done (and, I think, this is one of man's more endearing traits). The result, however, is that a good deal of review space is given to "good" reviews, leaving the appearance that there are not many "bad" books around. There are critics who would say that review space belongs properly to exciting books, that only the sickening PR job and the inflated reputation need comment in a review journal. Such a position—though I see its intention and its value— ignores, to my mind, the journal's need for the appearance of honesty, as well as honesty. It ignores also the instructive lessons that a sensitive examination of "bad" writing can afford the reader and undoubtedly other writers.

How is this apparent contradiction, between what I consider the need to propagandize small press and the need to call bad writing bad writing, resolved: briefly with an argument by metaphor—if our piece of ground is the richest farmland in the state, yielding the best produce around, we should not be afraid to say so, and loudly; at the same time, we recognize that weeds grow readily in the fertile soil, and need pulling,

Finally, the editor of the review journal, if he is serious about his and his journal's various prognosticating, evaluating, information-disseminating, and propagandizing roles, will formulate and implement programs of practical action aimed at correcting literary-political, literary-sociological, literary-whatever situations. If publishing channels are clogged, the editor proposes, examines, evaluates alternatives. If reviewing structures are inadequate, he shapes his journal as he sees the need. If bookstores are dead, he investigates the viability of other methods of marketing, proposes them, implements them himself where possible. God knows, at this juncture, the editor of the review journal must get his hands full of the crusty dirt of reality and practical action. The editor may not have the resources necessary to implement all programs he proposes; he ought, however, not be content to comment from his easy-chair, nor report from the press box above the playing field. Examination of theoretical possibilities is of great importance; but equally important in our current situation are programs of action, whatever form they may take. The New York *Times Book Review,* the *New York Review of Books*, and others, may not find such a course integral to their function, but for the review journal which intends to be effective in its work of extending the possibilities of literature, the need is obvious. Some review journals have already seen needs and have responded appropriately, by design or by instinct. Perhaps, however, we ought to be giving more careful extended consideration to the journal's practical role.

The good review journal does serve, then, diverse and sometimes apparently contradictory purposes, all of them valuable. It assesses the current literary environment and literary standards, creates new standards as they are needed; it presents information with the intent of making publications accessible (physically and intellectually), it propagandizes, it implements programs of practical action.

In making my various criticisms of existing structures, I am well aware, I'm afraid, that *Margins* does not—and in many ways does not—meet all my criteria. In setting down, as I have, what I consider the role and responsibility of the good review journal, I am able to mark off areas where *Margins* does not measure up. Such failings here should not deny the ideal, but rather indicate clearly the work that remains to be done—by *Margins* and by other of our alternative review journals. Not all editors of such journals will agree that these are sound working principles, I'm sure; and some do and have defined their purposes in other—more limited, or more open—ways. That *Margins* or any one review journal actually effects the delicate balance of the various elements I have outlined may be, ultimately, of lesser importance than I am ready to admit now. We may find, finally, that it is our alternative critical-reviewing structure *as a whole* which best assumes, in a fluid, natural way, the diverse roles I've envisioned for a single journal. Energy and experiment will tell. In the meantime, there is work for us to do.

1974

CCLM/COSMEP: A PARABLE FOR WHAT IT'S WORTH

A small, dusty town; hot sun overhead. Flies in the air with dust. Horses swat at them with their tails. Gray buildings, the sun brightens them. At the east end of town, a lone horseman rides in slowly, deliberately, a large full-boned man; mean, we have been led to believe, and rotten. At the west end of town, another horseman, smaller than the first, slighter, light and wiry, quick they say.

The horsemen dismount, each at his own station. Each tethers his horse. The street is empty. A few old men sit on the boardwalks in front of the stores and saloons which line the street. Some are talking quietly, some are whittling or carving pieces of wood. No one looks up.

In the saloons, cowboys drink, slapping each other on the back at each tall story. In the general store, a clerk is packing a large order for some rancher. In the dress shop, a woman fingers a new gown from out east, lovingly. She likes the feel of the fabric in her fingers. Smiles to herself.

On the street, the two horsemen face each other, squaring off, a show of guns now, a showdown. There is wind on the street, hot wind full of sun. The small wiry man hitches up his pants, adjusts his gun belt, wipes his nose. He ties down his holster with a leather thong. The full-boned man who came out of the east, tall and broad with thick fingers, clenches his hands into fists slowly, deliberately, wipes his brow with his forearm, touches his broad black hat.

The old men on the boardwalks still talk quietly, or whittle. In the saloon, drinks are being poured, stories told. The woman still caresses the fine dress, biting at her lip, wishing.

Flies buzz. Gunshots above the sound of flies. Clean full shots, you can hear them. No one looks up. Dust.

CYCLING/RE: A Viewing of Richard Kostelanetz's "Recyclings: a literary autobiography, Vol. I 1959-1967." (Assembling Press)

was time kostelanetz in lines however recyclings writes straight book his 1959-1967 but way is down grammar destroyed and result language from essays recyclings drawn quotes barthes fixed abolished cage demilitarizing kostelanetz breaking from usual straightforward favor more possibilities are significant are to imaginations manner simple it will however mathematical is to is criticism its footing it its context it its common sure are who say book but me that think more than reader are not kostelanetz's particular nor nor trends situations he contemporary craft and even and new american moves beyond is analysis what be is place discursive for reasoning critical cannot that require language to needs require method to goals goals are than analysis intent to material allow reader experience epiphany way critical sense is reader is to in gaps shape understanding raw kostelanetz providing don't that intends book be final not definitive about work i kostelanetz this be eye-opening for readers eyes frown and brains staid does it send searching ideas noticed can us for hidden that formerly us can permit reader return essays commenting two "bad the criticism this of age" "the art of no total" example on dimensions viewed this recycled arts be criticism this be criticism this can down can eyes have closed which wish remain this not only necessarily best or criticism should written it significant least would this anyone in breakthrough or we the garde you do you understand directions is context texture the today.

"OBITUARY"

We were distressed recently to learn of the passing on of a complex and sensitive writer. This prolific writer's demise came to our attention as we read his newest book, *South of No North,* a collection of stories recently published by Black Sparrow Press. Undoubtedly, readers of little magazines and small press books will share our sense of loss now that Mr. Bukowski—or Buk, to his many intimates—is no longer writing that sensitive and delightful prose and poetry we have come to expect of him.

Mr. Bukowski has been a giant among men, a writer who made his reputation and achieved his stature entirely in the small press world entirely on the strength of his concern for the language, the complexity of his vision, and his total devotion to his art; Black Sparrow Press's publication of his *South of No North* volume seems a fit and just climax— Buk would appreciate my choice of the word—to his steady and eventful career. As the biographical note beneath Richard Robinson's sensitive photograph of B. at the end of this volume notes so perceptively, Bukowski is "a major figure in contemporary American poetry and prose."

We take notice, reading B., of his handling of the English language. Nowhere in his work do we find such reckless and wayward prose as found in many of his contemporaries. His tenderness towards our language is evidenced by this carefully worked opening sentence from "You Can't Write a Love Story" in *South of No North*:

> Margie was going out with this guy but on the way over
> this guy met another guy in a leather coat and the guy in
> the leather coat opened the leather coat and showed the
> other guy his tits and the other guy went over to Margie's

> and said he couldn't keep his date because this guy in the
> leather coat was going to fuck this guy.

Seldom do we find in current literature writing that resounds so richly, tradition bearing heavy, bringing to mind passages from Gertrude
Stein and James Joyce, other giants. And more, the conclusion of "You
Can't Write a Love Story" reminds further of Joyce, of *Finnegans Wake*,
the story ending where it begins.

Where other writers have been content with the limited vision, dealing with only part of man's possibilities, B.'s vision is larger and more
far-ranging; the complexities of human experience do not elude him,
nor is he content with the easy characterization. The opening passage
of "A Couple of Winos" may serve to introduce us to both the complexities of B.'s vision and his careful techniques of characterization; I
quote the paragraph in full:

> I was in my 20's and although I was drinking heavily and not
> eating, I was still strong. I mean, physically, and that's some
> luck for you when not much else is going right. My mind was
> in a riot against my lot in life, and the only way I could calm it
> was to drink and drink and drink. I was walking up the road, it
> was dusty and dirty and hot, and I believe the state of Califor-
> nia, but I'm no longer sure. It was desert land. I was walking
> along the road, my stockings hard and rotted and stinking, the
> nails were coming up through the soles of my shoes and into my
> feet and I had to keep cardboard in my shoes—cardboard, news-
> paper, anything that I could find. The nails worked through
> that, and you either got some more or you turned the stuff
> around, or upside down or reshaped it.

Beyond the vision of life, beyond characterization, Bukowski seems also, in the paragraph, to be setting down for us his complicated vision of
art and its function: to turn the stuff around, or upside down, or reshape it.

B.'s vision is complex, as I've said, and more cogent than the obviously aimless wallowing of writers who claim to be searching roots of human
experience. He knows what he's looking for, he knows where to find
it, and he's not afraid to bring together disparate elements of human experience, joining them irrevocably (from "Politics"):

> I didn't want to do anything. I didn't even want to go to
> gym. In fact, the last thing I wanted to do was go to gym and
> sweat and wear a jockstrap and compare pecker lengths. I
> knew I had a medium-sized pecker. I didn't have to take gym
> to establish that.

And, the vision becoming more complex, the elements coming together (again from "Politics"):

'Some guys like to fuck bitching women, I don't.'
　'I suppose Pattie didn't bitch?'
'All women bitch, you're the champ.'
　'Well, why don't you go back to Pattie?'
'You're here now. I can only house one whore at a time.'
　'Whore?'
'Whore.'
　Ann got up and went to the closet, got out her suitcase and began putting her things in there. Jack went to the kitchen and got another bottle of beer. Ann was crying and angry. Jack sat down with his beer and took a good drain. He needed whiskey, he needed a bottle of whiskey. And a good cigar.

What other post-Freudian writer grapples with the larger emotions of man's existence so adequately, so sensitively, with intricate complexity yet crystal clarity. What other writer brings so much of actual daily living, as evidenced by the quotes above—the stuff of life, full human experience—to his writing. What other writer has taught us about ourselves so much that we might not otherwise discover.

What other writer indeed: not dead literally, only literarily.

THE OLD ONE

Reading David Middlebrook's *The Old One* (Urion Press) is akin to reading an old man's face—looking at the lines and wrinkles, you can see more than just the weathered skin, the creases around the eyes: you can see pieces of a life, each in place, and each suggesting far more than we might at first realize. *The Old One* is fairly straightforward narrative, crisp and tight with an economy of langugae that surprises almost to the point of dismay: you read, even if you read slowly, with a sense that you're passing over a lot of story and a lot of character so quickly. This is not to say the plot and characters in *The Old One* are poorly developed; they are handled superbly, and quite to Middlebrook's purposes in the novel. The reader may catch himself reading slowly, savoring each word, each syllable even, for all its juices. I found myself carefully exploring the rich texture of Middlebrook's cloth, exploring shades and shadows beyond the words in black and white.

The novel has three parts; the plot itself is uncomplicated and straightforward: things fit and fit well. In Part One, Peter (the protagonist, Shepp (Peter's archrival/new friend), Randolph and Chase (two of Shepp's friends) and Tot (the girl that both Peter and Shepp feel attached to) discover a secret room in a cave used centuries earlier by Indians. The chief characters in the novel are young when the story opens, between 12 and 15. You feel, reading *The Old One,* that Tom Sawyer and Huck Finn are kin-in-spirit to these young adventurers; and you feel also that Middlebrook is intent upon achieving far more than a good "story", that he wants to treat serious questions about human existence in a fully serious way, in all their complexities. In Part Two we find that Peter has apparently been killed by a bus while walking along a country road, coming back from the cave (we think we learn this), that he is indeed alive and moving in the world, and in mysterious ways.

Onto this simple framework, Middlebrook has hung myth and ritual, history and symbol. The myth, ritual, and history are essentially Indian. Middlebrook attempts to place the town of Shays in historical and cultural perspective, and perhaps to set down the central parable of the novel:

The Indians never saw Shays. They never saw a railroad or a white man. They lived too early and died too quickly to catch a glimpse—as later Indians did—of the people who would transfigure the land—what would grow and prosper, what would die. They decided to plant, even in the barren soil, and become the most peaceful of tribes. Few men journeyed into their isolated city and the members of the tribe who left to trade with the people of the east and south always returned. The end would come, the old men of the tribe could foresee, when their youths drew on the instincts of the hunt from the people to the north. The northern land provided mostly meat, but at the cost of war for the right to it. So their hills became like a vast body with canals and gates, places of storage, drainage and irrigation tunnels—all tiled to prevent the hills from crumbling beneath them. The breath of the city was rain. Rain then was more plentiful. When it did not fall, the city grew still and the old men chose leaders who decided what allotments of food should be given out; then they chewed a bitter cactus plant which for many hours drew them into the sight of the Great Spirit, making their bodies beat with a rhythm that seemed an intimation —if not of rain—at least for future happiness. Their Evil Spirit had brought the dryness, not their God. It would only be to satisfy the earth-killer to spill human or animal blood which —in any event—could not irrigate enough soil to grow even one ear of corn. The Evil Spirit was anything that killed, and the word for evil and the word for killer were synonymous. Violence among the young was not punished, simply ignored. By the time the children reached the age of fourteen years, the

need for violence disappeared. If not, youth or man could be
banished from the city. But the Indians lived in mistrust of the
very land which gave them bread. They named the stars, they
knew the winds, knew when the rain would fall and also when
the drought would set in. But they could imagine a place where
drought never was and where their religious enemy did not live.
A large poisonous lizard, extinct in the area now but plentiful
then, was their embodiment of evil. The lizards were trapped,
thrown into a pit and allowed to kill one another. This stink-
ing pit was known as the bowels of the Evil Spirit. It was a
strong contrast to the incense and flower-filled room in which
every boy and girl at the age of sixteen listened to the elder re-
cite the origins of the tribe—what manner of men they had come
from and what manner they had become. The boy was then
given a season in which to decide whether he would stay in the
city or leave it. Females were not permitted to choose. If the
boy decided to stay, he was introduced to the mysteries and initiated. An explanation of why men had been thrust from a
better place they could imagine into the land of death and poison was given by the Elders at this time. A lizard's body was
disemboweled and the long intestine dried and treated with
gum from a catus plant. It was then made into an instrument
producing a faint echoless music. In the ceremony itself, boys
and girls were initiated together and their bodies belonged to
the one mind which it was the Indians' purpose to be in constant communion with. Desire was considered to be holy and
the rules guiding love were complex. If a man loved a woman,
she received him into her house and fed him for two weeks. If
after this time she still did not love him, he was forced to
leave the city for the same period of time that he had stayed
with her; then he had to return and be re-initiated. If a man
loved an unmarried woman who was already living with a
man, the three of them shared her house for a period of a
month. During this time no lovemaking was permitted unless
the lover or the suitor withdrew. After a month's time, if the
woman still preferred her lover, the suitor had to leave the
city, return, and be re-initiated. Those men and women who
lived together for eight seasons and still preferred one another to all suitors could be married. No suitor could enter
their house. A woman was not allowed to enter the house of
another woman for purposes of love with a man.

When spells of melancholy came upon the Indians they carved
stones with a fitful jagged pattern or made tiles or composed
music on their instruments. Melancholy was, in fact, a characteristic of the tribe, as was the saving and transforming of all
things. Rocks, stones, beans, cornshucks, animal skins, metal

—all were transformed or worked into some kind of pattern.
But the men felt a sense of their smallness and could not see
how it was possible to transform the vast desert into a land of
their desire. At the time of their dispersal they had begun to
dig wells and troughs in a range of hills sixty miles distant. Their
lives never changed. Finally, a great drought, foretold by one of
their prophets, brought death and wandering to the entire city.
It took only a year for the water and food supplies to run out.
Many groups of individuals wandered away, hoping to find water and a place to wait for a few years, before returning. They
were either tortured by foreign tribes or initiated into their cus-
toms. Most of the Elders stayed on, using the cactus plant to
invoke visions of their future home. Old men dropped in the
fields, unintentionally delivering into the hands of the earth
the human blood which had been withheld for so long in religious abstinence. For years afterward, troughs and passageways
efficiently guided rain water to the fields of the eastern side
of the hills. A few wild crops flourished, but no Indians lived
to harvest them. Those members of the tribe who returned at
a later time had broken their pledge not to kill. Their children
were swept into the fire of change. Decades and centuries
passed. Tides of sand filled the wells and sealed the openings
of the tunnels, and the hills came to look like uninhabited
forms again. Buried jewelry, instruments, implements for cook-
ing, rooms with the skulls of the elders, went unnoticed though
men worked [in mines] just beneath them.

It is the heritage of these Indians that Peter, Shepp, Tot and the others discover—fall into; and they fall into the ancient rituals, by chance
(or it seems by chance, until we've read the full account), and all five
youngsters are deeply affected. Peter pushes Shepp through a hole in
the floor of the subterranean room; Shepp falls down and down, into
ashes, and surprisingly is able to find his way out of the hole, back into the room. Peter, Randolph, Chase, and Tot enter the hole in turn,
and return, through secret mazes. We learn that the youngsters have
performed part of an ancient (and lost) Indian initiation ritual, and that
they have been, not in fact, but in spirit and in the deepest places in
their blood, initiated into the mysteries that we can only partially understand. It is Peter who seems most deeply affected; and Part Two of
the novel proceeds without Peter, who has apparently been killed. The
youngsters are about two years older than when they first discovered
the secret room; the three remaining boys are to tell the story of the dis-
covery of the room to their schoolmates at an assembly, and to a professor of archaeology who is interested in the find. Tot is pregnant,
either by Shepp or Peter. The Indian history, unfolded in Part Two, is
revealed by Dr. Blicks, the archaeologist; the passage quoted above is

essentially his view of what Indian culture had existed in Shays area in ancient times. In Part Two, the reader is drawn to ask questions which go far beyond concerns about plot or structure of the novel: for forty pages we are left in suspense about Peter's ultimate fate, having no more than hearsay and rumor as evidence of his death. We are led to wonder about Tot, and her pregnancy, and its ultimate meaning. Details which in earlier passages appeared as merely isolated elements begin to seem more and more deeply interwoven into the fabric of mysterious existence; we begin to suspect that ancient ritual is modern ritual, that the Indians' adolescent initiation is a contemporary event, re-enacted now. The way that Peter held his arms in the secret room has links to the past. The atmosphere of the novel becomes as dense as thick fog, the mystery we feel around us as we read seems darker than the fullest night. And we are led to ask: what is good, what is evil—for the lost culture of the Indians, for the contemporary society of Shays.

In Part Three, some questions are answered: we learn the circumstances of Peter's apparent death, how he changed jackets with a boy of his own size and build who'd actually been hit by the bus, how the boy had been decapitated in the accident, how Peter found the head and buried it. Peter's parents identified the body as Peter's. We are led to wonder about an earlier reference in the novel to the boy who died as Peter's near look-alike: and by the time we read fully the meaning of "Peter's Testament" at the end of the book, we wonder even more: the cloth is close woven.

We learn, reaching the end of the novel, that:

> Peter had come to see. To see what would happen. He had popped up in the world and made his gestures and had helped to uncover the ancient city. He came and witnessed it. That was enough.

Peter transcends time and culture: he is not a youngster, resident of Shays, though he appears so throughout most of the book; nor is he simply the ghost of an Indian come back to haunt the ancient grounds. He stands beyond that; the shadows and the shades we've seen throughout the narrative are revealed more clearly now, bright and colorful and significant. This is Peter's testament:

> I want back the tree, the rock, and the ruby. I will never make them again the same way if they disappear because nothing has ever been made the way I wanted it. I couldn't control it. When I was left alone at first I didn't know what had happened. I was too heartsick to understand what was wrong. The first thing I did was I opened my mouth and that's when I found out I didn't have one. I found out that I didn't have any eyes or feeling. I might have left everything alone if it hadn't been for those things I couldn't feel anymore.

In the town of Shays, Peter is believed dead, and believed to have died mad and raving. His "testament" is his notebook, his words set down and given to Tot. They evidence serious schizophrenia—this, only at the level of common understanding, however, only in the "real" world where where vision counts for little. We begin to understand the cultural parable Middlebrook poses; we see links between past culture and myth, the present, the future of man. Fundamental problems of existence are Middlebrook's concerns; he is no John O'Hara to be examining the mannerisms and mores of a particular place, time, and social milieu. No. There is stuff in the world, good and evil, that our eyes cannot see, that the mind's eye refuses to accept. Middlebrook has touched it.

The Old One is a novel one cannot set aside easily once it's been picked up; it is a novel that you might think about long after you finish reading, to probe its meaning for more meaning; to go for the marrow of of the bone. It is a novel to take with you.

FIVE BOOKS FROM CAVEMAN PRESS (NEW ZEALAND)

The title of William L. Fox's *Trial Separation*, we are told in the jacket notes, "reflects his geographical dislocation from America to New Zealand during the latter half of 1971, and also refers to his failure to provide any clear dividing line between prose and poetry in this book." Whatever the nature of Fox's geographic dislocation, what is more interesting in this statement, and in the collection itself, is the lack of "any clear dividing line."

Prose, if it is good prose, makes use of many of the tools more proper to poetry. The ultimate distinction between prose and poetry—if we are pushed to ultimates—might lie in this: prose is linear in some or other sense—logical, narrative, psychological, conversational; prose is simile. Poetry moves, not with linear motions, but as process: as the tides move, by volume; by density of volume; by apposition, conjunction; by unspoken and mysterious (though not ambiguous) links; poetry is metaphor.

Fox's *Trial Separation* is difficult to categorize. Part of the difficulty lies in Fox's choice of materials, which are of two kinds. First, Fox observes and records bits of the world external to himself; he internalizes that world in his recording of it, as in this untitled poem:

> "someone has etched
>   a forest
> on my windshield
>   this morning
> all day i drive
> watching the leaves fall."

Or in this:

> "ridgepole poem
> is bearing more
> than it should.
>
> Smoked meat,
> axes, pots and
> pans, the roof.
>
> my family is
> breaking thru
> this house."

The second kind of material in the collection is that found entirely on Fox's internal landscape, a world which has no connections to an external world with its conventions and necessities, as in the first stanza of this untitled poem:

> "i can explain the egg
>   that's appeared
>   on my lawn this morning.
>   green and brown speckled eggs,
> small, out of a museum of childbirth."

And in the poem "free enterprise":

> "delicate is the frontier of the post-office
> half-frozen postmen huddling behind three
> blank walls
> and a roof promised by the government
> for next year.
>
> they receive more mail there
> than any other station in the free world—
> letters to lost relatives, queries
> from mystics about climate
> and availability of women,
> questionaires from commercial concerns.
> about space for rent
> and current population.
> the workers pass these among themselves,
> answering none, keeping only poems
> which ask no questions.
>
> when wolves come by for delivery

> they place bundles of envelopes
> in their mouths
> and send them over the border."

Fox's recording of his observations of the external are, I think, clearly poetry rather than prose; and some of them are, certainly, well-made poetry. They are clear views of objects and their attendants, in motion, in organic process, and they end being larger than the sum of their parts. They move easily by metaphor, leaping chasms; and we as readers can follow.

But Fox's poems from his internal landscape are another matter: first, that landscape seems to some extent dull and uninteresting as well as inaccessible. What Fox chooses to show us is not nearly enough to give us our bearings, to point us north. Without at least a well-placed landmark, without some perspective on the rest of what we see, we walk in circles; where we are going resembles where we have been:

> "the clothing stores are quietly producing clothes
> that fit no one. tailors are receiving measurements
> that belong to nobody we know: arms two feet longer
> than necessary, pants short by a foot, jackets with
> chest sizes twice their normal cut.
>
> all these are delivered to the best houses in town.
> there's no mistake, the boxes are clearly marked.
> my wife has the same problem, even with dresses from
> New York and Paris: too short, too wide, holes cut
> out around the genitals—she tells me the servants
> are getting suspicious."

Here, though we do not require linearity, we find it—though to what purpose? Though links may rightly remain unspoken, we are forced to ask ourselves the larger significance of these events—logically, emotionally, psychically, sociologically. I do not ask for cause and effect relationships into a world I know, and not for obvious parallels. But I do ask for significance in some human context; and, other than as mere literary exercise, and as an exercise of Fox's imagination, I don't find it in such a poem. Of what and to whom is Fox speaking? Throughout Fox's poetry of this second type we are left with that question.

We conclude that this second kind of poem moves entirely by the force of Fox's own intellect/psyche, and as such it stands dislocated from fuller human context. What we find sometimes is easy surrealism, recognizable. But more often the poem lacks the underlying psychological and emotional necessities and intensities that mark the best of surrealism. The poems, accordingly, seem to stand as simile, in one to one relationship, with Fox's interior landscape and to move according to necessities known only to Fox. We do not recognize them as process, apposition, metaphor in familiar senses. This is the weakness of these po-

ems, and one not found in Fox's observation/recording of an external
world.

II

Trevor Reeves is a poet trying, sometimes desperately, to link his ab-
stract realities to the concrete world he has observed; or to express as
subtle lesson what his observations have taught him. Throughout
Stones, we find tension, a deliberate tautness, between idea and image,
between thought and thing: when Reeves balances the two elements
properly, the poems are highly effective, as in "Trail":

> "dawn
> in ice
> red scented
> and rising
> fluffs
> at a touch
> of air
>
> till man's neighbour
> the nature
> of his scythe
> swings
> with steel fingers
> leaving the day
> frozen
> in the centre
> of passing"

Or in "Goldminer's Place":

> "The old chinese miner
> has gone
> his sluice gates are
> shut up
> rotted
> and weary deer now
> make their way
> down deserted raceways
> from the snows and
> ranking winds
> in a sun
> brandishing yellow
> halos, the grass
> I tread disperses
> like burnt paper
> towards the wrought
> fenced tombstone

> rusting, his life
> filed
> and harshly measured
> by ton and caught
> super gold,
> and now no name remains
> only a tarnished surface
> silence"

Reeves manages powerfully to pursue an object seen to where it leads, in these poems, and meaning explodes out of mere fact in handling. Reeves is able to explore nuance, shade of feeling as if searching the dirt on roots for secrets. When he is successful, Reeves' poetry is superb.

But his failures strike at both the ear and the intellect. "Apple (to Cezanne)" is one such:

> "The apple becomes an apple
>   in an orchard
>   but the sheen
> of these delicate strokes of red
> has undergone many processes"

There are a few poems in this collection which are less concerned with developing a meaning-unlocking tension between image and idea. "Quorum" is almost entirely concerned with "perspective and perception," for instance, and touches earth only to indicate it belongs to our world. And "Blurr" uses repetition effectively, with interesting results:

> "there's a pain in
> a pain in
> my head my
> head it grew
> into grew
> into a great great
> buzzing then buzzing
> flew away flew
> away fertilised
> a whole orchard
> of flowers"

Throughout *Stones*, Reeves' is poetry we recognize.

III

The poetry in Norman Simms' *Time & Time Again* is bloodless enough that—were we in a nasty frame of mind—we could label it purely academic. I have read any number of manuscripts by young poets who know—by generous estimation—one-tenth what Simms knows about the craft of poetry; and yet, the young poets, however ignorant of technique, are often able by sheer force of their vision and the urgency of their feelings to shape a powerful and human poetry.

Simms' poetry, for all its craft, is anemic by comparison; if it delights at all, it is not by insight or sweep of human vision, but by the delicacy of an intricate puzzle completed. "Your Mind to Me" is a prime example:

> "Your mind to me, a glossary of odd
> and ancient words, a hoard of similes
> and smiles, that like a toppled face of god
> defies interpretation. Yet I seize
> this moment out of time, and try this term
> and that, perform new rites or sing new chants,
> look you up and find you out, by firm
> or pliant means, although I know I can't.
> Your mind to me is a grand concordance
> of all the mysteries I've ever heard
> in love or life; still no analyses
> reveal the order, no patterns have recurred;
> and so, though centuries may pass beyond
> the errors of my text, only you will be
> my study, on you, my sweet pedantic love."

Or again, in "Fire in New Orleans: December 2, 1972," Simms constructs carefully, first indicating what it is he is not talking about, then what does interest him, and finally he makes a terse and disinterested observation that, given the material he is working with, seems particularly bloodless:

> "Lucifer fell headlong down,
> vaporous, to the icy lake of pain,
> and so too Titans, challenging
> the new commanding gods, swooped
> earthwards into another darker realm;
> and even sparrows, falling, are said
> to have a certain grace, a kind
> of providential meaning. But the ten
> who one by one tumbled sixteen storeys,
> skirts indecorously flapping over eyes,
> hands contorted, legs ridiculously
> swirling, look like pointless dolls flung
> by spoiled children out of windows, or
> bitter squid bored fishermen toss
> back at midnight from the chilly pier:

while a foolish helicopter flits here
and there, unable to be heroic or
to make hieratic bargains with the fire."

Simms is a poet who knows the craft of poetry. He is not, however, at least by the indications of this collection, a poet who knows the
stuff of poetry, and the stuff of life. He leaves us looking for blood,
elsewhere.

IV

Peter Olds stands in marked contrast to Simms; if anything, Olds'
blood flows too freely where Simms' doesn't flow at all. Throughout
the poems in the first part of this book, *The Snow and the Glass Window*, we find a concern for the small details of life (e.g. "And now it's
autumn-/ I hear that leaves turn red/and yellow, but up my street/they
look kind of sick grey,/ though I do see orange peel/now and again. . .")
though at times the interest is that of the conversationalist: content to
talk about what he's seen along the way, loosely and without making
tensions evident—either in what he saw, or in his own mind. Though
we find fault with Simms' bloodless craftsmanship, we find fault with
Olds' craftless blood, when it is craftless:

MORNING PRESS-UPS

"2 cups of tea
3 cigarettes &
one page of newspaper—
I'm staggering already.

I know I'm crazy—
the flies are getting at me
so I grab for the KILLER SPRAY
to do them in,
halfway thru a page on the indo-china war.
now, there are 2 books on the table—
one of Freud's INTERPRETATION OF DREAMS,
the other
Archibald Baxter's WE WILL NOT CEASE
& a fly buzzing, dying, hopping from
WE WILL NOT CEASE to THE INTERPRETATION
OF DREAMS

. . . I'm getting a bit sick of this,
I think I'll have another smoke."

I am not comfortable with recitation poems; there is no idea but in things, as Williams tries to indicate; but things must be given a context, must have shape and particularity that allows "thingness", the special character, to transcend "object" and suggest broader human involvement. All "things" have tentacles reaching out into a human world, have roots, if we consider them carefully; part of the poet's function, while not transforming objects, is to bare the roots for us. Olds often enough fails this task.

In the long title poem that closes the book, though, the poetry is far more successful. In the second section, for instance, the objects do belong to a world we can touch, though perhaps not at the gut level Olds reaches it at:

> "2
> He is alone in the room.
> The coal-range, shelf-clock and
> jam cupboard are quiet.
> He watches the light snow
> melt on the ground and
> it reminds him of mother's pastry.
> He watches the ice slide
> down the windy glass.
> It reminds him of mother."

And we are led, by the force of the poem, to accept a quiet vacancy, a tension between the world here and the world beyond the glass of the window, until Olds explodes towards anger and further tension. "Outside was not as rough/ as it looked from within:/ crabapples grew on nearly every tree. . . " Finally the tension creates climax: "In world confusion/not a sound worth noting was/heard. . ./ 'What have you lost? boomed/ the sky." The last section:

> "8
> 'What have you missed?'
> whispered earth.
> In controlled desperation
> He raised his fist and
> broke the glass."

When Olds is successful, he is powerful.

V

D.S. Long, with *Burrow Pit,* is perhaps the most interesting of the poets under review here. He is willing to take risks with his poetry, to show blood. But they are risks of a full professional and the blood is not spilled wantonly. Long shows us the vein or artery when he shows us blood; we can watch a living body. "Watershed," for instance, is minimal in its details, and especially in explanation of connections between details: but we find the links.

> "trace of a cloud
>   veins
>   in the eyes
>
> a dream in which you fall
>   in the fohn
>   grass heavy with dust
> the eyes too loose in the skull"

Or in poem "1210":

> "morning
>   light withering the trees
>   my own sounds
>   recoilless
>
> I am storing stones for winter".

And a world is cracked open before us. Long's poetry flashes and snaps with surprise; it feels faintly oriental in its revelations.

The only flaw in such a collection is the rare poem which doesn't spark. "1052" is one, and it fails, I think, because Long abandons the particularity he is so insistent upon in the rest of the collection.

> "light coming from the brutal trees
>   the eyes see too much
> of these hard images
>   the woman next door
> hangs out woolen sheets
>   an audible native song
> the pregnant throat
>   another interior imagination"

The vague generality of "another interior imagination" doesn't bring knowledge or insight.

But Long's failure here is rare: these are poems which need to be read to be fully appreciated; it is difficult to reflect their quiet power in a review: they thrust insight (Long's) outward (to us as readers). If we consent to read Long (and we should) we cannot ignore or pass off his revelations. And that is why his poetry moves us.

SOME POLEMICS, PRACTICAL CONSIDERATIONS
OR A MODEST PROPOSAL

Literature today finds itself in a very difficult position. Commercial publishers have published less and less "literature" in recent decades, and promise to publish even less in the future. Literature is not, it seems, a "saleable commodity" in our culture. On the other hand, we have come to value the independence, integrity and, sometimes, the "alienation" of the writer/artist. Thus, the writer today is faced with a choice: either to write "not-literature" which will sell; or to throw himself at the mercy of governmental, quasi-governmental or private funding institutions. The choice of either involves many tradeoffs: money for "art", freedom for security, etc.

Small literary publishing finds itself in a similar predicament. The small publisher's "wares", either magazine or book, cannot compete in the market place. Publications are produced at a financial loss; that loss must be made up out of the publisher's pocket, out of the author's pocket, out of government subsidy, out of some source other than the "commodity" itself. That which is best is not always that which sells.

2.

In the west, we have a tradition of subsidy for the arts—many painters and writers had "patrons" to keep the writer/artist's body and soul together while he produced his masterpieces. These patrons were often "private" as opposed to governmental. Subsidy of the arts—whether literary or visual—is at root a fascist enterprise. It becomes increasingly so the closer the control of subsidies moves toward government—i.e., the more directly subsidy comes from "tax" money. We realize of course, that all governmental activity is to some extent fascistic. In recent times, when tax money was being poured bushel after bushel into the war in Vietnam, the fascistic aspects of governmental action were most clearly seen. More recently, government money was poured into Chile to encourage and support the overthrow of Allende. The process which allocates money to projects with great potential harm for mankind is the same process that allocates money for the arts, potentially very beneficial. If a government is permitted control over funds for artistic endeavors, it is also permitted control over funds for less humane purposes. I am not questioning the "ends", whether good or evil; I am questioning the process by which the ends are achieved. The power to do good is the power to commit atrocities. If a writer/artist or small publisher concedes that the government has the right to fund his efforts, he also concedes to the government the right to defoliate the Vietnamese countryside. The process, in either case, is the same.

The funding of art/literature through private means, i.e., foundations, donors, or whatever we wish to call patrons of the arts, has fascistic elements as well. The choice to encourage one kind of endeavor over another seems an absolute choice which has ramifications for all of culture. It seems easier, however, to grant the private benefactor the right to do with his funds as he pleases. A well-educated and concerned person can allocate his wealth in any manner suitable to his tastes and disposition (and his income tax strategies), often for the benfit of many. We can and should wonder, however, about the injustices which may have been committed to build the wealth of a philanthropist. I can't help wondering, for instance, how many Americans were unjustly treated and unjustly paid to accumulate the donations which built our great art institutions, museums, performing arts centers, libraries, etc. Our most prominent cultural institutions have often been built of human flesh and bones and misery. For a writer/artist to accept "private" funding for his work may implicitly require him to accept social and cultural conditions which he opposes.

The most forceful and convincing argument for accepting either government or private funding for the arts is this: the money is available and might as well be put to a use which you think the most valuable and worthwhile, i.e., your own project; the money will be spent on something, in any case; it might as well be on your work, etc. Many of us accept this argument: let the money do what good it can for art/ literature, small publsihing, whatever.

If this argument convinces, one needs to recognize what else one accepts along with the money. And what one gives up.

3.

Man's impulse to art arises from the same source as his impulse to religion. Like religion, art should be separate from government.

Art and government are incompatible ways of structuring the world. Through art, the individual pulls personal order out of chaos. Through government, whether democratic or dictatorial, order is imposed on the world without regard to the necessities of the personal order of the individual.

When art and government mingle, it is to the detriment of art.

4.

Government does not owe the writer, artist, or small literary publisher anything. In our welfare state, we have come to think otherwise.

We seem to have forgotten about past artists starving in garrets.

5.

Easy money makes us fat: government subsidy spreads fat across the land. Good small magazines, handed money, can become sloshy, ineffectual fat ones. There are exceptions, of course; many small magazines have used funding wisely and responsibly.

Easy money, however, puts the publisher in a strange frame of mind: the publishing of a literary magazine is no longer a struggle. If and when funding stops, the publisher has forgotten how to make-do on his own. The magazine folds.

To pour money into literary magazines is to fatten them for the kill: when the money stops, the magazines die off/insidious censorship.

6.

Do we write, edit, and publish in order to eat/or do we do these things, & eat as we can?

7.

An alternative to funding small literary magazines directly would be to fund public and university libraries to establish a program for the collection of little magazines. Under such a plan, librarians would be required to use allocated funds only for subscriptions to small magazines; they would be provided a list of suitable magazines by CCLM or a similar organization. Magazines on that list would be divided into categories, i.e., mimeo mags, university quarterlies, small independent mags like *New* or *The Fault*, local and regional magazines, etc. The libraries would be required to select a certain percentage of magazines from each category, but would be free to choose which magazines in each category they would order. Only a certain percentage of funds, for instance, could be used for university quarterlies.

Such a program would have three beneficial aspects. First, it would make magazine publishers responsible for the money they receive: they would have subscriptions to fill. The money received from such subscriptions would support the magazine—perhaps not so fashionably as some editors would like, however; at the same time, the publisher would necessarily have to use his money judiciously. If he doesn't provide what he promises (by subscription) to provide, his magazine will not be re-ordered by libraries. Such a program would introduce a better method of financial accountability for magazines: they would have to deliver what they've sold. Currently, magazines are accountable to CCLM for funds received; whether the money was spent wisely is not a question that arises, only whether the money has been spent to support the magazine. If a magazine were to continue publishing under a funded library-subscription program, it would have to use its funds judiciously.

Secondly, such a program could allow wider and perhaps more equitable disbursement of funds. Instead of some magazines receiving the lion's share of the funding, the requirement that libraries subscribe to a certain number of certain kinds of magazines would spread more money among more magazines than presently receive funds through CCLM. Of course, each magazine would receive less—the growth of the magazine, however, would necessarily be "organic"; the magazine would not be gorged with easy money.

Hypothetically, if $250,000 allocated to small literary magazines were spread to 1,000 libraries, each would receive $250 for subscriptions to small magazines. If funding is accepted by libraries with the stipulation that no more than 10 per cent of the money could go into "administrative" costs, $225 would remain for subscriptions (or, of the total $250,000, $225,000 would remain for subscriptions). If the average subscription cost per year per magazine were about five dollars, each library would be able to obtain 45 journals. Requiring a library to subscribe to a certain number of journals from its region would insure support for local endeavors. If there were 500 magazines on the list from which libraries were able to select, each, potentially, would receive $450 in subscription monies. Normal library selection processes, of course, would be used to determine which magazines a particular library would obtain. This would put support for literary magazines on a broader base than it has with CCLM "grants" committees, in which favoritism/cronyism can be a factor. If, as the program is implemented, it appears that important magazines are being neglected by libraries, another category could be written into the selection-list, insuring that some of the neglected magazines, at least, would get support.

Finally, such a program would insure that, contrary to the present situation, "government" money would be used to make subsidized publications accessible to the reading public. As it is now, a magazine can receive $200-$5000+ in government money, and the entire run of an issue can remain boxed in storage. Present funding policies do not insure that subsidized literature will be read, only that it will be printed.

The alternative I'm proposing would, of course, need a good deal of work in order to be implemented. For instance, it may be necessary to insure that libraries would not use this funding in order to subscribe to magazines they would order in any case. Such a plan, however, appears to me to be more desirable—for the three reasons I've enumerated—than present programs. Such an alternative, I think, should be examined. thoroughly.

8.

When money is being discussed, when money is being handed out, there is seldom much agreement among the parties involved. Money does that to people, it seems. There are no solutions to the problems of funding writers, artists, and small publishing ventures. Only more questions of the kind we've seen raised in discussions on grants. Pandora's box.

THE PROSPECTS OF INTELLIGENT WRITING

I read and admired Rachel Carson's *Silent Spring* a few years after it appeared, in the heat of the controversy about pesticides. Shortly after reading Richard Kostelanetz's *End of Intelligent Writing* (Sheed & Ward) I chanced to pick up Frank Graham, Jr.'s *Since Silent Spring* (Houghton-Mifflin, 1970). Graham's book is an account of how Ms. Carson came to write *Silent Spring*—the reluctant crusader—and about the controversy which swirled around her for the few remaining years of her life and around the book after Ms. Carson died. *Since Silent Spring* is an intriguing book, uncovering the vested interests of many of the "critics" who attacked and damned *Silent Spring* as inaccurate, misleading, and downright false. Certainly, few chemical companies producing residual-persistent pesticides were happy when portions of the book appeared in *New Yorker* magazine, and fewer still when the full book was published later. There was big money in pesticides, to be sure, and furor over the long-term effects of DDT, aldrin, dieldrin, and other such substances on human health would cut corporate profits. The chemical companies, moving to reduce the influence of Ms. Carson's book, mounted vigorous publicity campaigns against it. More insidiously, supposedly reputable scientists, who had been studying the effects of pesticides *with grants from the chemical companies producing the toxic substances*, uniformly attacked the book and defended pesticides in the face of the compelling evidence Ms. Carson had gathered. "Reviews" by such academic critics, to all appearances disinterested third parties, appeared in reputable journals. *Silent Spring*, however, withstood the onslaughts of the chemical corporations and the research scientists directly or indirectly on their payrolls. Today, more than ten years since *Silent Spring's* publication, Ms. Carson stands vindicated as DDT is more and more widely banned.

There is a lesson in this. Richard Kostelanetz's *The End of Intelligent Writing* is going to be widely labelled as inaccurate, misleading, and downright false. That is predictable. Those with vested interests in publishing-as-it-is are going to strike out in influential journals of all sorts. The New York literary mob doesn't exist, they'll say, except in the wild imagination of a paranoic Kostelanetz. There is no "white collar mugging" in New York they'll say. Kostelanetz is through as a writer, they'll say. And *that's* the reason it took him years to get this expose of commercial publishing into print.

But, certainly, *The End of Intelligent Writing* will survive publicity campaigns of the "literary-industrial complex". It will survive the venom of "supposedly reputable" critics. Whether or not Kostelanetz's compelling evidence "proves" that there is an actual living-breathing conspiracy against intelligent writing in this country is not the truly vital question. Rather, appearances suggest that there is such a conspiracy. The kind of books commercial publishers continue to produce indicates there is such a conspiracy. The effects on the reading public are the same whether the conspiracy is actual or only apparent. The details of what takes place behind the closed doors in editorial offices in New York are of relatively minor significance. What matters is: young writers or avant garde writers or iconoclastic writers cannot pass through those doors. Their manuscripts sit boxed in desk drawers, in closets. Writers are giving up in frustration, or resigning themselves to publishing their work piecemeal in little magazines, just as much of *The End of Intelligent Writing* appeared in little magazines before it was brought out in book form.

Kostelanetz, fortunately, did not resign himself to publishing piecemeal only, but persevered. Sheed & Ward, Inc., is to be congratulated and admired for accepting the literary and cultural responsibility that American publishing seems to have shirked. Kostelanetz's is a persistent voice, the voice of a reluctant crusader who saw what needed to be done and accepted the challenge.

2.

Part One of *The End of Intelligent Writing* includes chapters on "Locating American Literary 'Establishments' ", "The Dynamics of Literary Politicking", "The New York Literary Mob", "Cultural Prosperity and Its Perils", "The Forms and Functions of Literary Power", "The Leverages of Collaboration", "Literary Rule and Professional Violence," "The Rule of Corruption and Repression", "The Rationales of Suppression", "The Literary-Industrial Complex", "The Rules of Ignorance and Philistinism", and "Double-Standards and Pseudo-Culture". These are, certainly, some awesome bulls to take by the horns. Kostelanetz handles himself with skill. He cites examples from his own experience and the experiences of other as evidence of "the end of intelligent publishing". The evidence is compelling. There is corruption in American publishing. We might nit-pick over particular items entered into evidence and particular criticisms, but we certainly have to admire the sturdiness of the whole cloth of evidence Kostelanetz presents.

3.

My initial response, after reading Part One, was: *well, so what? So what should I care about collusion behind NY publishing's editorial doors? So what if established publishing is shirking its responsibilities? Why is that important? Doesn't the work that independent small publishing has undertaken make whatever goes on in NY irrelevant to some degree?* That initial response was greatly tempered, however, by considerations about the power of information and the power of those in a position to produce and disseminate items of information. NY publishing presently owns and controls many channels of information in this country; it is NY publishing which fills those channels with the information it chooses. Therefore, though I believe that NY publishing may be entirely sterile in a matter of a decade or so, the corruption in publishing during the interim has serious cultural ramifications which cannot be ignored now. Though "alternative publishing" has grown and continues to grow, though it increasingly accepts America's cultural burdens, until alternative publishing is more visible than it presently is, until we see the other nine-tenths of the iceberg, until we change *status quo* prejudices, we have to concern ourselves with the corruption in present channels of communication. Such review journals as *Margins, Small Press Review, Booklegger, Shocks,* etc., simply do not reach and influence the audiences that the NY *Times Book Review* and the *New York Review of Books* touch. Until our own audiences are wider, we must be concerned, if we are serious about our cultural missions, about what information and what ideas are allowed to reach intelligent readers in America.

For myself, I have no desire to place a book with a NY publisher. Many small press folk of my acquaintance have no such aspirations either; these are serious, and many of them important, writers who have chosen the small press as the medium for their messages. "Alternative publishing" is no longer a stepping-stone to big-house publishing; little mags are no longer the proving grounds (or, a baseball analogy, the farm clubs) of mass circulation journals. This condition is not so much a change in the functions of small presses and little magazines, rather, a change in the way many writers are viewing publishing. Such a change of outlook is a significant breakthrough for alternative publishers and journals: more widely than in the past, alternative publishing stands not as the reverse image of NY publishing, but as a significant (and increasingly viable) force in its own right.

The most valuable cultural enterprises, clearly, are not always nor necessarily those which turn the best profit or have the greatest short-term impact (often this is obviously not the case). The best-seller, which has everyone talking for a few weeks or months, may be forgotten in a year or two. Art, generally, is allowed to touch only an elite few: our present cultural necessities require that. Our educational, social, and political structures reinforce the fact. I'm not one to believe that art requires an elite only. Rather, I firmly believe that a wide range of Americans could and would appreciate what now seems the province of a cultural elite. As things are, we see commercial publishers hyping schuck, then saying that's all the public will buy. We see them saying *this wouldn't sell* and *that wouldn't sell*, all the time ignoring the self-fulfilling nature of their prophecies. If we are serious surveyors and commentators on the current publishing scene, we have to be aware of the present circumstances in which information is produced and disseminated. We have to realize that if Americans are not offered intelligent writing, they cannot buy it. Part One of *The End of Intelligent*

Writing documents the end of "intelligent publishing" in the "literary-industrial complex". It should serve as a spur for thoughtful alternative publishers to take up those literary and cultural responsibilities abandoned elsewhere.

4.

Part Two of *The End of Intelligent Writing* moves discussion of literature and literary publishing beyond the established channels of publishing and dissemination. Chapters here include: "New Literary Periodicals", "Alternative Book Publishers", "The Nature and Fortune of Newcomers", "Young Writers in North America", "The New Poetries", "Innovations in Fictions, Dramas, Essays", "The Possibility of Rejuvenation", and "What is To Be Done". The first two chapters, "New Literary Periodicals" and "Alternative Book Publishers", provide an overview of alternative literary publishing in North America. These are two fairly lengthy chapters, totalling about 55 pages, yet they can do little more than sketch out the alternative publishing scene. They serve as a summary introduction to what is being done and give brief, sometimes cryptic indications of Kostelanetz's assessment of various publishers and periodicals. The chapters are not in-depth studies of particular presses or journals, and they were not intended as such. Whatever detailed discussion there is of particular presses or journals serves to identify and clarify characteristics of small publishing.

Given the literary situation exposed in Part One, these two chapters are intended to show us where to look for indications that intellgent writing and responsible publishing have not come to an end. In-depth commentary on alternative publishing would be a difficult feat for any writer: full and accurate criticism on the scene is a continual and challenging task, as many small press commentators will testify. Further, to do justice to the alternative publishing being done today, a writer would perhaps need to compile a book the size of *The End of Intelligent Writing* itself (480 pp.). There have been those who, as parts of the book appeared in various periodicals, complained of Kostelanetz's shorthand treatment of their journals or presses. But I've yet to see anyone else, *anyone*, attempt a survey the scope of Kostelanetz's. Alternative publishing is a broad canvas, and Kostelanetz's treatment here is an attempt to sketch in its general shape and characteristics.

The chapters on periodical and book publishers should serve as ground work for further commentary by interested writers. Kostelanetz looks at aspects of alternative publishing and what is being attempted. Canadian book publishers get some treatment, but deserve far more in an extended study, as do the feminist presses, the third world publishers, and others. Certainly commentators may latch onto parts of these chapters as bases for expanded and detailed studies of various categories of publishers. The full work on alternative publishing still needs to be written, of course, but Kostelanetz's treatment is a first large step. If *The End of Intelligent Writing* has the circulation it deserves, intelligent readers across the country will have clear indications of where to turn to find intelligent reading materials. I'm almost inclined to think that Part Two of *The End of Intelligent Writing* may spell the most trouble for NY publishing. Part One serves to expose some of commercial publishing's shennanigans; but Part Two guides the reader to non-commercial publications, and that alone should fog some bifocals in NY editorial offices.

5.

Publishers, in our culture, decide what can be read; the influential review journals what will be read. Distributors, booksellers, and too often libraries, largely follow the lead of the few influential but sometimes biased, idiosyncratic, or irresponsible decision-makers. The dissemination of information, in America, is unfortunately intricately bound with the production-publishing of information. The result: alternative reading in America is not easily accessible. Established publishing not only controls the production of books, but also the distribution, selling, and ultimately the reading of books in this country.

There are poets, fictioneers, playwrights, and essayists who are writing in America, and who continue to write despite the fact they are not published or are published piecemeal. Kostelanetz says:

> Although disorganized and distraught, young writers manage
> to exist, study, write, and occasionally publish, their works
> getting some circulation; and though their impact is far small-
> er than either the quantity or the quality of their numbers,
> it is clear that literate and imaginative young people have not
> all become journalists and film-makers, as the old-boy exclu-
> sionists would sometimes have it, but novelists, poets, play-
> wrights, and critics too.

He enumerates the names of many such writers in a list seven and a half pages long and makes a challenge: "Though I suspect that most of their names are unfamiliar even to each other, any 'critic of contemporary writing' who cannot identify works by fifteen percent of them should, perforce, retire into the Academy and lecture on people and periods past." Works by these writers would be our "alternative reading", were they to reach cultural daylight. Certainly, work by many such writers, those named in the list and those missed by Kostelanetz, is rarely published by commercial presses, and even more rarely reviewed by the influential review journals. Says Kostelanetz:

> Nearly all young writers are still "underground", whether
> they want to be or not, because they lack free access to the
> aboveground media; and though most of them were temper-

amentally (if not economically) unprepared for this disillusioning reality, the fact that so many should remain independent, uncynical, and productive is amazing as well as gratifying. Lack of literary talent or achievement has never been their problem, though the obstacles of literary politics and literary business are and will continue to be.

Whenever young writers are reviewed by the influential media, they are customarily handled by rear-guard literary "minute men" with an abandon akin to that of a kid plunking tin cans out behind the barn. And such plunking is passed off as serious cultural enterprise.

6.

Such a situation, and other points raised in *The End of Intelligent Writing*, turn up some essential questions about the nature of publishing in America, about the cultural values this country holds, about information, its value and its dissemination. More and more, information is power. Information shapes attitudes and cultural values. The person who holds information holds one of the most potent cultural weapons available.

We are led by necessity, therefore, to question the cultural responsibility of influential journals which allot review space on bases other than a book's full importance (or lack of it, bad books often serving as instructive lessons when properly discussed). Kostelanetz speaks out about *The New York Review of Books*:

> Literary reviewing media have the power. . . to decide what will (and will not) come to their audience's attention, and the possible power of a particular medium depends upon the quantity and quality of its readership. Although the *New York Review* has become the most powerful American cultural organ in the sixties, the publicizing purposes apparent from its beginnings have persistently favored Random House-Vintage produce in several ways. Since its editorship has neither changed not been diffused among assistants, only two people have ever officially chosen books or reviewers, or apportioned space: Robert Silvers and Barbara Epstein; and they alone must be judged initially responsible for the striking, if not shocking, disparities. For instance, in all the 1968 issues as surveyed in 1969 in Harry Smith's *The Newsletter*, "17 of 73 books singled out for individual review (more than 23% " were published by the Random House conglomerate— far more than any other publisher received, and more in sum than those from such quality-minded houses as Viking (one), Holt (two), Grove (one), Harvard (one), and Princeton (one) combined. . . . While it is true that Random House's multiple imprints make it larger than most of the other firms lis-

ted in the above comparison, the latter ten published more than six times as many titles in the previous year (3618 to Random House's 586).

Earlier in the book, Kostelanetz gives one indication why, or apparently why (the results being the same) Random House may receive preferential treatment; Jason Epstein was first in charge of Random House's Modern Library and then of its Vintage paperbacks, as well as serving as a senior editor in Random House's trade division. This is the same Jason Epstein who helped found *The New York Review of Books* and who frequently contributed reviews and letters-to-the-editor. There is evidence that "Epstein would. . . hang around the [*New York Review's*] office in the earliest days, opening the morning mail, writing headlines, and even soliciting reviews." Kostelanetz continues:

> The first "Statement of Ownership", published in the issue dated October 22, 1964, lists him [Epstein] among "the stockholders owning or holding one percent or more of the total amount of stock"—the others were his wife Barbara, [Robert] Silvers, Elizabeth Lowell (nee Hardwick), Robert Lowell, the *Review's* publisher A. Whitney Ellsworth, the poet James Merrill, and Blair Clark. . .

It is, without a doubt, culturally irresponsible for a publisher/editor who selects what can be read to have further advantage of selecting what will be read, via the pages of his own review journal.

The New York Times Book Review, which nearly monolithically gathers commercial publishing's advertising dollars (witness the demise of the attempt by the *Washington Post* and other papers to establish another weekly book review), selects books for review on grounds other than cultural significance. Kostelanetz again quotes a survey by Harry Smith's *The Newsletter*:

> which concludes that the medium's largest advertisers command reviewing attention disproportionately greater than their advertising space, while smaller advertisers suffer disproportionate neglect. "Most of the book companies placing more than 20 pages of ads had a review total approaching the ad page total [and they] tended to receive more than half as many review pages as ad pages", says the survey. For instance, Random House, with 74½ pages of advertisements, had 58 pages of reviews; Harper & Row, with 29¼ pages of ads, had 22¼ review pages. Little, Brown, also had 29 review pages. Less endowed advertisers received proportionately less attention—numerically measured either by reviews or review pages to ad pages—except Oxford University Press with seven reviews for 13½ pages of ads. Lippincott had 3¾ for 16½; and Harvard University Press had "negligible" notice for 9¼ pages. In more ways than one,

> therefore, reviewing space has been indirectly "for sale"; he
> who pays a piper gets at least a tune.

Such ratios, if they are not actually cause and effect relationships, at
least suggest that factors other than a book's merits impinge upon the
review editor's decisions about what will get space and what will not.

Further, the *New York Times Book Review* treats books as "news".
Kostelanetz points to the fallacy of approaching books this way:
"news" is what people are talking about and interested in; but the journals receive galleys of books well before actual publication; they have reviews in hand before anyone can be talking about or interested in a book
because the book is yet to be available on the street. Thus, the books
that are "news" are the books publishers' publicity departments hype
the most. The books that are talked about are the books the influential
journals choose to talk about. This is cultural serendipity, at best; at
worst it spells the end of intelligent reading.

The books distributors and booksellers handle are books that are reviewed (favorably or unfavorably—at least someone is talking about the
book, putting it in the public eye, making it at least visible). The books
librarians make available to their patrons are those which come to their
attention: often, with good but neglected books, the silence is deafen-
ing. The result: books that Americans should have readily accessible—
at least in their libraries—sit stored in publishers' warehouses or are
remaindered to butcher shops.

Journals such as *Library Journal* exist as safety valves: although *Library Journal* is nearly as biased against alternative publishing as are the
more popular media, they do give (however brief) attention to commercial books neglected by *New York Review* and the *Times Book Review*.
Unfortunately, in *Library Journal*, alternative publishing is treated as a
special province, getting space once a year in Bill Katz's small press
round-up. Would librarians' heads be turned around if a small press feature appeared in each issue? I'm inclined to think so.

In *New no. 24,* I say:

> I have some respect for the idea of libraries as "repositories
> of culture" but it is a secondary respect. Primarily I see li-
> braries as institutions we can use for cultural and social
> change. If we can change librarians, we can change the
> world (or at least the task will be easier).

If information is power, and it is, librarians can serve as an effective
channel of communication; it will be necessary, of course, for alternative publishing to get the attention of harried librarians and the task is
not easy. Even sympathetic librarians are strapped by restrictive institutional policies and restrictive budgeting. Reaching and changing librarians may not be a primary concern of alternative publishers, but it has to

be a serious concern and needs to be given thoughtful consideration. There seem to be few allies of small press more powerful than concerned, sympathetic, activist librarians. It seems wise for us to put some effort into communicating with them.

Certainly, there is merit to the argument that some presses and magazines must remain guerrilla enterprises, inaccessible to all but the initiated few; and they will. The 'hit-and-run' publisher can have significcant influence on the shape and trends of alternative publishing. But the influence will be self-abusive and masturbatory if none but the initiated few are affected. The more accessible publishers, I should think, are duty-bound to move the best of the guerrilla tradition into the mainstream of alternative enterprises.

For guerrilla publishing to be effective at all, however, we must have effective channels of communication. Constructing such channels, and keeping them open, is a central task of the alternative review media, but further, a primary task of all alternative publishers.

Certainly we can wonder whether a large part of the American reading public would have a new view of the books truly available to them if the *New York Review* and the *Times Book Review* changed their restrictive reviewing policies. Or would American publishing fall apart if its books were judged solely on merit?

Even the kind of alternative book publishers, the alternative weekly or bi-weekly newspapers, are sadly neglectful of alternative reading and have not contributed significantly to the construction of new channels of literary communication. Indeed, of some of them we may ask whether they forged any channels of communication at all. I've read—most recently in *Saturday Review*, that reactionary journal of the literary minute men—that literature is going to survive the young; that the pop books will pass. I quite agree. However, what the literary minute men— of many ilks—fail to recognize is that the books reviewed in the alternative newspapers aren't so different from those reviewed in the straight media: commentators in both media fail to look beyond what NY publishing is dishing out. How many truly alternative press books have been reviewed in the pages of *Rolling Stone*, or in the pages of your local alternative weekly. We must begin to wonder how long the "alternative" [formerly "underground"] papers can retain that classification when what they offer their intelligent readers is nothing very different from the usual. Political rhetoric does not an alternative make. Rich Mangelsdorff published his "Small Press Communications" regularly in the highly esteemed but now defunct *Nola Express*; beyond such efforts by Mangelsdorff and the editors of *Nola Express*, and by a very few others, the "alternative" in "alternative newspaper" seems pretty empty.

What Americans read, unfortunately, continues to be largely determined by a small number of ignorant (a condition that can be corrected with information) or stupid (a hopeless condition, I'm afraid) commentators. The coming bicentennial celebration of the American revolution seems as appropriate a time as any for overthrowing philistine ignorance with solid and comprehensive information; *The End of Intelligent Writing* arrives in time to call us to the task of making the necessary preparations.

7.

Where is the new writing, neglected by the influential journals, being reviewed? Often, only in little magazines with small circulations and small but interested audiences. Do the usual cheap shots about the way poets review other poets apply? Sometimes. Often enough. Much of the commentary on new writing is subterranean. There are some journals whose intent is to review/overview the new writing, and these too have failings—but not nearly so gross as the *NY Times Book Review* or *NY Review of Books*. Kostelanetz mentions some of the journals and indicates why he sees them as ineffective:

> All this activity [in little mags] creates the necessity for new
> periodicals about new literary periodicals; but these, too,
> are likely to reflect the limitations of the scene. One key
> weakness of Len Fulton's *Small Press Review* (est. 1967),
> Noel Peattie's *Sipapu* (est. 1969), and Richard Morris'
> *COSMEP Newsletter* (est. 1969), as well as the reviews in
> Peter Finch's *Second Aeon* (est. 1967, in Wales) and the *Al-*
> *ternative Press Index* (est. 1969), is a trade-magazine-mind-
> edness that avoids, but default, any head-on confrontation
> with the larger literary-political predicaments.

A more generous appraisal, as I would be inclined to make, would be to say that given the "limitations of the scene", the apparent limited interest in alternative writing (I say 'apparent' because only the tip of the iceberg that is alternative publishing has been seen and status quo cultural values are difficult to change), and the limited finances of these review journals, as well as the nature of their intended purposes at the outset (*COSMEP Newsletter*, for example, is an informational newsletter for COSMEP members; recent issues certainly have confronted larger literary questions, i.e., the state of literary grants in this country, though that is not the journal's primary purpose)—these journals constitute fairly remarkable statements about literary-political conditions. In another context, Kostelanetz says "Until better critical media emerge, the best way to learn about small press books is through the annotated catalogs of their distributors. . . " I venture to suggest that catalogs less openly confront literary-political predicaments then the above-mentioned journals, though catalogs may well provide acquisition information on more books. The very existence of these review magazines makes some communication possible and makes confrontations inevitable. And making information potentially accessible is, itself, an act of confrontation with literary-political predicaments, of course, whether in book catalogs or review journals.

I would venture further that "better critical media" are emerging, that new channels of communication are being constructed. Kostelanetz points out at the end of his preface that "The history documented in these pages stopped with the date at the bottom of the page", i.e., January 1, 1973. New organs which are assessing alternative publishing and which deal with broader literary-political questions are now being published. I assessed *Booklegger Magazine* in *Margins* in these words:

> Throughout *Booklegger*, the editors and contributors are taking positions, and strong positions—a concern for people, for ideas, for creating a humane, inhabitable world. The material here is oriented towards other activist library workers, but the concerns are broader: *Booklegger* is for all of us who put down *NY Times Book Review* (if we read it at all) still wondering what's going on in publishing; rich in information you've always wanted to know about but were afraid to ask. *Booklegger* will tell you: it's your world too.

The Canadian journal, *Open Letter,* is essential reading for anyone interested in contemporary writing. The condition of publishing is one of its many concerns; if it seems to neglect "American" concerns in favor of "Canadian", consider this: how often is Canadian writing given the attention it deserves in this country?

Richard Morris' sporadic *Camels Coming Newsletter* is a journal vitally interested in experimental literature and, further, in experimental criticism. The slightness of its format (newsletter) serves as no indication of the significance of the writing in its pages. There are few enough competent experimental critics working today; *Camels Coming Newsletter* should be spurring some of them to their task. Unfortunately, Morris is as poor as the rest of us; that fact, and the paucity of good experimental criticism apparently available, may hold *Camels Coming* to its format.

A newer but less exciting journal recently appearing and including at least as part of its purpose discussion of the alternative publishing scene is *The New York Culture Review*. By August, 1974, it had published eight issues in newsletter format (mimeo, set on typewriter, 8½ x 14 inches, most recent issue 12 pages). I would hope the *Review* can move beyond its format and editorial weaknesses and begin to pack a heavier wallop. We sorely need a full-blown journal in the east.

Nor are the older journals, *Small Press Review* and *Sipapu,* to be overlooked as necessary forums. Although *SPR* has appeared rather sporadically of late, I expect it to continue and raise some significant challenges; likewise, *Sipapu* continues, publishing short interviews with important figures in alternative publishing, and other matters relevant to alternative publishing. ⅰ

As the number of books alternative publishers produce increases, so some little magazines have increased the amount of their space devoted to reviews. The "Views" section in The Crossing Press's *New* has been expanded and is an important forum for review and comment. *The Shore Review*, formerly mostly poetry, now gives nearly half its enlarged issues to commentary and criticism. *The Minnesota Review* reviewed nearly 25 small press books in its most recent issue. *Poetry Now* reviews (so to speak) many new books by printing poems from them and providing acquisition information.

Few of these publications have "wide" circulation. *Small Press Review* and *Booklegger* claim 2,000 circulation. The circulation of most other journals, I suspect, is even more limited. Yet it should be clear that there is intense concern for assessment of what is being published, and for making it available. If any or all of these journals do not (or cannot) confront the literary-political predicament fully and head-on, they are, at least, carrying on the war with what arsenal they have. It would be difficult, at this point, to ask for much more—the task is one of slow building, moving as time, energy, and resources permit. There is considerable work which needs to be done, but perhaps we are not yet prepared—as writers, editors, publishers—to take it on all at once. The mere existence, however, of such forums and the continued attention they give alternative publishing serve to make alternative reading materials accessible to some, and available to all who can penetrate the cultural barriers.

What we may wish to see are several journals modeled on Stephen Vincent's *Shocks*, a magazine published in San Francisco. Said Vincent in *Margins: 9*:

> I started it [*Shocks*] because I felt the need for a journal that would help create a critical vocabulary and consciousness of the vast amount of work being written today. My feeling was that art without any critical sense of itself ends up an unmade jigsaw puzzle. Some of the pieces stick together as they did for a while in Bolinas, or among the women's movement, and now gays.
> However, little has been done to look at the individual pieces to find where they relate and where they disband. I tend to believe there is a relation among the various parts, that 'natural fact' poems have dream counterparts, that a literary knowledge of history will find its local occasion, as well as its participation in the larger flow of tradition(s).

Shocks is an intensely local or "regional" critical organ; I say "regional" in the fullest sense of the word. The magazine is concerned with defining the characteristics of its own; finding interrelationships among the work being done in the San Francisco area. Says Vincent:

> I've been speaking generally about what I think is a global
> condition. *Shocks* is in one sense a local matter, though I
> hope not in a neo-provincial way.

And he explains why:

> The whole [San Francisco] area creates a diverse and contra-
> dicting sense of identity. . . . [W]hat can appear as spectacu-
> lar variety has not been enough. The idea of *Shocks* grew
> from being torn by the enormous diversity of the kinds of
> writing [in the area].

This sort of regionalism—concern for assessing the shape of writing in an
area—will, in the future, become an important approach to assessing the
literary situation. Not only will review journals become increasingly regional in their concerns; so will literary periodicals and book publishers.
We've already seen several "area" anthologies. Anthologies of the
"Young American" variety are becoming suspect and increasingly
less useful as gauges of important literary activity. More and more, literary periodicals and book publishers are springing up, like *Shocks*, to
serve the concerns of their areas. Such a situation is healthy, if it en-
courages (as I think *Shocks* does) rather than curtails literary communication.

8.

All too often it seems that the labels "regionalism" or "localism" are
the last defenses put up by critics who cannot or will not come to terms
with work they haven't taken the time to understand. To call a writer
"regional" is, for these critics, to say: he or she doesn't deserve our attention; to say the writer's concerns are regional is to dismiss them as
insignificant and not worthy of further attention. This attitude generally springs from snobbery and insensitivity (two conditions which are
not unrelated): it is the snobbish and insensitive intellect which refuses
to evaluate and value material that, on the surface, may seem foreign.
The committed and probing intellect finds value wherever it may lie—
whether high on the bush or low in the weeds; it measures significance
in terms of full human needs and human involvement and chases the human spirit wherever it soars.

But all too often, it seems, commentators drop breathless in the
chase, faulting the "material under consideration" rather than their own
short-windedness. It should go without saying, at least to anyone who
reads with a discerning eye, listens with a careful ear, that good regional
writing transcends its boundaries and rises as the human spirit rises, as
all good work springs from the common ground of human experience
into the realm of human value and the better part of human tradition.

While it is certainly true that some writing labeled "regional" does
not and cannot stir a wider interest, it is also true that a good deal of
the writing intended to be cosmopolitan (read: "interesting to a NY

editor", or some such) fails entirely. Such writing often loses contact with truly human concerns; it does not touch the human condition except perhaps tangentially; does not set down roots in any soil, on any ground. Such cosmopolitan writing appears as a disembodied voice calling out in the darkness, and we cannot place it or gauge it or know it.

The irony is: many of us have been hoodwinked into thinking the fault is entirely our own: that we are too provincial, too regionally-oriented to fathom the mysteries of a "cosmopolitan" voice. The hollow voices of literary minute men have dominated the various institutions of our culture, to make such hoodwinking possible.

"Regionalism", as I use the term here, is meant to identify not only that writing with roots in a particular locale; there is writing with roots in other particular areas of experience as well. Experimental writing often occupies a territory all its own, the writers being concerned with both radical and incremental innovations in an art. Feminist writing has its province, as does literature by native Americans, blacks, etc. These are areas of particular concern; the labels are not boundaries meant to separate or to denigrate. Rather, as "midwestern" may identify special characteristics and directions inherent in some writing, so other "regionalisms" identify other particular concerns.

Too often such regionalisms, and the values and traditions they embody, are not permitted to enter the "defined" mainstream of literature, though of course in fact they feed from and into the mainstream and intricately blend with it, as tributary waters into a river. *The End of Intelligent Writing* suggests many of the obstacles between particular concerns and the "mainstream". Fault lies with the hip locutors of *Time*-ese and *Newsweek*-speak, and with the sinfully powerful *Times Book Review* and *New York Review*, and with American publishers. Fault lies also with the supposedly more informed and astute scholars in our universities. Such scholars would write and publish, too often, on a literature they have not experienced themselves nor allowed themselves to experience, thus effectively removing the "literary experience" from the human experience and thereby strangling it. Strangely, those in the university who are concerned with contemporary experience seem fascinated only by the literature of "nausea" and the absurd. To put current experience into full perspective, however, it seems necessary to include some of the wealth of writing that is being done now, beyond the absurd, and available often courtesy of alternative publishers.

Those in our universities live in a "publish or perish" environment created by a variety of circumstances, an environment in which the "acceptable" is as carefully delineated as the undesirable. It is easier to ask the "professor" to step out of the mold than for him to do so successfully: those who try often end up out on their ears, the cold pavement drawing blood. The "scholar" is no longer his own man, no longer a professional; he is an employee who meets not his own standards but those of his employer, not those set by other professionals, but those he's paid to meet. This is, in part, the reason for my frequent comment that writers generally do not belong in the university. The university, as an institution, often exists as a skeleton only; tradition, literary tradition included, ought to be bones, the bones of a living, breathing, moving animal. Instead, what we often find in universities is only bones and little flesh, little life. We need places of learning, but learning requires "engagement". And that, I fear, is where our universities fail us: wisdom has become a commodity, acquired passively, and is no longer a living body of knowledge, of information, insights and ideas.

I speak about the condition of our universities in order to show that the "end of intelligent writing" is not a matter only of American publishing. The condition of American universities seems as much a symptom of what is wrong in our culture as is the condition of publishing. And universities are just as much carriers of the disease.

What promise does a new "regionalism" in publishing hold for us? It would, first of all, get new writing out to the immediate interested audience; often, a writer's most interested readers are those in his own locale or those of similar concerns; regional publishing would serve that immediate audience and, further, may expand the audience beyond the usual poet or writer types in a community. On another level, regionalism would break the stranglehold New York has on books and information. Regional publishers, if they can survive, and if they can publicize (not hype) their efforts in their locales, may stir the interest of area mass media, booksellers, libraries, etc.; so far, many publishers have been unsuccessful in this regard. The resistances are difficult to break down, the task is not easy, resources are few. Mass media, in spite of their oft-stated good intentions, still shirks responsibilities. As a first step, it may be vital for each region to have a literary news sheet, with information about area presses, new books, literary and artistic events, and writers, for each literary-artist community. There are already several journals showing what can be done. But why not such a journal in every area where two or three are gathered together?

A new regionalism promises new regional organizations to meet the needs of publishing folk in particular areas. Already the New England Small Press Association, COSMEP-South, and the Committee of Rhode Island Small Presses are in operation; and a COSMEP-Southwest is in the planning stages. Such organizations might prove useful and powerful force in making literature accessible locally, and may undertake projects such as cooperative distribution schemes, informational mailings to librarians, conferences with librarians and others interested, discussions with area media about small press activities, etc. The San Francisco Book Fair, the New York Book Fair, etc., are significant national "book" events, but book fairs need not be nationally-oriented: regional organizations might undertake similar projects on the local level and bring attention to their work.

We run the risk, of course, of expending all our time and energy on organizational matters, to the neglect of the actual work of publishing. This is the risk of individual/small-group enterprise: the secondary work can kill us if we let it.

Perhaps the greatest result of regionalism in publishing will be in aiding the creation of literary-artistic communities where there have been none, where there have been poets, fictioneers, artists working in isolation. Community is a strange need for writers, who are often loners-as-artists by necessity. Community, however, and the communication which accompanies it, will bring support and encouragement to writers otherwise frustrated by lack of audience, of readers, of interest. It may also allow the recognition that the intrinsic purposes for writing have little to do with commercial success, publication in "prestigious journals", etc.; that a piece of writing has to be successful in manuscript first, and beyond that, in the minds of the readers a writer can attract, through whatever channels.

Regionalism, as I have said, is a matter of literary-artistic concern as well as of locale. We would do well to learn from both successful regionally-oriented publishers and those such as current feminist publishers, whose activities have a good deal to teach us.

In the end, regionalism (of place or mind) holds the promise of putting literature into the hands of everyone; no longer will the opinions of a few create standards of taste for everyone; no longer will New York be able to determine what we read, or when, or if. Centralization of information, of power, of responsibility spells the demise of intellect. Alternative publishing is up to the task of breaking down the stranglehold on literature, and such publishing will continue.

9.

I don't mean to imply, throughout my discussion, that alternative publishing is everything that commercial publishing is not; or conversely that commercial publishing is always and necessarily philistine. Commercial presses do provide significant and essential books that are beyond what alternative publishers can presently hope to undertake, at least on a regular basis. And alternative publishing is not without its flaws. There are writing and publishing coteries which serve no larger responsibilities; there are publishers who are irresponsible—one commentator on small publishing has told me that he is becoming increasingly reluctant to send money for books he would like because he too frequently gets neither the books nor his money returned. There are books being published by small presses which are without literary or artistic merit; some small presses are editorially irresponsible in other ways as well.

Commercial publishing has provided important literature to a large audience in the past and presently continues to provide some. But as

Kostelanetz points out again and again, the channels are closing up. Just recently I read a newspaper account which quoted a NY publishing executive who indicated that, because of the high costs and low profits, less experimental writing, less fiction, less poetry will be published in the future. The accountant becomes editor.

Whatever their shortcomings, present alternative publishers have accepted those responsibilities which NY publishing has most flagrantly shirked. New poetry has long been the province of the alternative publisher. New fiction is increasingly becoming its province as well. And experimental writing of all sorts has generally been neglected in NY, to be self-published or handled by small publishers.

The commitment of the alternative publisher is to information, to writing. Not to the ledger. Individual small publishers will come-into-being and pass-away, but alternative publishing as a tradition will survive and increasingly flourish, not in a financial rather in a cultural sense.

10.

Kostelanetz holds a singular position in contemporary literature. He is both an informed critic of innovative literature, and a prolific editor of such work. Several of his anthologies are available, and his introductions to them serve as some of the best critical comment such writing has received. *Breakthrough Fictioneers* (Something Else), for instance, is a landmark anthology, though it has been nearly universally neglected by the established reviewing powers. His introductory remarks likewise constitute landmark critical assessment of the directions of new fiction. The whole of *The End of Intelligent Writing* serves to delineate the reasons, first, why the task of compiling such anthologies falls to Kostelanetz—there are so few who are both competent and willing to take on the task; and second, why Kostelanetz's critical work on innovative writing ended largely as introductions—there are few journals willing to permit discussion of such literature in their pages.

Kostelanetz's treatment of the new poetries, fictions, dramas, and essays is an overview of the innovative work. Few other critics are willing to recognize, much less attempt any assessment of breakthrough writing. Rather, many "critics" are not critics at all, but flags in the wind, indicating merely which way the wind blows. Sustained criticism of new writing can be done only by commentators who are sensitive and perceptive enough to see the past in the present, the present in the past, and both past and present as it moves into the future. Intelligent criticism, even as broadly brushed as Kostelanetz's necessarily is as he attempts to survey new and neglected literatures ("The New Poetries", 23 pp.; "Innovations in Fictions, Dramas, Essays", 20 pp.), finds the relevant strands of literary tradition and intricately weaves with them the significant accomplishments of new writing.

Some would say criticism of experimental writing requires a "sympathetic" (they mean "biased") approach; in fact, however, it requires no more than criticism of any other sort of literature. Certainly, there is poor writing that is passed off as "experimental"; and poor writers often enough can get away with such bamboozling, for we have so few perceptive critics willing to speak intelligent though dissident opinions. The current state of literature, unfortunately, seems to encourage Sir Galahads defending anything and everything that is new—doing battle with the literary minute men at every turn rather than performing their full critical duties. The lucid voice of the perceptive critic attempting to cull out bad writing from the truly new is often ignored entirely or met with hostility.

Kostelanetz is both an informed and a perceptive critic of new writing; his past commentary on innovative writing has encouraged innovators to keep him aware of new developments and Kostelanetz thus has access to work not generally available. More important, perhaps, he is able to see across particular artistic boundaries; as more and more new work crosses or transcends traditional boundaries, the transmedia critic will become increasingly necessary. It has been said (again, I believe, in *Saturday Review*) that literature will survive such flirtations; I say, yes, it will survive, but because of them. Our age, perhaps, is an age of exactness, or precision. A good deal of 20th century literature has been concerned with identifying precisely certain perceptions, with exact statements. Literary history has its ages of "exactness"; it also has its more free-ranging "inclusive" periods. Minimalism, which Kostelanetz gives attention to, is an inevitable outgrowth of our tradition of "exactness"; innovations here can rebound to all of literature, infusing new life and possibilities. Both minimal art and visual art, either poetry or fiction, affect the way readers "read". Reading becomes more than a matter of understanding: it becomes a matter of perception as well. The reader is stimulated to participate in the creative act, to make connections which are not immediately obvious, or to create "narratives" out of sequences.

As with his discussion of literary periodicals and small presses, Kostelanetz's treatment of innovative writing is a stimulating overview. If anything, his discussion here leaves us wishing for a book-length study of innovative writing, its relevant traditions, its particular areas of concern, its relationship to the visual arts and musical arts, etc. I think such a full-scale study will be forthcoming. In his discussion in *The End of Intelligent Writing*, Kostelanetz emphasizes the major innovative writers, the best of the innovations, the significant directions. These need to be further explored; we need critical examination of related areas of writing, of minor technical innovations and how these relate to more major changes. Further, there has not been enough work done to relate the innovations in one art to those of others. And I would be interested in discussion of the implications present experimental work has for the future of intelligent writing. Kostelanetz gives us the intimations that his purposes and the space of *The End of Intelligent Writing* permit. I look forward to further discussion on his part.

11.

The End of Intelligent Writing is a provocative, stimulating book. The ideas, the possibilities Kostelanetz unfolds excite and drive the reader to the tasks needing to be done. Though the book is an expose, one written by a justifiably angry man, it finally is much more than that: the second part of the book suggests that the work might better be titled "The Prospects of Intelligent Writing". The prospects seem good indeed, if all of us, editors, publishers, readers—confront the challenges we face and accept the responsibilities that are ours.

✳

1975-76

LETTERS THE POETRY EDITOR WOULD LIKE TO SEND:
Mark Vinz's Letters to the Poetry Editor (Capra Press)

Dear Confessorial Poet from Decatur—Sorry to hear there's not much to confess in Decatur. Could I sell your mother, the librarian, some books? Or perhaps get a good deal on a used car from your father? Sincerely, etc.

Dear Suffering Poet—Please add this rejection slip to the 3,000 you've collected in the past five years. Perhaps you can do a collage of them, but ah! that's been done, I guess. Sincerely, etc.

Dear Freelancer From Manhattan—I don't publish poems that can be bought, alas; this isn't *Cosmopolitan* or *Field & Stream.* You should know we can't pay hacks. Sincerely, etc.

Dear Shithead Yrself—Make that a total of 19 poems I've rejected this spring—please find the five you just sent enclosed. Mostly, I'm pleased not to have poems like yr nineteen appearing in the mag. If that's bad taste, so be it; we don't eat magazines much around here any more. Sincerely, etc.

Dear Pleated Poet—Enclosed please find the letter you sent; if you want the poems returned, man, you'll have to send me an envelope big enough to hold them, and correct postage. The Post Office will just send the whole pile back to me if you don't, & the sanitary engineers in the neighborhood don't take kindly to heavy-duty garbage. Sincerely, etc.

Dear Prolific Poet—Yeah, I recognize yr name, & confess I recognize the 37 poems you sent, only when I read them they had different titles. Sorry to cut against the current & slow down yr appearance in print, but the poems are returned, enclosed. Sincerely, etc.

Dear 90 Year Old Poet—Thank you for sharing your wisdom with me, esp. the ode to your 75th birthday; but I'm afraid these are too wise for the narrow pages of my magazine. Sincerely, etc.

Dear Rhymer—If in these poems lies your heart, this, I fear, is where we part. Sincerely, etc.

Dear Worrier—I've not yet received the poems you say you sent over a week ago; I confess the post office is getting worse & worse; perhaps it's the reason you're not yet through the D's in the directory, or more likely it's editors like me, alas. In any case, when your poems do arrive, I'll have to return them to you, as *Denver Quarterly* probably wouldn't look very favorably upon my submitting them for you. Sincerely, etc.

Dear Self-employed Degenerate—Yeah, kiddo, you're a helluva man— yr mother was right, though she didn't step back far enough. If you can take it raw, the poems stink. Returned, enclosed, Sincerely, etc.

Dear Wild Food & Organic Things—Your perfect life there in the woods is a remarkable achievement in these days of post-Nixon depression. Yr kids are beautiful, you're beautiful, your poems are returned, enclosed. Sincerely, etc.

Dear Lifetime Member of the SPCA—No one's poetry could be as bad as you characterize yours to be, though I admit the verses you sent—returned, enclosed—come close. Sincerely, etc.

Dear East-of-the-Hudson-River-er—Yeah, we got barns & blizzards & Indians way the hell out this way; sorry you've not been west of the Hudson, sorry yr poems are so bad. Sincerely, etc.

Dear Poet—I am a *man*, alas, but I use Emily Dickinson stamps, too. Mousefully yours, etc.

Dear Comrade—I laid yr poem bomb against the petty bourgeois myth. There was throwing done, fer sure, but *up* not *over*. Sincerely, etc.

Dear Young Poet from Decatur—Give a young editor a break, man. Poets should cease to submit the bogus wisdom of *Freaking Out*. Sincerely, etc.

Dear Friend—No, I'm not Jewish & thank you for the five issue subscription. If you insist on sending a cake, I'm fairly partial to German Chocolate. Yr poems are returned, enclosed, Sincerely, etc.

Dear———, I don't have any mutual friends, sorry, nor do I recall any parties *c.* 1972 in Cincinnati. Yr poems returned, enclosed. Sincerely, etc.

Dear Fellow Regionalist—Thanks for letting me see your work, esp. the 16 portraits of yr neighbor's Uncle Josh at work with *Red Man* snuff and whittling knife. But there is a difference between regional writing & local color, isn't there now. Sincerely, etc.

Dear Ethnic Poet of All Shades—I'd be interested in seeing yr Indian (Tlingit group, please) and yr Polish ghetto poems (I need a token Totem Pole for my pages!). Sincerely, etc.

Dear Inspirational Poet—No, I'm afraid there is not much Beauty left, nor Contentment, Nature, Love and other Aesthetic things. My aim, as yours should be, is to retire. Sincerely, etc.

Dear Grace Ray—Thanks again for the shelter you offered my night in Fargo-Moorhead; and thanks too for the nice illustrations in this volume. Especially the mouse. Sincerely, etc.

Dear Mark Vinz—You've parodied very nicely the kinds of letters little magazine editors often find with submissions, yes, and with some charity, as you've hoped. On the one hand submissions made without letters seem so cold & impersonal; on the other, many of the letters accompanying poems are better left unwritten. Ever notice how it's always the editor at fault, whether submissions aren't returned in a week, or returned folded the wrong way in an envelope half the size it should be, or whatever. You don't tell anyone you have to read submissions on the sly, at two in the morning when your daughters are asleep, because that doesn't shock the corn, does it. Anyway, I just wanted to say that *Letters to the Poetry Editor* is as precise a little book of (serious) (light) [pick one or part of each] verse as I've seen in a while, cutting with a keen edge at one of those annoyances editors of poetry journals face day after day. Sincerely, etc.

THE SMALL PRESS BOOK CLUB

"As anyone looking at the yard can tell: the grass is knee-high and spreading. I've wanted to put a new shower in the bathtub for six months now, but can't find the time; also, have over a hundred bucks worth of copper pipe hanging on the back fence for the past three months—planned to put in a new water line from the street, but again: haven't got around to it! Now damned near all my free time goes to the club."

So says Bob (Robert R.) Miles, founder and proprietor of The Small Press Book Club. Miles is a 47-year old longshoreman who first broached the idea of a small press book club to me in a letter dated January 19, 1974. Said Miles: "From everything I've been able to read on the subject, the number one problem of small presses in this country is distribution. And I take 'distribution' to mean 'getting the books into the hands of the paying customers.' And the number two problem seems to be getting reviewed in the straight press. And number three, or thereabouts, is getting a buck or two into the hands of the various publishers." In his letter, Miles outlined some of his ideas for the book club, saying he believed it would be a workable way to solve two out of three of those problems—he felt a small press book club could both get small press books before an audience and get money into the pockets of some publishers. Closing that early letter Miles said, "Now as for me: I'm willing to blow some money on such a venture in order to try it out ....Don't have to work too much in order to make ends meet, really don't care a hell of a lot for the usual possession-collecting, so have the necessary time to devote to such a project." I responded to that letter quickly and enthusiastically, believing a small press book club could hold any number of benefits for small publishers, all the while wondering what the hell a longshoreman was doing to think about investing time and money into the promotion of small press literature.

But, as Miles himself puts it, "Like everything else, there are longshoremen and longshoremen." A flurry of letters was exchanged following that initial one, and I was witness to the birth of an idea and a reality: a book club geared to meet the needs both of the small publisher and the interested reader. Miles said, early on, "We're not selling ballbearings by the pound; we're selling small press books one title at a time. There will be a problem now and then. But we'll do our best to solve it quickly and to the customer's satisfaction."

Customer satisfaction seems an important concern for Miles. When I asked him why he elected to start a small press book club instead of, say, a wholesale distribution service, he said, "The 'book club' concept would allow me to choose just a few titles each period, and then promote *them*—and since I'm more of a promoter than a businessman-of-the-normal-stripe, this appealed. Also, this qualified the number of titles carried-in-stock, whereas in wholesaling it would be tough to take a publisher's good titles, but stiff him on his not-so-good titles. But *most important*," Miles emphasized, "I would be dealing with the people on a one-to-one ratio, whereas in wholesaling I'd be dealing with companies in one form or another." Further in one of the blizzard of information sheets, flyers, printed memoes, etc., that are a part of the book club's workings, he says, "We despise computers. Your requests will be read by real-live-people, letters written with plain-'ol-human intelligence. And if we foul up somehow, you'll be complaining to a person—not some idiot machine."

Why would a man, and one who despises computers at that, want to undertake the strange task of promoting small press literature? "I'm pretty much like most Americans in this respect," he says. "Nine times out of ten they'll root for the 'little guy' (versus his huge impersonal opposition, say). There's a hell of a lot of good publishing that never gets a chance to be seen, and most of it is coming from alternative publishers. . . . If I can get these books a bit of exposure that's fine—and if I can get a few sold, that's even better."

Miles admits he was fairly uninformed about what small presses were doing until he started "to read *Margins* and *Small Press Review* a bit over a year ago." He has become knowledgeable about the literature appearing from small publishers, however, and spends a good deal of his time keeping abreast of what is becoming available. "For sure I'm missing a lot of titles that I simply do not know exist," Miles says, "but as the club becomes better known, these 'misses' will become fewer. . . . Some titles I request publishers to send (review copies) because of reviews I've read, others from the publisher's own puff sheets, and some titles are chosen as selections because the publishers have sent review copies cold and when I eventually get around to reading them, I find I like them." Miles says he selects titles for the club on the basis of his own taste, although he seeks the advice of folks knowledgeable in certain areas. Further, Richard Kostelanetz chooses the "neglected classic" title for every other list, and Don Dorrance picks and reviews the selections that make up the "mag-bag" (a cloth bag containing a variety of little magazines, alternating with the "neglected classic" offerings). Miles also tries to "balance" each list, offering a few titles from the big small presses, "Black Sparrow, Capra, Scrimshaw", a few from the medium-sized small presses, and a few from the smallest of the small. "I try and have each selection list as balanced as I can," he says, "i.e., a few fiction [titles], a few poetry, a few non-fiction, one kids book on every other list at least, and an addition to the Small Press Reference Shelf (titles to fill holes)." He continues, "And sure, I choose a few titles that I figure won't sell very well, but since I dig them for one reason or another, they're 'selections'. Everyone, I expect, would like to be 'king' for a while, so as long as it's my 'store', I'll handle a title or two that won't pay."

The book club has enjoyed some success, although Miles says "I sure had no experience in book clubs heretofore, believe it! Experience in a very small retail book shop in a 100% summer-tourist town, but no book clubs—and that book shop experience was 30 years ago." He believes, however, that "it takes a certain kind of person to be in a retailing operation—just as it takes a certain kind to put out a magazine. Not *anyone* could run even a very small book club. My god, of course there must be a hundred people who could do it—but don't make it sound too simple, since I don't feel that would be doing anyone any favors."

"The main problem here," he says, "is the same problem throughout the entire small press scene: the necessity of operating a business (in a capitalistic society)—and usually those 'operating' the business either have had no business experience, or are intellectually opposed to the entire business basis, or (again) are simply opposed to it. I only mention this because if ONE book club selling small press proceeds to rip-off mail-order (retail) customers, regardless of their reason for doing so (ignorance, spite, whatever), then every other small press club will have to work like hell to overcome the resulting bum publicity."

Despite such fears, Miles has freely offered advice to others interested in setting up small press book clubs, mostly on a regional basis. "Naturally, they would compete with me," Miles thinks, "but to what degree remains to be seen. I personally think price cutting is dumb (and no doubt it'll be tried even more than it is currently) and usually hurts the outfit trying it, since there simply isn't a large enough margin in books to begin with to allow a living of some sort together with discounts. But I have, and will continue to, answer questions from people who are considering setting up their own clubs, because I don't think you can say you're for small press on one hand, and then try and discourage someone from selling small press books on the other."

Miles does have strong reservations about possible grant financing for competing clubs. "Now say one of the large funding agencies laid several thousand bucks on someone to set up a book club, I'd squawk like hell—but frankly I don't think it'd work in the long run, since I feel that giving a writer or an artist, or even a mag or a press, money like this is one thing, but giving money to a retailing business would be another—and I'm not talking about profits-as-incentive, but rather about politics-in-organizations. But we'll see; I've been wrong before. . . ." Miles believes that "the 'grantor' has strings of one sort or another on the money, and so I'd prefer to bypass these strings (and the eventual possibility of having to lie [in order to continue receiving grant money])." He adds that "It also seems to be human nature that what is worked for is given more value than what is received as a 'gift'."

Miles states that when he started the book club, in March, 1974, "I had a shade over a thousand bucks to lose, and was surprised to find when I took inventory the first of this year that it came out to a bit over $1300." In April, 1974, the first month of actual operation, the book club picked up eight members and grossed $67.95 In May, 16 members were added and orders totaled $138.30. By July, 1974, the book club had a total of 84 members and did gross business of $585.10 for the month. From August through November, membership in the club increased steadily, 26 members being added in August, 33 in September, 45 in October, and 38 in November. Gross sales for the period totaled $2,260.75. Six new members were picked up in December, 1974, 36 in January, 1975, 91 in February, and 30 more in March. The size of the average order—usually between six and nine dollars—swelled to $11.85 for November and to $12.85 for December when Christmas orders were placed.

On January 19, 1975, the *New York Times Book Review* mentioned the book club in its "Book Ends" column, and response was large and immediate. By the end of January, 190 requests for information were received; by the end of February, another 110 information packets had been sent. In February, the book club grossed $1086.35, its highest gross to date.

In the first year of operation, the club acquired a total of 389 members. Gross sales for the year amounted to $5,845.20; says Miles, "that's quite a few small press titles sold at that!" When expenses for the year were balanced against income, Miles says, his "tax man showed where I lost $1,929.47".

Miles' expenses undoubtedly ran high because of the promoting he did for the new venture. He indicates that "the club ran a total of 28 inches in the *New York Review of Books* (one inch each issue minimum, plus one four incher, and three three-inchers) on a yearly contract; this has expired and I don't see any reason to renew now—received a lot of requests from the ads, and they seemed to establish our credibility. Also they're a pain in the neck to keep up correctly, since camera-ready [copy] is naturally required, and this takes time. I also ran a total of three classifieds in *The Atlantic Monthly* that weren't worth the effort—mainly, I think, I didn't explain [the book club] satisfactorily. Just started a five-line classified in *Wilson Library Bulletin*, and the first insertion has pulled eight responses so far, with one library already sending in its first order, which has paid for the first ad."

Miles intends to continue efforts to make libraries aware of the club. He says he wants to use "a mailing to at least half of COSMEP's 2,000+ library list (after trying a test on 100), and if that pays, use the rest of that list." He is also participating in "three book fairs this year for the first time (New England, New York, San Francisco), but have no idea what to expect here". Miles believes the biggest promotional break the club has had was the mention in the *NY Times Book Review* "Book Ends" column. He says it "gave us still more credibility since we use a copy of the piece in mailings, etc." He adds that the club has "received ongoing listings in Beyond Baroque *NewLetters*, mentions in *Coda*, *Northwoods Review, Literary Sketches,* a full page in *West Coast Poetry Review,* plus two helpful notices in *Library Journal* and *Wilson Library Bulletin*".

Requirements for membership in the book club are minimal. "There is only one 'requirement' for remaining a member: you must agree to purchase a book every six months—from more than 50 titles made available. And since many of our books are priced at a dollar, this shouldn't impose too great a financial strain on anyone".

The club sells no "book-club-editions"; each volume is from the publisher's regular stock and, unless otherwise indicated in the selection list, is a first edition. The book club guarantees to accept returns for any books which arrive in damaged condition and offers to pay postage costs plus one dollar for the customer's inconvenience.

Most members, Miles thinks, like the club; "very few seem to drop out. And when I started stapling the 'this is your last selection list unless you buy something this time out' form onto their selection list, the response has been good—though I don't have firm evidence yet. The results from the second batch of expirations indicate that 34% bought another book or so, keeping them in the club, while 66% simply were no longer interested. I think this will be the pattern: early excitement and larger-than-usual purchases, tapering down, and with a certain number, then no purchases at all. I'll bet this holds with the big clubs too. (Of course, many members remain, making a purchase now and then as a title or so appeals to them)."

"Also, just today turned up a rather monumental screw-up on my part: the guy paid for books, I apparently cashed his check, but either I didn't ship, or they were lost; anyway, I wrote him an airmail letter this afternoon and will get this cleared up pronto—but if he hadn't answered his 'this is your last selection list' form letter by informing me WHY he hadn't bought any more books, I would have known nothing about it. How this 'one book every six months' requirement affects the size of the average order, I don't know. I expect it doesn't help any, but as yet I have no hard figures. Also, *no one* has *ever* complained about having to buy one book every six months". Customer satisfaction, again, seems a paramount concern.

Miles offers this advice to anyone who might be considering undertaking a project similar to The Small Press Book Club: "Prepare to work long hours, have a fine time doing it, and cope with a million small details. Book-keeping is imperative", he says, "and being able to read figures and what they seem to be saying will help. A certain amount of money will be needed, a certain amount of taste, ability to be a bit of a promoter without shucking, something of a business-head, too. Knowledge of elementary printing practices, and so onandonandon. And most important, a certain amount of responsibility: to your members, to those you buy books from, and even god save the mark, to your friendly banker. Because what we're talking about here is primarily a business, and if it's not run like a business, regardless of what a person thinks of the business-trip, eventually it's going to fall on its face".

Miles modestly tempers his advice, however: "here I'm talking like a big glittering success of some sort—hell, man, wait until the club has a thousand members and it's moving a couple hundred titles at a crack—then maybe I'll be able to talk with a bit of 'authority'!'"

Miles' success, glittering or not, has not come by serendipity, it would seem, but by his strong business sense and by hard work. "I do all the letter writing and answering, book wrapping and returning", he says, but adds, "whenever it's putting-out-the-next-selection-list-time, my wife, my mother (who'll be 78 on her next birthday), and my 17 year-old son all pitch in—and it still takes the better part of three days to get the damned thing finished and in the mail! Currently, address labels are a bottle-neck, but I hope to get a used Addressograph, or somesuch, shortly. Also, I haven't decided on a format for sure, so I waste time with that too. Things *are* getting easier all the time, I'm making fewer mistakes-that-consume-extra-time, so optimism reigns. As usual. . . . "

What of the future you might ask. Will the book club continue operations, and for how long? "When I checked February's figures", Miles says, "that did it: the club is here to stay. Don't even think of not going ahead with it any more. Still occasionally wake up in the middle of the night now and then, wondering what the hell I'm doing, but things continue to look great in the light of day. Can't really see anything on the horizon that could stop it now. . . . "

MILWAUKEE LITERARY ACTIVITY:
A LOT OF ENERGY IN ONE PLACE

It may have been someone from Wichita, Kansas, who wrote me some time back: "It looks as if there's a renaissance going on in Milwaukee" (or words to that effect). That, perhaps, is one view of Milwaukee's literary activities.

From the basement office where I work—where *Margins* and Margins Books are produced—I'm unable to determine whether the energy and motion I see constitutes a "renaissance" or not; I'd prefer to think it is merely the Milwaukee manifestation of the literary and small press energies surfacing all over the country. I've said elsewhere that you can *write anywhere,* and that you can run a small publishing operation anywhere—in Dekalb, Ill., or Fargo, N.D. New York publishing houses have no monopoly on talent. Rich Mangelsdorff, a native Milwaukeean himself and the most persistent American critic of small press literatures over the past ten years, puts it this way: "There's a lot of small press activity going on in Milwaukee, no matter how indifferent people are to it. Why Milwaukee, then? Why not? Most small press business either is or could be conducted via the mails—in distinction to most other arts, small press activity can be effectively carried on most anywhere." No matter how indifferent Milwaukeeans are to it, the literary scene here is vigorous and thriving. While we may not have a "renaissance" on our hands, there is a lot of work being done.

The nature of the midwest personality, perhaps, is partly responsible for the character of the Milwaukee literary scene; the often-acknowledged rugged individualism of the midwesterner ("They're independent cusses," I've heard said) is evidenced by the lack of any sense of a "larger" community within the city. There are, to be sure, poets and writers who run together, who see each other often, exchange information, opinion and gossip; but none of the groups is very large, none dominates the scene, and none seems intent on creating any literary dynasties. Pat Wagner, who managed Milwaukee's small press bookstore, Boox, Inc., for some time, put it in her own tongue-in-cheek way, reflecting the talk on the street: "Street Poets, The Elitists (a name given—in derision —to include the editor of *Margins*), The English Department, The Shore Guys and the Radicalesbian Feminists." There is some truth in such a view of Milwaukee's literary activities, although any implications of cutthroat competition and overt hostilities do not seem warranted. In 1972, when Martin J. Rosenblum was editing *Brewing: 20 Milwaukee Poets,* perhaps the competition was more than a little fierce, but many of the animosities stirred up by the publication of *Brewing* have since cooled, some four years later. The cover photo on *Brewing* is a group picture of 16 of the 20 poets included in the anthology; my own question when the date for gathering for the photo had been set was: how much blood is going to be shed by the time a suitable photo is taken? There was no blood, and so far as I know, has been none since. Although one always has the impression there *could be* some.

The common meeting ground for writers in Milwaukee appears to be poetry readings, those held at Boox, Inc., under the auspices of the Fly-By-Night Coffeehouse, and the Cream City series at the University of Wisconsin-Milwaukee. The facilities at Boox/Fly-By-Night are open to any poet who'd like to give a reading and is willing to take matters into his own hands—doing scheduling, promotion and the detail-hassling that surrounds getting an audience in front of a poet. The Cream City reading series is under the direction of project coordinator Mary Zane Allen, a poet formerly of Oshkosh, Wisconsin, now studying at UWM. The Cream City readings are weekly or near weekly. Milwaukee poets Wladyslaw Cieszynski, Mitchell Lechter, Sheila Bowler, Mike Balisle, Rocco Ditello, Sue Schneider, Martha Bergland, Debra Drilias, Jim Hazard, Sue Firer and Pat Bieth, and Wisconsin poets David Steingass (Stevens Point), Bruce Taylor (Eau Claire), John Judson (La Crosse), and J. D. Whitney (Wausau), are among those who have read in the series, as has James Liddy, an Irish poet in residence at UWM this year. Mary Zane Allen indicates that Cream City is checking into the possibility of a grant to tape the series for broadcast on educational television. The Fly-By-Night readings at Boox are more sporadic than Cream City's. This spring, Angela Peckenpaugh and Tom Montag from Milwaukee and

Todd Moore from Belvidere, Ill., and D. Clinton from Manchester, Michigan, presented their works. In addition, Michael Tarachow of Pentagram Press sponsored a monster one-time reading at a local pub on May 29th. At the Saturday afternoon affair, 18 Wisconsin poets read, including: Martin J. Rosenblum, Tarachow, myself, Jim Hazard, Susan Firer, Antler, Jeff Poniewaz, John Price, David Clewell, Barbara Joffee, Judith Wittig, Walt Cieszynski , Mary Zane Allen, Angela Peckenpaugh, Ron Slate, Bob Borden and Ruth Glassner.

The audiences at Milwaukee poetry readings tend to be small, despite promotional and publicity efforts. And over and over, you see the same people attending the readings. Milwaukee, as a city, is not very receptive to its poets. The city is not *hostile*, rather it simply ignores most literary activities and endeavors. In living memory, the daily *Milwaukee Journal* has devoted none or very little space to local publications or poets. The daily *Sentinel* published a small feature on Milwaukee poetry in 1972, and nothing since. The alternative weekly, *Bugle American,* which almost begrudgingly publishes an irregular poetry-page (presently edited by Michael Tarachow, formerly edited by myself, and before that by Martin J. Rosenblum), seldom prints reviews of local books. *Bugle American* did, however, give attention to Milwaukee's small press community in an article in 1974, and to *Margins* in a piece published last year. Poets have also read and discussed their works on the local educational station occasionally, but never on a regular basis. Unfortunately, when all is said and done, one gets the impression that Milwaukee finds poetry about as useful as teats on a boar.

Boox, Inc., Milwaukee's small press bookstore, serves as a small oasis on Milwaukee's wasted landscape, making available not only the local magazines and books, but also a wide selection of small press titles from around the country. The bookstore is beset with staffing and financial problems at present (and as usual), but plans are underway to restore some of the energy which has existed at Boox in the past. Boox shares space with Milwaukee's experimental theatre, Theatre X, and with the Milwaukee Mime and Improvisational Troupe, the Fly-By-Night Coffeehouse, an art gallery, and other projects; the whole complex is in the process of being brought together administratively under the umbrella of the Water Street Arts Center.

Two anthologies, *This Book Has No Title: An Anthology of Milwaukee Poetry* (The Third Coast/Amalgamated Holding Company, Milwaukee, 1971), edited by Roger Mitchell, Roger Skrentny, and Kathleen Wiegner, and *Brewing: 20 Milwaukee Poets* (The Giligia Press, Lyme Center, New Hampshire, 1972) edited by Martin J. Rosenblum, captured and recorded some of the Milwaukee poets of the early 1970s. Both anthologies are useful. *This Book Has No Title,* which presented work by 30 poets and allowed each a page or two or three, gave the broad sweep of the Milwaukee scene as it existed in 1971. *Brewing* presented fewer poets but permitted each writer more space, adding a "depth" to *This*

Book's breadth. But, so far as I know, there are presently no plans for an anthology as ambitious as either *This Book* or *Brewing,* although there is enough good poetry in the city today to justify one.

And the fact that the face of poetry in Milwaukee has changed considerably since *This Book* and *Brewing* were published would be reason enough for a fresh anthology. Several of the poets in the earlier books have either stopped writing or moved. At the same time, several poets have moved to Milwaukee and indigenous new talent has surfaced. Kathleen Wiegner, certainly an important force while she was here, is now in California; likewise, Roger Mitchell has moved. Morgan Gibson and Barbara (Gibson) O'Mary are gone. Jim Sorcic, publisher of the seminal Gunrunner Press, is now in New York City; Steve Lewis lives in New York state. Bob Watt seems to be headquartered in Madison these days. Celia Young has moved away and not kept contact with Milwaukee. To replace those lost, poets such as Wladyslaw Cieszynski, Martha Bergland, Mary Zane Allen, Kathleen Dale, and Mike Tarachow—to name but a few—are making appearances in print and at readings. Although few faces on the Milwaukee scene have been changing, the level of literary energy seems to remain constant.

Some of that energy has been diverted to publishing enterprises, not all of which survive. Milwaukee's *Kaleidoscope,* a highly literate underground paper for part of its existence, focused a good deal of attention on local poets in the mid to late 60s. Milwaukee was home for several more strictly literary ventures which have since moved away or folded:

**Gunrunner Press, edited by Jim Sorcic in the sixties and early seventies, was a nationally recognized small press whose work was (and remains) invaluable, however unsung that work goes today.

**Amalgamated Holding Company and The Third Coast, which co-published *This Book* and which separately sponsored readings and publications, have disappeared from view.

***The Other,* an attempt by Rich Mangelsdorff and others to create a literary review distinct from the university, published several issues and disappeared.

**Albatross Press, edited by Martin J. Rosenblum, published small "road-map" editions by several writers and folded (and/or was transformed into Lionhead Publishing).

***Harpoon* and Harpoon Press, founded by Dave Buege in 1972, existed long enough to publish one issue of its magazine and three poetry pamphlets.

***Erratica,* edited by Don Dorrance, published a number of issues from Milwaukee before Dorrance moved to South Milwaukee and before his untimely death in September, 1975.

***Lakes & Prairies,* established by Edward ("Ned") Haggard in 1974, published and continues to publish a large number of Milwaukee writers, although Haggard has now taken his journal with him to Chicago.

***Minnesota Review,* which Roger Mitchell brought to Milwaukee when he took over the magazine from New Rivers Press' Bill Truesdale, is in the process of moving to Bloomington, Indiana, where Mitchell has a teaching position.

Several publishing ventures survive in Milwaukee, however, despite the lack of a large local audience. *Amazon,* a feminist monthly which recently changed its format from magazine-size to newspaper-size, appears to have a better local readership than Milwaukee's more strictly literary publication. Likewise Milwaukee's monthly magazine for the gay community, *GPU News,* not incidentally, conscientiously publishes poetry by gay writers and prints well-considered reviews of small and large press books by and about gays. *Cream City Review,* the independent publication of a group of people associated with the writing program at the University of Wisconsin-Milwaukee, has published a fairly strong first issue which contains work by many UWM and Milwaukee poets. *Cream City Review's* impact on Milwaukee remains to be determined. The magazine, which is open to submissions from writers around the country, is intended to appear two times a year, and more frequently (three times a year) if finances permit. For the first issue, UWM's Union Activities Board subsidized some of the costs of publication.

Most other small magazines and presses in Milwaukee are more visible at the national level than at the local. *Paid My Dues,* edited by Dorothy Dean, is a singular quarterly journal devoted to the work of women in music and radio. Hit Man/Broadsides, a new Milwaukee guerrilla imprint, has thus far published five broadsides in two series; Hit Man's editor prefers to work anonymously. The broadsides have not been offered for sale as yet, but have been distributed to a select mailing list. Lionhead Publishing, an outgrowth of Martin J. Rosenblum's defunct Albatross Press, has issued a "postpoems" series—an anthology of poetry postcards. Cities Investigations surfaced last year to issue John Jacob's novel *The Chicago Report: Ward of the State;* the imprint appears to be temporarily inactive. Joshua Kesselman's Ziggurat imprint continues, sporadically. *Ziggurat Two* appeared last year, having been in the works some six or eight years; plans are underway for *Ziggurat Three,* I'm told.

Ed Burton, who operates Morgan Press (named for his daughter), seems to be an editor who is loathe to sell his publications. Burton's first love is making books, and his care with them and his expertise on his various letterpresses and offset machines is evident in each issue of *Hey Lady* and the individual chapbooks on his list. Burton could, quite possibly, justify a claim to being, if not the oldest, one of the oldest surviving small press operations in the city.

The Shore Review, edited by Kenn Kwint, continues to appear, though on a more irregular basis than in the past. No. 14, the most recent issue, is 140 pages and contains work by 47 contributors. The amount of space *The Shore Review* devotes to critical essays and reviews in its past several issues gives evidence of the increasing concern for critical discussion of "current (not 'modern')" poetry on the part of little magazine editors around the country. Kwint's The Shore Press issued over the past several years a number of books of poetry, the most notable being, perhaps, those by Kwint himself and *Six Eyes Open,* an anthology of work by Kwint, Jeff Woodward and Harley Elliott.

My own imprint, Monday Morning Press, produced the bulk of its list in 1972, when French-folded broadsides by nine Milwaukee and three out-state poets were issued. Other publications include a "mini-anthology" called *Sorts,* and chapbooks by Don Dorrance, Doug Flaherty, Brian Salchert, Karl Young, Barry Russal, Amy Powers and myself. The only Monday Morning Press title presently in the works is a collection of poems by Paul Mariah. I also edit and publish *Margins: A Review of Little Magazines & Small Press Books* which appears (or, rather, is supposed to appear) monthly. Margins Books is an outgrowth of *Margins'* critical concerns; books presently in production include Robert Peters *Great American Poetry Bake-Off, The Younger Critics of North America,* edited by Richard Kostelanetz, Kostelanetz's *Twenties in the Sixties,* an as-yet untitled *Margins Reader* edited by John Jacob and myself, a smaller reader edited by Jacob and *The Coleman Symposium: Alternatives in Poetry, Publishing and Design* edited by Stephen Wiest and Denis Boyles. Several other critical books are in the editing or planning stage.

Pentagram Press, edited by the young and energetic poet Michael Tarachow, is perhaps Milwaukee's newest press. Pentagram released seven books, four chapbooks, three broadsides, and a series of postcard poems in the past year. Tarachow's list includes work by Carol Adler (*Arioso*), Joel Dailey (*Exploring Another Leg*), Harley Elliott (*Sky Heart*), Doug Flaherty (*Near the Bone*), Tom Montag (*Making Hay & Other Poems* and *Ninety Notes*), William Matthews (*Sticks & Stones*), Steve Lewis (*Exits Off a Toll Road*), Michael McClintock, S.L. Poulter and Virginia Brady Young (*Jesus Leaving Vegas*), Robert Peters (*Shaker Light*), Michael Tarachow (*Sunrise*), Diane Wakoski (*The Fable of the Lion & the Scorpion*), and Martin J. Rosenblum (*Scattered On: Omens & Curses*). Tarachow's plans for the future include books of poetry by William Kloefkorn, David Clewell, and Ted Kooser, fiction by John Jacob, and critical essays by myself and Richard Kostelanetz. Tarachow recently purchased a small letterpress and, once he has issued the books currently in progress, plans to confine his publishing to handset letterpress chapbooks and broadsides.

If Ed Burton's Morgan Press is not the oldest surviving small press in Milwaukee, then Karl Young's Membrane Press is. Membrane Press is probably, also, Milwaukee's most well-known small press. Young has his own small offset machine in his basement and, like Burton, does all his own printing and binding. Young has so far issued two numbers of the journal *Stations,* and books by Toby Olson (*Vectors, City* and *Changing Appearance*), Martin J. Rosenblum (*Home* and *The Werewolf Se-*

quence), John Shannon (*Each Soul Is Where It Wishes To Be, Hyde Park, Hosea Jackson,* and *W Tungsten*), Kathleen Wiegner (*Encounters*), Barbara Einzig (*Color*), Hilary Ayer (*Variations on the Hermit*), and Tenny Nathanson (*The Book of Death*). Membrane has also produced a large series of postcard poems, with work by Young, Rosenblum, Olson, Jerome Rothenberg, Charles Doria, Harris Lenowitz, Nathaniel Tarn, Carol Berge, John Taggart, George Economou and others. Young's upcoming titles include work by Berge (*The Unexpected*), Olson (*Home*), Rothenberg and Lenowitz (*Gematria 27*) a book of Jackson Mac Low's Gathas, and Young's own *Elephantine Fragments.*

Tarachow's Pentagram Press and Young's Membrane Press are—at least in terms of the size of their respective lists—Milwaukee's most ambitious and enterprising publishers of poetry. Young's and Tarachow's tastes differ considerably, but the two editors have one thing in common: each is intent on taking care of the business he has cut out for himself. In contrast to the continuing work by Membrane and Pentagram, Milwaukee has several one-shot imprints which are used to issue work self-published by some Milwaukee poets. Happily, poets in this city are not reluctant to self-publish when that is the most useful option open to them. A popular format is the French-folded broadside which I originated here in 1971. This format allows a poet ample space and an attractive medium in which to present his work, yet is inexpensive to produce. Other poets have self-published chapbooks and small books which are available to the public at Boox, Inc., and a few other stores around the city. Most poets here, those with books out from established small presses and those who are self-published, are only too happy to sell copies of their works at readings; and most Milwaukee poets swap their books and broadsides rather readily. The work does get passed around. If the average Milwaukeean ignores the city's poets, the poets themselves seem to remain keenly interested in the work of each other. And that, I think—despite the fragmented and sometimes abrasive nature of the literary "community" here—is a clear indication of the good health of the Milwaukee literary scene.

Some poets, perhaps, thrive under adversity and can remain to write in a city which chooses to ignore them. Other poets must move elsewhere if they are to continue doing their work. Some poets here have, unfortunately, simply stopped writing or otherwise disappeared from view. Whichever encyclopedia calls Milwaukee the "Naples of the Midwest"—and I'm told one of them does—is wrong. Yes, we have Lake Michigan and the shoreline and the harbor, but the city gives its poets little more than that.

OUT OF THE VIETNAM VORTEX

James Mersmann's *Out of the Vietnam Vortex* (University of Kansas Press) is "a study of poets and poetry against the war". It is concerned primarily with the work of Allen Ginsberg, Denise Levertov, Robert Bly, and Robert Duncan. Mersmann attempts "integrated discussions of the full canons of four chosen poets, relating their protest poems to their poetics and other work in order to discover the common techniques, attitudes, and images that have shaped the poetic outpourings against the war." The book is, so far as I know, the first full-length treatment that poetry against the war in Vietnam has received. Mersmann is an assistant professor of English at the University of Alabama, Birmingham.

Mersmann first reviews briefly the protest poetries that past wars spawned, and briefly compares them to the kinds of writing which came out of the greenhouse sixties. He then discusses the work of Ginsberg ("Breaking Out"), Levertov ("Piercing In"), Bly ("Watering the Rocks"), and Duncan ("Irregular Fire—Eros Against Ahriman"), and includes a survey chapter dealing with other poets against the war. His concluding chapter is "against concludings".

Mersmann confines himself chiefly to "compare and contrast" questions: he is an astute enough reader of contemporary poetry to discern trends, motifs, and techniques in the work of the writers he is primarily concerned with, however much we might disagree. He deftly interrelates facets of the four poets' work. The book seems as good an academic treatment of protest poetry as we are likely to find.

However. Where is the fire, where is the blood? Where are the eye teeth into flesh? The passion of the sixties lies dissected on the table, the autopsy showing little that I'm intensely interested in seeing. What fire burned the poets, bringing them to cry out? And with what impact: did Bly's readings against the war bring young men to burn their draft cards? Did those readings, those poems put bodies on the line, at the maw of the monster? Did poetry do anything, anything at all to end the war? and if so what? These are the kinds of questions "out of the Vietnam vortex" which interest me. Mersmann provides few clues towards an answer for these questions; his approach is cool—he's a scholar, not a fighter. He is not "engaged".

I am of course being unfair to what the author intended: I doubt that anyone could do justice to the 'fire and blood' questions about protest poetry, that of the sixties, or any. Certainly I would hesitate a great while before attempting a full length investigation of the questions I've posed: the answers cannot be formulated easily in discursive, critical language: the fire and blood of protest poetry is in the poetry, beyond that, in the complex interactions of the mind and eye of the individual in society, and the complexity of the workings of society itself. Readings against the war didn't "end the war": I'll venture that. The word in this case was not efficacious. But why? The question stands.

Out of the Vietnam Vortex, if not the book I wanted to read when I picked it up, is a good book and essential reading for anyone interested in the temper of the sixties. For those wanting the fire and the blood, we must recommend the best of the protest poetry itself.

SHAMP: One Long Whistle

Jaimy Gordon's *Shamp of the City-Solo* (1974) must stand as a special marker in current alternative press publishing. Len Fulton's *The Grassman*, a full length, powerful and sensitive novel, is a tale told more or less traditionally. Curt Johnson's *Nobody's Perfect*, a narrative which should be dear to the hearts of little magazine editors, and Jerry Bumpus' published fiction, while laying open the traditional narrative on the strength of each author's style, do not push narrative technique into the far frontiers of the new. Ms. Gordon's *Shamp*, as perhaps George Chamber's *Bonnyclabber* does, moves the novel, or at least the language of the novel, into some new territory.

In terms of the necessities of publication, *Shamp* evidences special care in production, and meets big-house publishing on what would seem its own grounds: that of excellence of the artifact (even without consideration of artistic criteria). Johnson's, Bumpus', and Chamber's narratives, as books, are well designed and well-produced (though one might question the inclusion of several apparently gratuitous nudie photographs in Johnson's book, but these might well be justified on "artistic-philosophical" or "artistic-political" grounds); Gordon's novel, produced in an edition of 950 trade paperback copies and 50 signed/hardbound copies, utilizes three production processes: silkscreen, letterpress, and offset. The number of pages (140) belies the actual length of the novel, the typeface being (it looks) nine-point, as opposed to the more commonly selected larger faces. The book has not been "puffed" in the process of production. We find the silkscreen work on the cover (black, white, green, red, and blue) by James Aitchison (who also does several attractive drawings to accompany the text), silkscreened by Adam Gordon. Having done some silkscreening myself, I appreciate the register, the texture, the sensitivity of Adam Gordon's work. The title page is letterpress, blue and brown on white. The book is nine inches tall and five inches wide. The artifact is worthy of the art.

The novel itself draws energy from many sources. At root, the tale is episodic, though the themes and subthemes of the story are developed/amplified by the insights unveiled in the episodes. Structurally, the novel is solid, and Shamp's opening musing over a grave is paralleled by his closing considerations: "For in the end I have one real pleasure, and that is my joy to be quit of whatever, to have nothing but my hole [where Shamp actually lives] and the meadow at the far end." The novel starts "in the hole" so to speak, and thematically arrives there again. We do not read *Shamp* solely for the story told, however; this "narrative" is far richer than that.

This is joyful story-telling, in the fashion of John Barth's *The Sot-Weed Factor*, though Gordon's work seems less baroque. The narrative elements of *Shamp* are not so complex as those of *The Sot-Weed Factor* though the gists of the two tales are similar.

In his story, Barth proposes that history itself is a dishonest story-teller and opens the possibility for the reader's realization that "true facts", i.e., history, are not as they seem. *The Sot-Weed Factor* is an historical novel, its basis is in factual material—the "hero", Cooke, did exist and did write his own "Sot-Weed Factor". The voluminous details about Lord Baltimore and the history of Maryland which Barth unfolds are as persuasive as the different version in the history books. But are they "true"?—the pieces of history come apart and fall together very artificially in the telling. Yet the history in *The Sot-Weed Factor* is as faithful as the history of the historians.

Barth is willing to admit history as artifice, to admit that there could have been and were motives, influences, and coincidences that not even the participants of the historical events could be aware of, that forces move beyond the grasp even of the most careful narrator (and reader). Eben Cooke claims to be a "poet" and "virgin" and he attempts to find his identity in these terms, despite the evidence that his poetry and his virginity become quite clearly tattered, grotesque caricatures. In the end, Cooke is reduced to silence, desisting in his claims to be either poet or virgin, and ultimately he lives and dies outside those labels meant to sum his essence.

The importance of *The Sot-Weed Factor*, I should think, lies in its disjunction of history and "actuality", of identity and language; the novel leaves us with the clear impression that we are not seeing out of both eyes clearly when we look around ourselves, or that we may be peering through the wrong lenses, that we cannot, even at great effort, find "identity" in the words with which we would define ourselves, not necessarily find "meaning" in our culture and history, that what lies outside ourselves may ultimately be more complex than all the artifice of words and grammar can grasp, that what we call "reality" may be only another culturally-perpetuated illusion we have been living all along.

In *Shamp* we are drawn to similar conclusions, though they are expressed in terms greatly differing from Barth's. Shamp's ultimate pleasure, his joy in "being quit of whatever", is evidence that he has resigned from his previous attempts to find meaning, sense, identity, in himself as grappler-with-philosophical dilemmas or seeker-after-*topos*-and-*tropos*. Ultimately, Shamp's tale comes to silence, as it must. But the silence is not the more usual silence coming when the story-teller has told the tale and has nothing more to say. It is the silence of a man who recognizes language cannot contain the stuff of "the world", who is aware that grappling with "philosophical dilemmas" can often be an urgent and powerful stimulus to the intellect, but cannot satisfy the "whole" man. Shamp is a man who wants, ultimately, to *live*. He and his name-sake, Shamp the younger (though not Shamp's offspring) "wander down the tracks, lose the time, sometimes coming over a green hill like the others to Bosky Point, the mouth of the Sump, the bay and the open sea." To "lose the time".

Shamp's acceptance of silence is not a "sour-grapes" resignation: "What is there, earnest lector, if a man be more than his topos and tropos, more than his points and tracks, his comings and going and the stations of his mail? Is there no more to reap the likes of Shamp, who lets it all go but the field it flows through? Nor can a field be empty but fills with his passing whistle, the breath that escapes him as he goes down the track all solo, one long whistle banding, filling, overflowing to the summer sky."

The philosophical questions raised, grappled with, and left aside by Shamp are not new. "All philosophy is but footnotes to Plato," I've heard; if so, there are some important footnotes and some more interesting than the text. In *Shamp*, the sources seem recent. There are Nietzchean overtones here, as Shamp and Shamp's three masters reach for power and fame in the city-solo. Existential "faith" and "bad faith" are in clear evidence as Gordon delineates her characters and the situations in which they find themselves. There are elements of Sartre's "nausea" and Kierkegaard's "fear and trembling". *Shamp*—on this level—is a philosophical novel. It takes on and disposes of, with Shamp's acceptance of silence, some of the most primary ideas of modern philosophy.

If *Shamp of the City-Solo* is not to be read for the story Gordon tells, neither is it to be read as a novel of ideas. The full richness of *Shamp* lies in the language of the narrator.

Gordon—in *Shamp*—finds herself in a philosophical dilemma of her own. I'm not sure that she would argue, as I.M. Copi does, that "the universe is not a vain capricious customer of ours. If the shoe fits, this is a good clue as to the size of the foot. If a language is adequate to describe it, this indicates something of its structure." Throughout *Shamp*, we find indications that if the "shoe does fit the foot", we cannot have a full idea of the size of the shoe. Joyce O. Hartzler, in *A Sociology of Language*, says "by means of words properly organized, men are able to identify, objectify, describe, standardize, classify, and universalize all their different types of experience." Hartzler states further that labeling or naming is one of the fundamental functions of language, that language determines what we, the speakers, perceive of our environment, that it functions as our means of perception. In terms of the world we think we live in, language may serve these functions, and perhaps we must admit as much; but in terms of Jaimy Gordon's artistic necessities, the requirement that she get her story out and set it down, we might find ourselves arguing about Gordon and her art, that—as Burlingame says in *The Sot-Weed Factor*—"One must needs make and seize his soul, and then cleave fast to't, or go babbling in the corner; one must choose his gods on the run, quill his own name on the universe, and declare, 'Tis I, and the world stands such-a-way!' One must assert, assert, assert or go screaming mad."

Gordon's language, that is, the language of Shamp as narrator of this novel, if it has any model, probably is related to the language of Shakespeare's Falstaff. The "words" are not the same, of course; what is similar is the joy that both Falstaff and Shamp take in language, in sound and sense of words strung together to affect the people around them. There has been no cursing in literature so creative and joyful as we find in Falstaff; less intent on the sense of the word itself than on working the word in relation to other human beings, Falstaff speaks loudly and joyfully, with—often enough—some brew to loosen his tongue. Shamp's language, given the necessities of his world, probably does enable inhabitants of that world to "identify, objectify, describe, standardize, classify, and universalize all their different types of experience." But we, as readers, can at best understand Shamp's experiences only analogously. It is not our own experiences of a world, it is like our experience. Rather like the world of Barth's *Giles Goat-Boy*, Shamp's world has but few obvious points of contact with our own. Unlike Giles' world, however, Shamp's seems whole and integrated. Where Barth abstracts our world to create cardboard imitations intended as allegory, Gordon intends little as allegory; her interest, rather, lies in conveying the full nature of a world she has seen, in relating the goings-on of the "language" and some of the very interesting "characters" (both senses) in that world. Shamp's experience is *like* our own; his language is *like* ours. The philosophical dilemmas he faces, when he does face them, are *like* those we face ourselves now and again. But they are not ours, and we can only read them analogously.

We find, reading *Shamp*, that Gordon's first intention is not to create a world resembling our own, though we can reach it; it is not "to teach", but rather to entertain. The moral lessons to be learned, if there are any, are secondary considerations. Barth's *Goat-Boy* world does not often touch ours, but it does imitate it. At best, I find for myself that events in Shamp's world—when juxtaposed against events in my own experience, and moral predicaments—stir my sense of irony. This novel is not an allegory in the sense that *Giles Goat-Boy* appears to be one (and the moral lessons in *Goat-Boy* are less obviously drawn than in Barth's earlier novels), though *Shamp* does have in some places and for myself as a reader, allegorical elements. Shamp's world, however, is not built out of cardboard boxes, as parts of *Goat-Boy* seem to be, whatever the tradition of allegory.

What, finally, has Ms. Gordon achieved? We might put the answer in these terms: what has Joyce's *Ulysses* achieved, or his *Finnegans Wake*.

Why does a child learn to whistle?—in order to have the tune? We set our children loose in a meadow and they return with flowers. Jaimy Gordon wanders off into a world she has seen, she returns speaking a language she has heard. The challenge to the reader is to hear it: "Nor can a field be empty but fills with his passing whistle, the breath that escapes him as he goes down the track all solo, one long whistle banding, filling, overflowing the summer sky."

CANADIAN LITERATURE

Frank Davey has written what may well serve as the standard survey of the sixties' Canadian literature for some time to come; Davey, editor of the first-rate journal of contemporary criticism, *Open Letter*, has attempted what would seem an unmanageable task: to fully overview a decade of Canadian writing. And, fortunately for us, Davey has succeeded. *From There to Here* (Press Porcepic) is 288 pages of tightly written criticism and bibliography. Davey's method is to thumbnail the development and the especial characteristics in the art of the sixty writers he considers the most significant in the Canadian sixties; he provides thorough bibliographies of works by each author (books, essays, & interviews), and further lists a number of essays on and reviews of the writers—these appearing primarily in the Canadian press. In the 3-4 pages generally allotted each writer he treats, Davey highlights the writer's innovations and his special contributions to "Canadian" writing. Davey's foremost interests, and these come through page after page, are nationalistic Canadian literature and "innovative" writing. As a survey of recent Canadian literature, *From There to Here* is an invauable guide; but more importantly, I think, Davey's book stands as a "declaration of independence", an independence asserted in a clear, controlled, and reasoned voice.

On the surface of it, the "culture" of the United States seems monolithic and pervasive. Commercial publishing in the US, perhaps with malice and forethought, perhaps unintentionally, sometimes helps to perpetuate the impression that there is a "standard" American culture; there may be a "mass-culture" in this country, but it is far from standard and far from pervasive. I am, to be sure, weary of seeing the same authors discussed in academic journals, the same myths perpetuated in the classroom, the same assumptions nodded to and accepted again and again in the popular press, in films, on television. I am weary of reading about New York as the "big apple" in/of/for our culture(s).

And *I'm* a citizen here. I can sympathize with Davey's nationalistic feelings in his critical stance—"American" books out-number "Canadian" books in Canada at the moment, I'll wager, and most of the "American" books in Canada aren't ones I'd be particularly interested in; I can't see that Canadians should be any more interested in them. Yet a good many "Canadian" publishing firms are subsidiaries of American firms; and the largest book distributors in Canada seem ideologically American rather than Canadian. The situation is at best unhealthy and, at worst, detrimental to literature both in Canada and the United States. Nationalism itself, of course, is generally debilitating, but seems presently the best option for ensuring Canadians protection against American money and American "culture", ideas, books, and credit cards.

I've often called for an emphasis on "regionalism" in literature, believing that such emphasis serves to underline the roots, traditions and affinities of our literatures, allowing each both full context and space to move beyond particulars. The old saw urges writers to write what they know best; the kernel of truth in that saying cuts sharply against any notion that literature can be made at much remove from the writer's surroundings & deepest understanding. What cuts against "regional" writing is usually the assumption that there can be one and only one literature that is vital to the dominant and apparently monolithic culture of any particular political entity. An emphasis on regional writing can help ensure artistic freedom for the writer by promoting literary diversity. If Canadian "nationalism" frees the Canadian writer from any overbearing influence of "American" literary taste while not encouraging monolithic, uniform "Canadian" literature, such nationalism can be a valuable catalyst. When nationalism—American, Canadian or otherwise—impedes rather than frees the writer, however, literature suffers. Literature suffers further when the best writing from one country is disparaged or neglected in another, especially when there are obvious affinities. Canadians would do well, I think, to "write Canadian", but would be poorly read were they to assimilate only Canadian literature; and—here is my complaint—American readers are sadly negligent if they ignore the literature of Canada.

I do not intend to imply here that Frank Davey is a rabid Canadian nationalist. His prose is level-headed and well-considered, only very occasionally shrill about Canadian/non-Canadian matters. Most often, Davey is a well-read, sympathetic, yet judicious critic, even when discussing the most "provincial" literature. His comment on George Elliott, for instance, reads in part:

> George Elliott's single work of fiction, *The Kissing Man* (1962), concerns a perennial subject in Canadian literature, the small town. In a number of ways *The Kissing Man* invites comparison with the classic of Canadian small-town fiction, Stephen Leacock's *Sunshine Sketches*. Both are set in rural Ontario in the early part of this century. Both are collections of stories which are arranged to form a whole which is arguably a novel.

... [H] is stories speak poignantly of the limited success-
es these characters find in seeking the love and understanding of their fellow townsmen. The theme of *The Kissing
Man* is that man should act affirmatively toward life—should
view life as an active and joyous process rather than as a
waiting for death. ... Elliott's stories centre on the few
characters who have worked to create love and joy. ...

His prose, despite occasional awkwardnesses, especially
in the opening story, is extremely delicate in texture. A tendency to withhold all but the most essential details gives
the stories an air of insubstantiality close to that of fantasy
or dream. The stories are thus as liberated from the unin-
spired materiality of daily life as Elliott would have his characters be.

Always, Davey's eyes are alert to nationalistic considerations; about Henry Kreisel, for instance, he says: "Kreisel's 'Canada' is often culturally
indistinguishable from the rest of North America". Davey quite consciously examines the various relationships the writers he discusses have
with "Canada". He recognizes as well the larger issues involved and can
succinctly state them while introducing discussion of a particular writer:

Dave Godfrey has been among the most energetic of the
new wave of Canadian literary and economic nationalists in
the 1960's and 1970's. Recognizing that those who control
a country's media also control its culture, he began working
toward the wresting of a significant portion of the country's
book publishing industry from foreign control. He helped
to found three of the period's new nationalistic commercial
publishing houses, House of Anansai, New Press, and Press
Porcepic. He became one of the principal initiators of the
Independent Publishers Association, an association of Cana-
dian-owned presses which have bonded together to form a
political lobby and to attempt to solve common distribution problems. His conviction that a country's literary independence is tied to its degree of economic independence is
reflected in his being not only a co-editor of *Read Canadian:
a book about Canadian books* (1971) but also co-editor, with
nationalist economist Mel Watkins, of *Gordon to Watkins to
You* (1970).

Equally as valuable as his nationalistic concerns are Davey's interests
in innovative literature. A healthy nationalism can serve to free writers;
likewise, an atmosphere in which literary innovation is respected, where
breakthroughs are fostered, can and will help to keep a literature vital
and significant. In the US, we find that literary innovation is usually
confined to small-circulation journals. If Davey's concerns are in any

way indicative of the literary atmosphere in Canada, the situation Canadian literature finds itself in is far healthier than that of the US.

Davey does not take a limited view of "innovation"; *From There to Here,* whole-cloth, charts the larger course of "changes" in Canadian literature, for the writers Davey is discussing range in age from the very young to the older established writers. If a writer influential in the sixties did his most significant or most innovative work in the forties, Davey says so. Davey appreciates *literature,* he appreciates *Canada,* and he appreciates *past and present breakthroughs* which allow today's literature and keeps it vital, moving toward tomorrow.

As a critic of innovative literature, Davey aligns himself rigorously with no particular school or style; he knows the flow of the various literatures around him, but has not chosen to swim in one river only. His allegiances as a poet are undoubtedly far more limited than his concerns as a critic overviewing a decade of Canadian literature. His broad appreciation of all the significant literatures he is discussing is enviable; indeed, the breadth of his appreciation, both the more traditional and the more innovative, is a primary virtue of Davey's book. Yet just as he concerns himself throughout with "Canada", so Davey examines the writers of the sixties for what they may have contributed that is new and necessary. Looking at the innovative writers, he finds bonds among them, and places each in perspective. Of Gerry Gilbert, for instance, he can say:

> The most extreme (and therefore least publicly known) example of the movement of Canadian writers to multi-phasic, relativistic, and phenomenological forms has been the work of "Canada's National Magazine", Gerry Gilbert. Gilbert chooses the most recalcitrant of subjects: the ordinary breakfast-to-bedtime experience local to his own life. He presents these in their random sequence because it is exactly this sequence that he wishes to make substantial to his readers.

Davey places Gilbert against two contemporaries also discussed in the book, George Bowering and Daphne Marlatt:

> He avoids even the minimal amount of 'packaging' that gives shape to a George Bowering or Daphne Marlatt lyric; neatness, conciseness, or rhetorical form would directly betray the randomness of reality he seeks to evoke, and merely duplicates the various institutional and political structures which he believes to distort life and oppress men.

Davey further recognizes the relevant literary traditions which inform many of the innovations which interest him. Of bpNichol he says:

Of the many experimental poets of the last decade, only bp-Nichol has consciously adopted a symbolist and semioticist attitude to language and form. Nichol's work, however, is utterly unlike any Canadian symbolist writing of the previous decades. It takes its inspiration not in the asceticism of William Morris or in the deliberately charged image structures of Baudelaire and Mallarme, but in the linguistic experiments of Dada and Gertrude Stein and in the semiotic experiments of European and South American visual poetry.

A healthy innovative literature requires an aggressive and interested criticism. Davey's criticism throughout *From There to Here* will serve, I think, to foster a spirit of innovation in the Canadian writers of the seventies and beyond. It will further, undoubtedly, encourage writers to closely examine the soil from which their writing springs, to take and to hold the best in the literary traditions infusing writing in Canada, to write not what has been written before, but what needs to be written.

* * *

W)here? The Other Canadian Poetry (Press Porcepic), edited by Eldon Garnet, is not "criticism" nor is it entirely an "anthology" of Canadian poetry. It is, we might say, a critical, or more properly, a polemical anthology. Garnet is interested in writers who "have published their work in the small presses, with the expected result that their work has had poor general distribution."

In the rare moments when their poetry is heard it is often tuned out because of the strangeness of its sound. The poets may break poetic barriers & open new territories of poetic expression, but the last boundary they have yet to shatter is the silence imposed upon them by a lack of audience. They will pass through the sound barrier from unsounded to sounded when the Canadian reader opens up, catches up & meets the new poetry.

In his introduction to the anthology, Garnet immediately serves notice to the reader expecting a "traditional", familiar literature: "I feel that a poet who makes no effort to innovate, & therefore to add something new to what already exists is no poet." The poets collected in *W)here? The Other Canadian Poetry* do make efforts, fully conscious, to make "new" literature, and to make literature new. If the work here seems difficult, it is difficult because it is unfamiliar. I am reminded that Eliot's "The Wasteland", which today is discussed over coffee by the newest of English grad students, baffled very astute critical minds when it was published. William Carlos Williams, of course, recognized that "The Wasteland" set American poetry back fifty years. "The Wasteland" perhaps improved critical thought more than it benefitted subsequent poetry; whatever the case, the poem has been assimilated into literary tradition and the techniques which initially appeared difficult are now commonplace. The thirteen Canadian poets in this anthology no doubt are incrementally creating future Canadian poetry. I would think too that their works will spur adequate critical discourse.

I sometimes think that the most rewarding reading is that which is most difficult, that which encounters an entirely new literature. There seems little challenge in reading what has already been read, and little reward in mastering the familiar. There are, of course, familiar joys which no doubt give pleasure, and these cannot be denied. There is also, however, a special exhilaration which results when a difficult puzzle is solved. I'm told that higher mathematics holds such joy for the minds which can pursue the equations to conclusion; I find that a good piece of "new" writing can bring similar intellectual excitement. More often than not, the poets Garnet anthologizes—David UU, Joe Rosenblatt, bpNichol, Daphne Marlatt, Gerry Gilbert, Maxine Gadd, David Dawson, Frank Davey, David Cull, Judith Copithorne, Victor Coleman, bill bissett, and Nelson Ball—lead us to read beyond the limits we have customarily set for ourselves. Their works, in this sense, are instructive lessons in how-to-read; and the result is often a joy in reading-as-exploration.

Eldon Garnet, I said earlier, has compiled a critical/polemical anthology here. In addition to his testy and very useful introduction, Garnet has included an informative running commentary on the poets and poetry in the book. His "criticism" serves to identify and define, as much as one is able to within the limits of Garnet's own premises: *Boundaries are not allowed. To set up fixed parameters is to deny openness, to deny the possibility & value of experimentation. Every statement made above (& very soon below) is a garrison which must be broken."* Garnet shows us, we might say, where these rivers of words are flowing at present, what directions, what speeds, without prejudice to future shifts in the course of each river; he is apparently fully aware that commentary on the text, to be most useful, needs to be at once descriptive and polemical. Of Joe Rosenblatt's sound poems, for instance, Garnet says:

> These "sound poems" with their rhythms of repetitions demand to be read out loud for their cumulative effect to develop completely. If they are to be read only with the silence of the eyes they will never take on their full life; it would be like watching a movie without the sound track. Rosenblatt's vigorous rhythm, which embodies many qualities of the chant, takes the reader quickly & easily into & through the poems. The dithyramb—the wild, passionate,

choric hymn sung in honor of Dionysius the Greek god of
fertility—is a fitting description of Rosenblatt's exuberant
rhythm.

Garnet says of Judith Copithorne:

> Copithorne does not illustrate poetry, rather she draws
> graphic poems; the graphics & the words do not stand on
> their own, but together they form the poem. She is not at
> her best when she attempts to write a poem & surround it
> by graphics, but only when she completely integrates both
> elements.

We can see the truth of Garnet's analysis when we read Copithorne's endearing poetry.

Garnet's conciseness and clarity in describing the works of a poet as
multifarious as bpNichol is admirable; indeed, his commentary is more
informed than that of most, if not virtually all, literary "critics":

> .... Nichol utilizes basic elements of langague and alpha-
> bet—sound & shape—in an attempt to remake poetry from
> the roots. ...
>
> Throughout his work Nichol has been concerned with the
> concrete, visual representation of the poem. At times he
> has experimented with the shape of the printed work on the
> page, bending, expanding & stretching out the letters to cre-
> ate new words & new verbal images of printed language. At
> other times he has abandoned letters & words completely
> & drawn his poems. ...
>
> In a similar manner in other books Nichol works to-
> ward the oral source of poetry. In these he plays with
> sound, raising his voice in excitement, chanting, or holding
> his mouth open as one letter is sounded in a steady stream
> of sound. ...
>
> Searching for the primitive roots of poetry, Nichol also
> becomes involved in the minimal poem—a poem articulated
> in the briefest & least dramatic series of words possible. Mi-
> nimal poetry, like minimal art, where a white line on a white
> canvas constitutes the painting, is deliberately low-keyed.
> A poem may be a single word appearing in small type in the
> middle of a white page, as it is in the poem "em ty". In the
> form of the one word graphically represented is contained
> the feeling which is the poem. The tone of minimal poetry,
> subdued & seldom changing, runs throughout much of
> Nichol's work. ...

Garnet, in four short paragraphs, is able to give us a minicourse on the concerns not only of bpNichol but of a good many contemporary writers. It is difficult to find such astute and careful commentary *anywhere*, much less in an anthology. However, saying what has not been said before, or not often enough, is one of the primary characteristics of Garnet's discussion.

I have said, it seems, more here about Garnet's approach in *W)here? The Other Canadian Poetry* than I have about the poetry itself. It may be, perhaps, that Garnet has said the best of what can be said in his commentary; or perhaps the task of full appraisal of the poetry will fall to a commentator other than myself. I am intrigued by the "polemical" nature of this anthology, and excited about Garnet's method. The poetry, certainly, is often superb and very often exhilarating. A taste of what is in store for the reader should suffice; I close with "part I" of Nichol's engaging "dada lama" (unfortunately the only part of the six-part poem reprinted in the anthology, obviously incomplete as it stands alone) and leave you (the reader, after all) the task of acquiring the poetry and teaching yourself to read again. "dada lama (part 1)":

```
        hweeeee
        hweeeee
        hyonnnn
        hyonnnn

        hweeeee
        hweeeee
        hyonnnn
        hyonnnn
        tubadididdo
        tubadididdo
        hyon
        hyon

        tubadididdo
        tubadididdo
        hyon
        hyon

        ffffffffffffffffffffffffftsssssssss
        ffffffffffffffffffffffffftsssssssss
        ffffffffffffffffffffffffftsssssssss

        hyonnnnnn
                unh
        hyonnnnnn
                unh
```

SALTHOUSE

In an editorial note in the first issue, *Salthouse* editor D. Clinton says he "hopes to publish poetry with an emphasis on the primitive leaving that a very open field & space for the magic to happen. . . . I figure with proper encouragement *Salthouse* will be a lot of interior geography, map making, sea expeditionary poetry, reprints from *National Geographic*, reports on the killer bee, the sexual patterns of zoo feeders & an open warm dedication to Marlin Perkins & the hope that poetry knocks us over." By the second issue, Clinton is re-examining and changing the emphasis of *Salthouse* slightly: "shifts in the focusing are already at work. Leaning more toward a histories geographies fieldbook & all the peripheries that circulate around those things." *Salthouse* is subtitled "A Little Magazine of Field Notes".

What Clinton is doing with *Salthouse* is precisely what many little magazine editors fail to do: he has given his journal a special reason for existing. Many new little magazines come into being simply to publish "the best available writing we see", etc.; I would not quarrel very seriously with such a reason for publishing a little magazine, at least not until any deluge of little magazines proves counter-productive. But publishing "the best available writing we see" tends to make one little magazine look more or less like another, or several others. Few have the peculiar stamp of an editor, few mark out territory as their own. Clinton has staked his claim in "histories, geographies, field notes"; like *Alcheriṅga*, a journal of ethnopoetics which lays claim to a particular kind of poetry and an editorial vision all its own, *Salthouse* gathers a kind of poetry not usually brought together, and sometimes not even considered "poetry". There is a paradox in an editorial vision such as Clinton's, one I think we can readily see: while taking pains to identify the particular poetries he's interested in, the editor is opening himself to almost endless possibilities, an interest in field notes, histories, geographies, I would think, is underwritten by a special concern for open, expansive poetries, some perhaps unlike those we are accustomed to seeing.

In practice, it is interesting to see such an editorial stance worked out. Contributors to *Salthouse* no. 1 are: Carolyn Forsche, Peter Wild, Jeff Olma, David Shevin, Michele Birch, and Mark Berman; those to *Salthouse* no. 2: Stewart Lachman, Dan Raphael, Galen Green, Christtine Zawadewsky, Stephen Legget, and Gordon Anderson. The contributors seem amazingly diverse. The range of poetries is from Stephen Legget's very tight "Roots" (*Salthouse 2*) through Gordon Anderson's tight though expanding "North America" (no. 2), Peter Wild's four poems (no. 1) and Stewart Lachman's "The Buttonmaker" (no. 2), onto Carolyn Forsche's exquisite "Northport" and "Caliche" (no. 1), to Jeff Olma's light/serious linguistic workings called "the wet deck poems" (no. 1), onto David Shevin's fantasy-catalogue with acknowledgements to history, geography, and politics, "When They Caught the Murderer,

He Was Sitting Pretty in the Only Ghost Town in Kansas" and his "suppose" exploration entitled "The Gaon's Meditation" (both in no. 1), up to Christine Zawadewsky's essentially surrealistic "biographical" prose-poem account entitled "When the Snow Was Blue" (no. 2). The work of the other poets included in the first two issues of *Salthouse* fall into place in this ordering as well.

Legget's "Roots" is a precise exploration:

> Digging up the cactus,
> a tiny blunt root
> nails it to the earth.
>
> Pale white roots
> of wild grasses, cattail,
> milkweed.
>
> The floating roots
> of water chestnut.
> Wherever we go:
> roots.
>
> Take root.
> Grow out of.
> Grow in.
>
> Bending over the earth
> our hair comes back,
> catches on roots,
> our quick thin fingers
> finger dart down
> into darkness.
>
> Raddish.
> Ra.
> Root.
> Snout.

Legget finds meaning in roots; in "North America", Anderson searches particulars looking for myth (a brief section from the long poem):

> . . .
> and
> the horse came to North America
> there were no wheels.
> guns
> other weapons: club antelope bone.

wife washing clothes, taking the children to grammar school and
    nursery school
one long flow
of water
north to Hudson Bay
south to the Gulf
search for metal
deeper and deeper into the earth
molten hot
climbs on the surface along the
Atlantic Ridge
someday another continent
the Americas and Europe drift.

Both Legget and Anderson are examining roots, particulars, and are finding something larger; Peter Wild starts at roots, moves into history, and
beyond, as in "Lewis and Clark":

At Lolo Pass Lewis and Clark
lay down their guns before the escarpment,
which twitched like women's legs,
silver potatoes that put down roots,
into the flooded soil. as they shaved
they saw fierce Sacajawea naked on the hills
working her mandibles, and ships lost in the Orient
backing out from glacier cliffs.
behind them farmers already screamed
like the dawn, corn exploding from furrows,
at their wives who had gone to live
in the stone library at Hamilton, for
their daughters speeding on the Snake
in jet boots. they felt their chins
smooth as China plate, limp quills
raining out, thinking of Jefferson counted
the trinkets, that leapt through their
fingers in the light of Missoula
ten miles away, a cave, a honeycomb
reversed, ranchers
    applauding around the girls,
bellies going in and out, throwing
their breasts around their heads like
silver lassos, from Sweden, Greece, and Egypt.

Wild marks the contrast between the America Lewis and Clark dreamed
of, sleeping, waking, and the America which actually inhabits the land
these explorers traveled across. Lachman's "The Buttonmaker" is root-

ed in history as well, though French history, and the life of a button-maker. Carolyn Forsche finds other contrasts to make in the details of one kind of American life; this is "Northport":

> I smelled the montreal chop of the hardwood (the way
> the big-hand logger laid her on the hay barn floor, house
> dress up around her waist).

> We'd felt the woods that day (all the coffee), burnt wipe
> of October through birch peels. Slicing rounds off felled
> trunk pitched into the cellar, underside spinning bug nests.
> Arrows sped wind to the deer flank. I cooked chili in the
> mason canner pot, they brought drums, tin pans, made noise.
> It was Northport Boogie Season, deer killing, gourd picking
> time. Before snow when breath crawls out your face and you
> lug cheese, night oil by sled from town.

> I felt like getting pregnant by one of those men who'd pull
> away with the logging camp. I'd be alone, someone to suck me.
> It felt like the time in my life, went with putting up pickles
> in salt brine. I would want him to hang around, having me
> boil his shirts, beans, water.

> I went to the houses that smelled of stale blood, spittle,
> pablum, asked how it felt. They said

>> Like taking a big shit, feeling the back of your belly
>> in a meat sieve, your breasts swell hard, for once you're
>> full bosomed, at first you'll heave breakfast then sleep
>> on your back. Have someone to help you, heat water, make
>> broth. Be afraid if your child is in the woods, with men,
>> guns. Certain times they shoot what moves, have their dogs
>> flush it out. Not a pretty sight, baby coming home in the
>> jaws of some hound.

> Then these women smile, say it's worthwhile, cup baby droppings
> in their hands.
> One more winter, ice scars, fires smell up sheets, dust
> stokes the sun. I stare at my naked hands, flat belly, I know
> what I will say when a young woman asks me.

Jeff Olma's "the wet deck poems" are at once perhaps an exploration of American life and a journey langague can make; from "Cutting a Captain's Log":

"Beneath the prow, no damage to the ship if the
flooding amidships has anything to do with it.

"the day's first business was a public flogging of
Navigation, witnessed by the crew
and a majority of officers:

"it is hereby judged inhumane and masochistic
to sail by the stars, in lieu of the fact that,
the vessal has an aviation incapacity.

"therefore, i—captain—have elected to measure
the voyage by sea birds, should they be sighted.
i will insist that land is near by, regardless
of position and prevailing winds.

"also, while i think of it, i crave swiss cheese."

The four additional poems from the sequence, published here, give further evidence of the kind of tricks Olma is up to. That Olma will accept
no "givens" on his expedition except those he chooses to create ("i will
insist that land is nearby") prepares us for the fantasy-interior geography of David Shevin's "When they Caught the Murderer. . ." ("and
there has never been a Presidential assasination in Kansas before.") and
his "The Gaon's Meditation" litany of

Suppose a man were to marry a peri
and between them they begat a bear
and soldiers came to steal the bear etc.

At the far end of the possibilities presented in *Salthouse* is Zawadiwsky's
"When the Snow Was Blue", which examines interior landmarks as a
way to come to understanding, in contrast to Legget's real roots spark-
ing knowledge within the poet. Zawadewsky's prose-poem ends:

When he found someone's crushed mitten trampled in the
snow, when I heard the click of the lock as I walked away
and saw the dogs sniffing between his legs, I laughed and
laughed. Or I wish that I had. As the string of thorns
around my breast expanded. An entire life of this:
climbing up the threadbare stairs, sitting at the
kitchen table and staring through the window at the
cemetery in the snow, its long curved trees like
scythes, dull blades that'll never know wet flesh
or slaughter. From a distance misery resembles beauty.
But when the earth is as fragile as a Christmas tree

ornament, when the pear-shaped earth is my belly, his
sun, he screams like a rat who screams like a child,
I pretend to kiss a leper and I love him. And I fill myself
with snow.

That there is poetry in history should come as no surprise; history
begets myth, and myth is the stuff of poetry. Personal myths born out
of personal experience can produce a poetry similar to the historical-
geographical if the poet is willing to use his materials as the starting
point for explorations such as those we find here. When historical texts,
incidents, or biographical details are used as a basis for poetry, the poet's responsibility is to find the mythic dimensions in the material. Even
a poem such as Legget's, found in first-hand personal experience, suggests mythic qualities in his handling. Similarly, the sheer narrative
flow in David Shevin's fantasy-poems, the nature of the story-telling
lends the poet's personal vision a sense of the legendary or mythic.

There are, no doubt, nearly endless ways to deal with (and nearly
endless ways to discuss) the kinds of "histories, geographies, field notes"
that make up Clinton's concerns in *Salthouse*. My own remarks here,
and the poems I have quoted, are meant to help delimit the range of
Clinton's vision. Nothing has been said yet of the basically *flat* nature
much of the poetry here; and I do not use *flat* in a derogatory way.
With certain exceptions, much of the poetry here does not crack with
thunderous imagery nor peal with lyrical smoothness of language. There
are other places those poetries can be published. Rather, the poets
here, by and large, find their imagery in the common stuff of ordinary
existence, they make their music in the patterns of daily speech. In
such poetry, the poet's hand is most evident in the ordering, the structuring of his materials; by careful placement of details, with an eye to
the larger sense of the poem, these poets are able to suggest to the
reader the special significances they find in the unadorned particulars
of existence, in the common phrase turned uncommonly. There is music, to be sure, as small linguistic surprise follows surprise in ordinary
speech, in the litany-like chant, action following action. The poetry is
not "primitive" in the same sense that we might describe the poetry in
Alcheringa as primitive. Neither is the poetry "raw" in the sense that it
hasn't been carefully worked, for it has. Rather perhaps much of the
poetry in *Salthouse* is related to other poetries as Truman Capote's *In
Cold Blood* is related to other novels. Raw perhaps in the sense that a
documentary is "raw". Yet, we are all the while aware of the artistic
sensibilities underlying the poems.

The first two issues of *Salthouse* seem larger than their 36 (no. 1)
and 32 page (no. 2) sizes might indicate. This is a measure of the poetry
in the magazine. We could wish, though, for larger issues, if only to be
able to see what other "field notes" are being written now, what other
terrains are being explored. Our interest is aroused: what other territories can the editor as scout and guide lead us through?

JAYHAWKING WITH THE VARMINT

"Everything
is out of an ordinary
that never really was"
—*Varmint Q*, p. 134

Charles Boer's *Varmint Q* (Swallow Press) is said (on the front cover of the paperback edition at least) to be "an epic poem on the life of William Clarke Quantrill". This "subtitle" does not appear on the title page, page, and I tend to think Charles Boer would not want us to read it as a true subtitle nor as a fair indication of the full nature of his long narrative poem. A common definition of "epic" suggests that it can be: in the first sense, a long narrative poem in elevated style, recounting the deeds of a legendary or historical hero; or in the second sense, a work of art resembling or suggesting an epic; or in the third, a series of events or body of legend or tradition felt to form the proper subject of an epic. While *Varmint Q* contains some elements proper to each of these definitions, it is difficult to deduce from *Varmint Q* that the poem is fully and fairly an epic, at least in the traditional sense. Or, perhaps we ought to start with the premise that it is, and allow Boer to carry us through his narrative in order to destroy or at least radically reformulate our sense of what an epic is or can be.

We grant, at the outset, that *Varmint Q* is a long narrative poem. Further, we can read Boer's "An Invocation to John Greenleaf Whittier as an Aside from the Author", which opens the book as prologue, as one attempt in *Varmint Q* at "elevated style". Or if it does not suggest elevated style, the invocation is high-blown self-appreciative strutting by the narrator-Charles-Boer (as distinct from the poet-Charles-Boer). Yet the prologue is not high-blown self-appreciation either, since the invocation undercuts any significance we might attach to John Greenleaf Whittier, and any self-importance we might find in the (actual and metaphorical) strutting and preening of our narrator, the fictitious Charles Boer. The invocation to Whittier concludes with the line "you are the only poet we'll read anymore" and we realize *we've been had*.

The real Charles Boer listens, yes, only occasionaly interjecting a comment or two of his own to undercut his narrator, and he is amused not only by the antics of his story-teller but also by the uneasy squirming of his readers or listeners as they become aware they are being played with, *put on*, teased, taunted. The real Charles Boer is also amused by his material, the life and deeds of the violent William Quantrill. Quantrill's is an interesting story to play with. If Boer were directing a movie, which he's not, we would hear his actors complaining that he contradicts himself about the way they are to portray the characters; the actor playing Quantrill, I would think, would throw up his arms and walk off the set, mumbling something about having to depict two contradictory personalities (or several) simultaneously. The real Charles Boer would smile, no doubt, his eyes would probably twinkle, and he would find another actor for the lead. Further, Boer-the-director would film the actors complaining, and these incidents would appear in the final version of the film.

For what Boer-the-poet is attempting in *Varmint Q* is an identification of "hero"—what, exactly, constitutes a legendary or historical hero, one to be written about; what does it mean to "recount the deeds" of such a figure. Boer-the-poet is trying to find out.

First, you need a legend or history.

Add:

2 parts fact

2 parts gossip

½ part newspaper story

1½ parts recollections by participants in the events you are writing
  about.

Stir well.

Let set overnight.

In the morning, read the truth.

I say *that, Boer* doesn't say *that*. Yet Boer-the-poet attempts to un-cover, by putting together Quantrill as hero, the way we choose our he-roes, to reveal the uncritical need Americans (perhaps all humans) have to *construct* heroes when none are readily at hand. That need. Quantrill is an historical figure; we have record of his being "a well-known and desperate leader" of Kansas raiders "who are known familiarly as gueril-las, jayhawkers, murderers, marauders, and horse-thieves". At least we are led to believe we have such record, that characterization of Quantrill and his band being attributed to Lucien J. Barnes, Captain and Assis-tant Adjutant-General at the Headqrs. District of Central Missouri, Jefferson City, Mo. (pp. 117-118, *Varmint Q*). If we felt the urgent need, we could consult William Elsey Connelley's version of the life and times of Quantrill and the raiders; Connelley's book is in the libraries, it is a matter of record, it is a source for Boer's narrative (in fact, one cri-tic, Susan Grathwol, charges that Boer is much too faithful to Connel-ley's version of Quantrill).

That Boer may be very close to Connelley's text becomes irrelevant, however, in the context of what the poet is attempting. In destroying our conception of epic and epic hero, Boer is intent on raising questions for us to ponder, questions which become finally irrelevant except inso-far as they have been raised:

1. Are we to believe Connelley when he says Quantrill's ancestors "endowed him with depravity, bestowed upon him the portion of de-generacy. In cruelty and a thirst for blood he towered above the men of his time. Somewhere of old his ancestors ate the sour grapes that set

his teeth on edge." (p. 7). Should we assume a man is not responsible for his acts; does a man's blood determine what he can become; is Quantrill merely acting out his small part in a larger and foreordained drama?

2. Should we believe Quantrill when he writes to his mother in January of 1860: "Though I have been quite foolish in my notions of the last three or four years, still I have been taught many a good lesson by them, and think I shall not regret it in after life so much as I do now, for it is now that I feel it the keenest, and can see the whole picture of my doings in one broad sheet, which may be rolled up and laid by to look upon in after life." (p. 49). Quantrill's reflection follows other, more pungent opinions which, we can assume, he thinks are not foolish notions: "You have undoubtedly heard of the wrongs committed in this territory by the southern people, or proslavery party, but when one knows the facts they can easily see that it has been the opposite party that have been the main movers in the troubles and by far the most lawless set of people in the country. They all sympathize for old J. Brown, who should have been hung years ago, indeed hanging was too good for him. May I never see a more contemptible people than those who sympathize for him. A murderer and a robber, made a martyr of; just think of it." (p. 48). One is reminded of the boy explaining to his father how he became involved in an after-school fight: "Nuthin' would have happened if he hadn't hit me back." We can pull elements from Quantrill's own words that cut back against Boer's "epic" and change its nature: "A murderer and a robber, made a martyr of; just think of it." Does Quantrill become the kind of martyr he seems to despise?

3. Or do we accept Jake Herd's impressions of Quantrill, known to Herd at the time as Charley Hart: "At first Quantrill appeared to be rather reticent, but after a time, crossing frequently [on the ferry Herd helped operate] as he did, he appeared to become more sociable. . . . He did not strike me as having any braggadoccio or desire to make any display in any way. . . . I don't think he had any very positive convictions on questions that were agitating the territory at the time; if he did, he certainly kept them to himself." (pp. 71-72). Herd does add a telling observation, one we keep in mind in reading the character(s) of Quantrill in the poem: "One thing is certain, he was always willing to go into anything that turned up that had a dollar in it for Charley Hart." (p. 72).

4. We might select John Dean's portrait of Quantrill as reliable: "I met *Quantrell* as a *now* known spie and *assassin*, working in connection with *many others* for *reward of Earth*. He was a *sensitive, falsely polerized,* or polerized to *Evil*. Your description of him was fair but not positively correct or sharply drawn. . . . his eyes were *uncommonly large* and full. He was quite *talkative* at times. Very *pleasant* as a studied rule, laughing and joking, not a loud boisterous laugh, but a rolling, rippling, quiet laugh. He was *acting* the spie in his connection with me

and of course much of his seeming character was 'put on'. . . . he was very temperate as I now remember, but did at last, or about 1861 begin to have his little times with a drink or two, did not use tobacco in any way as I remember, but was given to the worship of women somewhat. His time was spent much with those lawless and reckless neer do *wells* that abound in such times and places. When asked *why* he *did* associate with such characters, he claimed to be spieing *their* plans, with the intention of doing good. . . " (p. 82). The varmint is a weasel, spying and plotting, seeming to be what he is not. Is the weasel in his blood, or is Q.'s scheming the working of a world-wise mind? Or does the weasel work for money? Does the varmint reflect much upon an after life? Is a hero responsible?

5. The *Louisville Daily Democrat* contradicts Boer-the-narrator about Quantrill's capture (during which our varmint sustained the wounds of which he later died): "Captain Terrill and his company arrived here yesterday from Taylorsville. They brought with them the guerilla who bears the name of 'Quantrill.' It is not the Quantrill of Kansas notoriety, for we have been assured that he was at last accounts a colonel in rebel army under Price." (p. 147). We wish perhaps that we had similar assurances, or any assurances. We've been told by the narrator that the Kansas Q. and the Kentucky Q. are one and the same; we've also been told, this time by William Scott, the first biographer of Quantrill, that he and Quantrill's mother removed the varmint's skull from a grave in St. John's Catholic Cemetery in Louisville, Kentucky: "She identifies/a chipped side tooth/in lower jaw/on right side./She will not let me/take the skull back. . . " (p. 25). Does majority opinion rule, do we believe the Kansas Q. was killed in Kentucky because we have the narrator's and William Scott's word for it, against only the report of the Louisville paper? Has the weasel escaped? What contradictions is history made of?

6. Or does Boer-the-poet give us the clue: "Everything/is out of an ordinary/that never really was"? I tend to think so. Throughout the narrative Boer has quoted letters, biographies, a newspaper story, recollections by eye-witnesses. Boer, perhaps, is drawing his epic hero from as many points of view as possible, each perspective different and intended to add to the characterization of Quantrill, however contradictory the details. Each line set down may be factual, and the poem does form a whole we can recognize, though the various lines or pieces of the work do not "fit" in a way we are accustomed to. Perhaps *Varmint Q* is to the epic as a cubist painting is to representational painting? We might think so. Yet there is no one William Quantrill to be found, only a multiplicity of historical perceptions; we are left with a truth, a history or legend "that never really was". Perhaps *Varmint Q* is a collage, Boer piecing together into a cohesive flow of narrative the contradictory evidence at hand; Boer does not give us, finally, a unified portrait of Quantrill, nor is his hero any larger than "an ordinary" man.

Boer-the-narrator doodles and embroiders upon the evidentiary collage, with the result that his hand is so much evident one can doubt *Varmint Q* is a true "collage". Certainly Boer-the-poet allows more levity into the poem than we might be used to in epics of a more familiar sort. Not only is his invocation of John Greenleaf Whittier finally humorous, finally a witty jest, but throughout the narrative we're treated to remarks which are funny or snide or both, no matter how serious the underlying intent. For example, in the section of *Varmint Q* entitled "The Raid on Lawrence", where we might expect some direct comment on the violence, on man's inhumanity to man (about 150 residents of Lawrence were killed in the raid), we find only oblique references to the violence and some reflection on the nature of the poem itself:

> Oh come on!
> This is not the time
> for lyric and rhyme.
> A song and dance maybe—
>   liar, liar
> your pants are on fire—
> to liven up the deadliness
> of every man's disorder.
> Just tell the story.
> Only the story is
> the whole poem!
> Just tell the poem.)

Or again:
> (and this too was not
> a part of the poem [of a man named Quantrill]
> because it rhymed.)

There is exaggerated abhorrence of the fact that the only Jayhawker killed in the raid on Lawrence was thrown into a ravine and left to rot:

> Pollution!
> That is what it is!
> The stink of this city
> of this city
> rotting
> upon its hill.
> The filth
> of this city
> stinking
> upon a hill!

Pollution indeed, the violence done, and we might worry about pollution? Boer misdirects his focus to a single telling detail for comic effect—the good people of Lawrence are little better than the Jayhawkers in allowing the corpse of one of the raiders to rot unburied, children stealing rings off the finger bones. The incident is deliberately set out of perspective, and we can chuckle at Boer's cleverness; as we laugh, though, we are knifed in the back: "the deadliness/of every man's disorder." Boer is smart for a poet. He often presents a light, playful surface though his intent is deadly serious. For example, in the passage in which Pelanthe, a Shawnee Indian, hears of the proposed raid on Lawrence and attempts to reach the city in time to warn the inhabitants, Boer punctuates the Indian's frantic ride with a flash of humor and a note of melodrama:

> . . . the horse, this sorrel mare,
> fell to a slower gait,
> then faltered, breathing hard
> again, and Pelanthe,
> who was smart for an Indian,
> took out his long knife
> and gashed its shoulders,
> took gun powder from his pistol
> and rubbed its wounds
> until it charged up suddenly,
> galloped a few more miles,
> then plunged to the ground,
> dead.

The two lines which strike one as contrapuntal to the seriousness of the narrative are the nearly gratuitous "who was smart for an Indian" and the obviously melodramatically placed final line, "dead". That Boer-the-narrator says Pelanthe was "smart for an Indian" gives us some sense of the historical reality, the place of the Indian in the frontier consciousness, the irony being that the Indian rides like a wild man in order to save the whites who think so little of him. Boer-the-poet smiles as the realization hits us. At the opening of the same passage about Pelanthe's ride, Boer uses repetition of words and rhythms to lighten the tone:

> Pelanthe,
> an Indian of the Shawnee,
> had heard the news from Bartles,
> a Red Leg scout,
> had offered to warn Lawrence,
> the city of refuge,
> said he would go along the Kansas River,

on the north side,
to avoid the guerillas.
Bartles,
the Red Leg scout,
said he would never make it in time,
took from the corral his best horse,
a Kentucky sorrel mare,
and Pelanthe,
this Indian of the Shawnee,
was off.

And the repetition continues. Boer, this smart-for-a-poet poet, knows how to pace his horse—his does not drop dead. The contrasting and contradictory tones throughout the poem, the refusal to paint a coherent portrait of Quantrill, the comic relief, these serve to underline what becomes the central assertion of *Varmint Q*: "Everything/is out of an ordinary/that never really was".

The surface of *Varmint Q* becomes increasingly deceptive, the narrative intent increasingly difficult to penetrate. We are constantly faced, on the one hand, with "the deadliness/of every man's disorder", and on the other, with Boer's insistent wit. The questions Boer raises for us, the the questions we find ourselves asking, lead us to re-evaluate the poem we think we've read and understood (to some extent, at least), lead us to wonder about other "heroes", to question the truthfulness of other epic poets, to question even whether the exaggerations of the Grade-B westerns we've seen are exaggerations at all, or if that matters. If anywhere, it is here that Eliot's dictum is true: we will never see the *Odyssey* the same way again, nor Michael Ondaatje's *Collected Works of Billy the Kid*, nor a John Wayne shoot-'em-up. Boer-the-narrator is attempting to reveal the *known facts* about William Clarke Quantrill; Boer-the-poet is undercutting those facts at every turn.

To return to our definition of the "epic": the style of *Varmint Q* is not generally "elevated", but more nearly common, conversational (though, of course, a good deal tighter than talk). The use of repetition, of line length and shape, these are stylistic matters, but always they reinforce the commonness of speech, rather than "elevating" it. The deeds recounted (if they are indeed "recounted", not fabricated by Boer or some historian) are those of an historical figure. Boer's poem suggests an "epic", yes, but rather than *resembling* the epic, we might say *Varmint Q re-assembles* it (which, I think, is part of Boer's intent). Finally, the life of William Quantrill may or may not form "the proper subject of an epic". Charles Boer-the-narrator would have us think so. Charles Boer-the-poet, perhaps, is not so sure. The poem ends with these lines:

And you see, the man
did die,
though the people
could not be sure
(the people
would never be sure),
because the poem of the man
went on
and on.
It was the poem of a man
named Quantrell.

The poem went on and on, we're told, at which point Boer's poem ends. The fact of the poem ending plays against what we're told, just as throughout *Varmint Q*, Boer-the-poet plays what his narrator is saying against what the poem is doing, where the poem is heading. The several questions raised by the poem remain as questions, unless we are able to say, as I think Boer intends, that *Varmint Q* is written out of an ordinary that never really was, that the deeds recounted are Quantrill's but also ours: "the deadliness/of every man's disorder". If everything we are told "never really was", we can say: yes, this is true, and this, and that, though they may be mutually contradictory. We can say, yes, Pelanthe was smart for an Indian—how witty—and how tragic, riding so hard, for whites who had little use for him. We can say, yes, Quantrill was a quiet man, not given to bragging, though he was a schemer, a murderer, a spy, though he was made a martyr of. We can say that Connelley's analysis is correct, that Quantrill's thirst for blood was in his blood; yet we can say that Quantrill was acting as a man responsible for his actions. We can say that the varmint got his due, shot down in a farmyard, though at the same time, we might exclaim, as Quantrill had said about John Brown—"indeed, hanging was too good for him. . . A murderer and a robber, made a martyr of; just think of it." A murderer and a robber, the hero of an epic poem; just think of it!

Boer-the-poet is smart for a poet: he wants to tell us a good story, to entertain us; he wants to raise moral and philosophical questions, to teach us; he wants to show us his virtuosity as a poet, and his wit, to edify and humor us. Boer does his entertaining, his teaching, his humoring within the framework of something generally familiar to us, the "epic", though at every turn of the narrative he undercuts the reliability of the facts and impressions he has gathered and set down. I doubt that we could easily specify what Charles Boer actually thinks about violence, about murder, jayhawking, whatever; having read *Varmint Q*, however, one may have a clearer sense of one's own position on violence. I doubt that we will know Boer's opinion about the accuracy of the historical records he uses as the stuff of his poem, or the weight of each piece of evidence presented; but we do have a clearer sense of the stuff history and legend and heroes are made of: contradiction and confusion. This is the paradox: Boer has 1) removed himself from the poem at such a distance that we cannot know what he may actually think; and 2) he has made himself so much a part of the telling of the poem that none of the details he recounts are as significant as the fact that the poem is Boer talking, telling a story, any story, with any hero, out of an ordinary that never really was anyway, out of the deadliness of every man's disorder. Epic, my foot: co(s)mic paradox; man the glory of the universe, man the varmint.

A LOCAL HABITATION

Alvin Turner as Farmer (Road Runner Press; reprinted by Windflower Press) was, until I read Ted Kooser's substantial collection entitled *A Local Habitation & A Name* (Solo Press), the single foremost book of "midwest" poetry I had read; Kloefkorn's poems are local and particular, yet universal & appealing as well. Kooser's work here will not change my assessment of Kloefkorn's work, but this volume might be placed alongside *Turner*: these are impressive and powerful poems that rise out of the heartland of our country, yet transcend the land from which they spring & move well beyond the borders of any locale and any particularity. "No ideas but in things", Williams urges. Or as Karl Shapiro, in the introduction to this volume, notes: "William Carlos Williams' dogma of the Local remains the touchstone of what authentic American poetry we have." Shapiro, further on, may praise "midwest" poetry at the expense of other kinds—I do think there is space & breath enough for several sorts of poetry; I don't think we have to elevate one poetry at the expense of another. What is called "midwest" poetry, as all good poetry does, reaches widely, to affect many sorts of readers. The poet, wherever he touches earth, touches man. And the reader, if he reads with any sensitivity at all, sees that & is moved. I have often confessed my intense interest in "regional" writing, especially the writing which comes out of the midwest experience. Several of my own poems are admittedly regional. My interest in midwest writing has frequently been challenged, sometimes by writers I consider well within the midwest tradition; I expect this piece will serve to re-open discussion. I don't intend to write here an apology for "midwest poetry" because I feel the poetry needs no such apology. I do intend, though, to explicate some central qualities of midwestern writing, and of Kooser's poetry in *A Local Habitation & A Name* in particular.

Ted Kooser is a well-published poet, and the magazine credits for his poems appearing in this volume show how wide an interest his work stirs. Some of the poems in this book appeared previously in Kooser's

Official Entry Blank, published by the University of Nebraska Press and
now out-of-print, and in his *Twenty Poems,* originally published in
the Best Cellar Press series. Solo Press's production of *A Local Habitation & A Name* is first-rate; the book is 79 pages long, printed on heavy cream/pale tan paper, perfect bound. The cover, designed by Peter
Langmack, is attractive, its mood in keeping with the spirit of Kooser's
work.

A *Local Habitation & A Name* is divided into two sections: the first.
"Red Wing", holds those poems which most clearly and most perceptib-
ly rise out of the land, which most intensely embody the essence of the
midwestern spirit. The second section, "Other Depots", shows Kooser
further removed from the earth and more personal; "Other Depots",
however, bears the imprint of a poet in touch with the land & himself.
The links between the poetry of the first & second sections are clearly
in evidence.

The qualities which identify "midwest" poetry are many & various;
key elements include: 1) an acceptance of the land as an impenetrable
force larger than ourselves, a mysterious force to live with, struggle with,
attempt to control while fully aware that such control is impossible; 2)
a quiet irony at almost every turn, whether the material at hand is the
power of the earth over human endeavor, the power of love, the power
of death; 3) a humor that rises first out of the quiet laughter one has at
oneself & one's own predicament, & only secondarily out of incongruities in the situations of others—humor, even at the expense of another, is very seldom malicious; 4) an openness to, & interest in, other
people; and 5) a conservatism, in poetic, & in tone & mood & intention
—the intent is to capture the spirit & a way of speaking, rather than to
create a new diction. There are other important qualities in the writing
coming out of the midwest, of course, but these I've mentioned seem
the most central & essential.

Kloefkorn's *Alvin Turner as Farmer* has such qualities in abundance:
"there is always the rock". Kooser's work, especially in the "Red Wing"
section, is clearly marked by acceptance of the land as that large a
force, one that can be read:

Abandoned Farmhouse

He was a big man, says the size of his shoes
on a pile of broken dishes by the house;
a tall man too, says the length of the bed
in an upstairs room; and a good, God-fearing man,
says the Bible with the broken back
on the floor below the window, dusty with sun;
but not a man for farming, say the fields
cluttered with boulders and the leaky barn.

A woman lived with him says the bedroom wall
papered with lilacs and the kitchen shelves
covered with oilcloth, and they had a child
says the sandbox made from a tractor tire.
Money was scarce, say the jars of plum preserves
and canned toamtoes sealed in the cellar-hole,
and the winters cold, say the rags in the window frames.
It was lonely here, says the narrow gravel road.

Something went wrong, says the empty stone house
in the weed-choked yard. Stones in the fields
say he was not a farmer; the still-sealed jars
in the cellar say she left in a nervous haste.
And the child? Its toys are strewn in the yard
like branches after a storm—a rubber cow,
a rusty tractor with a broken plow,
a doll in overalls. Something went wrong, they say.

The struggle between a person and the land is a difficult one, as any farm-er—from the Midwest or elsewhere—will tell you. The struggle requires a toughness and a determination; if these are lacking, the land can drive a family off. The struggle itself is necessarily ironic: man cannot "win" —he can only "make do". The irony is that generations of midwestern-ers have persevered in the struggle, the hand on the plow, on the reins; or now, on the steering wheel of a large combine or picker-sheller. Tech-nology makes the struggle easier, but does not, cannot overpower na-ture's weapons, the sheer vastness of the landscape ("It was lonely here, says the narrow gravel road"), the weather ("the winters cold, say the rags in the window frames"). Nor can it help to fathom the mysterious nature of the midwesterner's situation: "Something went wrong, they say". The central irony: we cannot survive the struggle & yet we must continue.

There are other ironies, as in "A Place in Kansas":

Somewhere in Kansas, a friend found
an empty stone house alone in a wheatfield.
Over the door was incised a ship's anchor.
There was no one to ask
what that anchor was doing in Kansas,
no water for miles.
Not a single white sail of meaning
broke the horizon, though he stood there for hours.
It's like that in Kansas, forever.

No one need ask "what that anchor was doing in Kansas". The land lies comfortable in its own shape, with its own strange necessities. The further irony is that not only Kansas is like that, forever; the "Red Wing" of the first section of this volume is Red Wing, Nebraska, 'forever' as well. And not Kansas and Nebraska alone.

"The Widow Lester" may be emblematic of certain aspects of the toughness of the Midwestern spirit, an acceptance of 'the way things are' required by individuals who find themselves in certain situations. The "coldness" evidenced by the Widow Lester exists, though we may not like to admit it: but then many of us, perhaps, have not felt the icy hand of larger powers-that-be: coldness, in the Widow Lester's situation is a human response; its purpose, survival. We may not wish to condone it, but at the least we must understand it:

> I was too old to be married,
> but nobody told me.
> I guess they didn't care enough.
> How it had hurt, though, catching bouquets
> all those years!
> Then I met Ivan, and kept him,
> and never knew love.
> How his feet stunk in the bed-sheets!
> I could have told him to wash,
> but I wanted to hold that stink against him.
> The day he dropped in the field,
> I was watching.
> I was hanging up the sheets in the yard,
> and I finished.

The sheets; the stink; the death. We survive with what resources we have available to us. We live with ourselves, finally.

Despite such instances of coldness, there is a warmth in the midwest as well—quiet, unobtrusive, sincere. There is concern, as in "Boarding House", but it is not worn on the sleeve like a badge, that toughness again:

> The blind man draws his curtains for the night
> goes to bed, leaving a burning light
>
> above the bathroom mirror. Through the wall,,
> he hears the deaf man walking down the hall
>
> in his squeaky shoes to see if there's a light
> under the blind man's door, and all is right.

The hallmark of much midwestern humor is that whatever small joke there is turns back on the speaker. In "A Letter from Aunt Belle", the speaker, telling of an explosion at the neighbors in which the woman was killed, said of her: "She always made me think of you,/but on that stretcher with her hair pinned up/and one old sandal off, she looked as old/as poor old me." The humor is quiet, the jokes nearly always small ones. The uninitiated, were they to read the surface of the words, might think the midwesterner more serious than he is. I am reminded of my father who, when asked by the county tax assessor come to reassess the land if he thought it was going to rain, replied: "It'll be a hell of a long dry spell if it don't". My father didn't smile, and you had to look close-ly to see the twinkle in his eye as his remark hit home; he had no con-trol over the weather, and no foreknowledge. He had little time to "make talk". To admit as much is to admit one's limitations in the face of nature & the work to be done; in context, the humor is double-edged, not malicious, but sharp as icicles along a barn's eaves. We live from mo-ment to moment, day to day, season to season, harvest to harvest. We stand open and vulnerable. That toughness.

"Wildflowers" shows the humor as well, in another light. But again the small joke is on oneself:

All of the flowers wilted into knots
of cotton stuck to sticks before we got
them home. That Chevy trunk was oven-hot.

The Queen-Anne's-Lace was spinach, and the rue
was ruined. The asters floated in a little blue
over the soup. Oh, how I laughed at you,

your shears still at the ready, and your jeans
crawling with ants and chiggers. That was mean
of me. I miss you now, your dear knees green

from kneeling in the pastures of the past.
We should've known the flowers wouldn't last.

The Midwestern view of the world is often a tragic one, and accord-ingly the humor seems wry, tragi-comic. The toughness demanded in what is a tragic world gives rise to the conservative aspects in midwest poetry. Survival demands that new ideas, new ways of acting, be tested gingerly; the tried and true methods of generations—which are known to work—are generally selected over courses of action one may be unsure of. Midwestern stock was immigrant stock, & once roots were set down in the land, the immigrants felt compelled to hold onto what they had. Midwestern poetry, while transcending the merely local, is still at its best a part of the fabric of the inhabitants of the land. The midwest po-et cannot rightly be faulted for not being chiefly an "experimentalist", an avant garde practitioner: there is breath and space enough for sever-al kinds of poetry. Competence, we can demand, and universal interest; we can demand that the midwest poet, if he is setting down the spirit that moves around him, be true to that spirit. And Kooser's work in *A Local Habitation & A Name* reads true; his intention is to capture, to record a world that exists, not to create—at least, not in the first place—a new world, a new spirit. If there is a larger intention, it is to show a people to itself, clearly.

Kooser has, here, a series of "Postcard Poems". Each is dated, i.e., "July 7, 1905", "April 1, 1913", "October 4, 1904", etc. These are most obviously midwestern in tone & in manner of speaking. They are intended to be read as, or may truly be, real postcards, actually sent. "Postcard: October 6, 1908":

> I wish you girls had
> been over to hear the
> singing this evening
> it sure was dandy.
> But I suppose you
> do not care to come
> to Bennett at night again.

"Postcard: December 31, 1914":

> Dear Velma. Hope
> you are having a
> fine time. Enjoy
> life while you can
> for when you get old
> you can't. Happy New
> Year to you. From
> Grand Pa.

"Postcard: March 1, 1910":

> I hope this will find you
> feeling much better and getting
> stronger every day. Have thought
> of you so many times
> and felt sorry you had to suffer
> so much. But I know you
> will be able to appreciate
> good health when you get
> strong again, and that is something
> to be thankful for. People
> who haven't been sick really
> do not realize how fortunate
> they are. Thought you would like
> a picture of this curious rock.
> It is about six miles from here.

The midwestern voices here are authentic. I have heard them before. I am torn between saying that Kooser has done an excellent job capturing the voices, and saying that he is fortunate to have been able to fashion these "found poems" out of actual postcards he's come across. The postcard poems are that true.

I cannot leave the "Red Wing" section of *A Local Habitation* without commenting briefly on the precision of Kooser's language and imagery. The many poems I've already quoted should give most of the evidence. Kooser has an economy of langauge that leads to a precision in the line and in the image. He has a keen clear way of seeing. He shows us the heart of the seed, and will not waste our time. "Field Studies" shows most compactly Kooser's powers.

> Coyote is white
> and gray.
> He runs away.
>
> Owl is brown
> and black.
> He circles back.
>
> Mouse is the color
> of a stare.
> He is not there.

The poems in the "Other Depots" section are more personal, & more removed from the land, than the poems in first section. There are poems "For My Former Wife, Watching TV, In the Past", for his son, for a man 'who never missed a day of work', for "The Failed Suicide", & others. This one is "Airmail from Mother":

> We're keeping the news of your divorce
> from Grandpa, who needn't know the truth.
> At his age (96) (and don't
> forget his birthday the 31st)
> he'll never need to know, so try
> to act as if things were the same
> as always, and if he asks about
> Diana when you visit, say
> she couldn't come. That's good enough.
> He'll never know the difference.

These poems, with few exceptions, are equally as good as the poems in the earlier section. In some cases, however, Kooser seems too close to the material for clear perception; "I Put my Hand on My Son's Head" seems a little maudlin for that reason:

> I put my hand on my son's head
> and grow suddenly older.
>
> His head is heavy and sun-warmed—
> a stone turned up in a field,
>
> an unopened geode
> crowded with beautiful crystals.

At times, the poetry in both sections of the volume, the similes & metaphors seem a bit contrived, e.g., "houses, freshly folded/and springing open again/like legal papers". But these are petty complaints against the power of this poetry. Kooser's voice is strong & clear, heavy as the smell of rain in air. Kooser knows his land, he knows his people. He knows the sound of iron against the rock. We can see his world, touch it.

The final commentary on *A Local Habitation* ought to be Kooser's; these poems have earned that for him. This is "Plain Song":

> I have been in my time only as far
> as the mountains to the west and there
> I was terribly afraid. My wife and son
> were with me in those days, but we were soon
> to be parted, perhaps my fear of things
> only as far away as my love gone out of me
> into a woman. Now I am very much alone
> here on my prairie. I think I must lean
> in my place like an old broken tree.
> If you are coming through one day, stop to see me.

LITERATURE & PLACE: Touching the Landscape; Reaching Beyond

What we touch moves us, can move us. As writers we are, perhaps, acutely aware of relationships as processes. In some sense, all writers, all poets especially, are regional writers: that which is at one's finger tips, at one's nerve endings, is first source, primary "material". The land, the shape of the landscape, the forces moving across the earth as wind rustling through an Iowa cornfield, these are sources for a literature which has yet to be fully discussed and given its place. "Regional writing" has often been considered merely the "local color" in our literature, the particularities of person and place that we endure while seeking out "broader" meaning and implications. As if, one would say, there can be any meaning beyond what we have experienced individually and as a species: all of us, writers and readers, are sentient, moving organisms, and what we have "learned"—I find—is what our senses are able to teach us, what we are able to take, beyond that, and shape as part of ourselves, a whole organism; and in a more extended sense, we "know" also what those who have gone before us have learned—we are able to pass on information in our genes, in our language, through our social institutions. Where we see movement, we can see process, or at least infer it, an interchange of material and/or energy; we *can* ". . . see the World in a grain of sand,/ And a heaven in a wild flower,/ Hold Infinity in the palm of your hand,/ And eternity in an hour".[1] Or we can make the equation that Wendall Berry has made: "What we have been becomes/ The country where we are."[2]

The literature which I most value is that which rises out of the process the writer finds himself a part of as he struggles to place himself in his world: out of "accomodation" or out of reflection upon accomodation flash the revelations which constitute the roots of all good literature whether we term it "regional" or not. I have short patience for writing as mere "game-playing" or as "decoration". The writer is, first of all, an organism; he acts; he is acted upon. He must necessarily touch that which is *landscape*, the tableaux upon which he moves, the natural elements, the markings of the land, the weather, the seasons. He must touch *person* or persons, the human presence which may mark the landscape and which is marked and shaped in turn. Finally, the writer touches *place* proper, both landscape and person, these in motion, in process, in a continual state of exchange and interaction; the writer touches place because he *creates* it out of the materials he finds on the landscape and in the human presence. The writer stands, of course, as both participant and observer; what he observes moves him; and when he moves, the tableaux changes. In moving on the landscape and in responding to human presences, the writer gains new perspective. He gives voice to what he has encountered. And if the writer is fully an organism and fully human, his voice will carry beyond any particularity of landscape or person or experience. The writer fully *of* his *place*, that which he has created, speaks to all men, and will be heard. Whatever "local color" his writing carries is the detail from which he extrapolates context and process and relationship, the stones—so to speak—with which he builds his abode. The scientist may be interested in studying one species of plant or animal in an ecosystem; but if he is to understand, he must see that particular organism in its multifarious roles—as a predator in the food chain, as food supply for another species, as habitat for insects perhaps, as transporter of seeds, as a presence marking the landscape while moving on it, and more. To understand any literature, one needs to be able to gather from it a set of contexts and relationships, a whole place out of which a piece of writing arises. The whole of what he touches moves the writer, moves the reader; the particular stands as marker in the *place* the writer creates.

Because there is no "real" world for any of us individually beyond that which we perceive and understand and that which our cells destine us to, beyond that we inherit in our blood and find at our nerve endings, the creative artist has a vital role both in bringing us back to ourselves as organisms, physical creatures in a physical universe, and in liberating us from the confines of our bodies. The observant writer can reveal a world to us which we may not have noticed; the fine colors of autumn leaves, if we've never lifted our eyes to see them, can astound, and the poet will point to them. He will be able to teach us to hear the sound of wind through the wheat of a Kansas field, or the babbling of a mountain brook, or the 'immemorial murmering of innumerable bees'. If the writer has a keen eye, he will be able to uncover the many particularities of the specific landscape he stands upon, a part of. Yet the successful poet is able to do more than point at a landscape and objects on the lanscape: he will reveal facets of it that we are not able to *see* with our eyes or feel at our finger tips. The color of leaves in fall, if read as part of a world in flux, have significance which relates to the cycle of the seasons, to weather and climate, bio-geographical development of the land, and more. The leaves fall, decompose, become mulch and enrich the soil. The full glory of fall colors may be even more suggestive: when the leaves turn color, the corn in Iowa is ripe and ready for harvest, or is already being harvested. The pumpkins are full and plump, orange as the leaves. The sap is beginning to run out of the trees, preparing them for winter. The air at night begins to take on a special chill. By suggesting the context in which the details of the landscape exist, by underlining the rhythms, the cycles, the motions these details are a part of, the writer moves toward creating a place his readers have perhaps seen often and yet not seen at all. The earth has rhythms, the land we work has rhythms, and the poet on the landscape is able to uncover and reveal them for us; in this way, he helps to break the bondage of the nervous system. For the writer's senses may be no more keen than anyone else's, yet he is able to find, or perhaps rather to fabricate, a *whole* out of diverse particulars.

The writer aware of himself as a physical organism will recognize earth- and bio-rhythms larger than those of his own body. Not simply knowing by the feel of his bones that rain is coming, he knows what rain on dry land signifies: to feel the earth soak up the rain, grasses and crops and trees swelling with moisture. If the writer cannot understand and refabricate such larger features of the landscape, he is not a poet of place. The simple nature poem, sometimes, remains nothing more than fine description; and, on the other hand, writers cognizant of context and process and aware of themselves as organisms may choose not to uncover the larger rhythms of the earth, attempting instead to find essential self-rhythms and the rhythms of their individual existences as social, psychological, or intellectual beings. In such matters of concern, we are able to recognize the *poet of place* as distinct from a poet of another type: i.e., the poetry of two individuals born and raised on the same landscape may have very differing characteristics, the one poet looking into himself and out to the social world around him, choosing to deal with essentially human matters, the other turning to the earth he walks on and its larger processes. For the truly regional poet, place is central to his existence, and is an essential component of his poetry. Even when he is writing chiefly of relationships between and among human beings, the poet recognizes that existence in a certain place, with its history and its physical necessities, colors, and sometimes even determines, the nature of the human relationships.

The most usual "regional" literature that I have heard discussed has been midwestern American writing. This has been, perhaps, because good midwestern literature bears somewhat peculiar stamps. Elsewhere, I have noted these among the primary concerns of such a literature: "1) an acceptance of the land as an impenetrable force larger than ourselves, a mysterious force to live with, struggle against, attempt to control while fully aware that such control is impossible; 2) a quiet irony at almost every turn, whether the material at hand is the power of the earth over human endeavor, the power of love, the power of death; 3) a humor that rises first out of the quiet laughter one has at oneself & one's own predicament, & only secondarily out of incongruities in the situations of others—humor, even at the expense of another, is very seldom malicious; 4) an openness to, & interest in, other people; and 5) a conservatism, in poetic, & in tone & mood & intention—the intent is to capture a spirit & a way of speaking, rather than to create a new diction."[3] These are not, of course, the only marks of midwestern American writing, nor are all of them entirely necessary to all specimens of that literature. They do, I think, stand central to the concerns of the midwestern poet. Often enough a particular piece of writing may lack one or several of these qualities while still being clearly midwestern.

Tom McGrath, author of *Letter to an Imaginary Friend* and *Movie at the End of the World*, may not evidence a conservatism of politics or poetics, or may be more interested in creating a "new world" than a "new diction". Yet McGrath, who has said "Dakota is everywhere", is certainly a poet of *place*. He has said "we've got a kind of tuning fork inside, and sometimes we strike a landscape that's vibrating at just the same frequency, and that's when something begins to happen. It's most likely to happen, perhaps, where you spend those times of your life that are most important to you. But it may be that you have to go around the world a couple of times to discover that place."[4] Elsewhere he indicates that he doesn't think his "sense of importance of place has to do with regionalism as such. I do think that if I lived somewhere else I would have the same sense of the importance of the place I was in, and I would want to know something about it. I would want to know it not just in a historical sense. I would want to try to live in the landscape of the place."[5] In his three part poem entitled "Used Up", McGrath is able to give us a place that is whole and has its own needs; he speaks

about "new-dropped colts in the time when I was a boy", and saw
later that the colts' "necks were circled/ With a farmer's need". In the
poem's third part, he shows us the horses being butchered: "Now, dead:
swung from the haymow track with block and tackle;/ Gut-slit, blood in
a tub for pigs, their skin dragged over/ Their heads by a team of mules. . ."
The poem concludes: "Three acts and death./ The horse/ rides/ Into the
earth."[6] Clearly, this poem could not be written out of the contemporary "urban" experience, nor perhaps out of the contemporary farm experience. The poem does flash from "a farmer's need" and its implications, a time and place past, as does the work in William Kloefkorn's
Alvin Turner as Farmer[7]. *Alvin Turner* is not a narrative poem in the
usual sense, though it is as full a version of the "farmer's need" as we
are likely to find. As the vignettes of Turner's life are etched, a lyricism
arises out of the revelations, out of the struggles against the rock-
marked land, against the illness and death of a wife, against the loss of a
daughter. The hidden rock blunts the plowshare: "Yet somehow I expected yesterday's blunted share/ To be the last. That part which I cannot see,/ I said, cannot reduce me." However, "There is always the
rock:/ That, first and last, to remember." In his second book, *Uncertain the Final Run to Winter*,[8] Kloefkorn's concerns touch on "farmer's
need", but are intent on engaging person more than landscape. In *Alvin
Turner*, there *is* always the rock, and it marks every one of the 60 poems in the volume; in *Uncertain the Final Run*, what interests the poet
is person and personality, the characteristics of the men and women gathered just beyond Alvin Turner, just beyond the rock, townspeople,
for instance, who provide supplies and services to farmers. The two
books share a certain tone, that resignation to the land upon which lives
have to be made, that quiet irony—the great forces of the earth, of love,
of death constantly standing against human endeavor. Certainly, the
human relationships in *Uncertain the Final Run* are deeply marked by
the necessities of the land, by the "rock". As with McGrath's "Used
Up", *Alvin Turner* deals with what happens close to the landscape. *Uncertain the Final Run* more closely parallels John Stevens Wade's *Gallery*
which, though not a "midwest" book at all, is essentially a book about
person and person-in-situation; *Gallery* is a "regional" book, but of another region, New England. Kloefkorn's description of "Elsie Martin"
opens:

> She's six of one, half a dozen of another,
> According to Stocker:
> Not a bad looker, for a widowwoman,
> But her face so knobbed with indecision
> You'd swear she has hemorrhoids.
> Heard of another case just like her,
> He said,
> Who starved to death in a grocery store,
> Comparing labels.[9]

Wade says of "Fanny Decker":

> There were too many warts
> in her church of the stump, but she
> believed, and this was enough
> for us to blame her. To look
> suspiciously at the moon.
> We didn't miss that witch
> who died believing in the hound's
> uneasy cry. But when
> the Sunday wash was on
> the Monday line, a few
> of her survivors, still looked
> at us. We didn't tell them
> the world had changed in the cracked
> looking glass of our eyes. [10]

My argument is that we cannot speak about people from other places in the same ways these poets speak about Elsie Martin and Fanny Decker. The characteristics evident in such descriptions arise as peculiar manifestations of a particular place in the world, with the necessities which such a place may require. In a similar sense, perhaps, the black poet writing of urban ghetto life might well be considered a poet of place, one far different from the place which Tom McGrath and William Kloefkorn write of, but a place nonetheless with its own givens and its own particular stamp on the personalities of the inhabitants. Or some of feminist poetry, we might say, arises from place—most often, of course, place as social station—but often enough we can read the particulars of such poetry as tableaux or landscape upon which the persona struggles. At other times, certainly, the struggle remains essentially social. But we might ask, where does the battle against the ghetto or against the kitchen as places leave off, and the battle against racism and sexism being? There are, undeniably, links between the place in which one exists and one's social station.

The urban poet, if his interests lie both in the essence of the city in which he moves and the nature of the personalities which move around him, can be a poet of place. Clearly, the city imposes demands on inhabitants which determine innumerable details of daily existence, just as the land does for the farmer. The city has its rhythms—the morning migration into the heart of the beast, the evening exits, for instance; or bus or subway schedules; or the hour bars close. These rhythms, day after day, can mark the urban personality as clearly as the rock marks Alvin Turner for Kloefkorn. The poet interested in such relationships in an urban setting would be a poet-of-place, however different his writing and Kloefkorn's would be.

We might venture that novelists have understood the rhythms of the city more clearly than the poets have. James Joyce, perhaps, stands as a particularly striking example of the perceptive urban novelist. The Dublin of his fiction is the same Dublin we can visit; we know who inhabits the city, we know which street intersects which and where. And not only does Joyce give us in his writing the physical details necessary to find our way around the city, he also gives us clear glimpses of the people we will meet on the streets. As midwestern poets such as William Kloefkorn have, Joyce has given us both the landscape and the human presence. His fiction cannot be set in a city other than Dublin, yet how much more than "local color" do we find in his work. And how much more we find in Faulkner's country, how much more at Thoreau's Walden Pond. We can claim these writers as writers dealing with particular landscapes and particular personalities; each has his place, yet each speaks to the world.

Writers do not fabricate places we can recognize; they reveal to us a landscape we have seen but not fully understood, they examine the human presence against that landscape, the interaction of place and person. It may be that the poetry of place is more easily recognizable when the landscape examined is a natural rather than a man-made one; other landscapes than the natural exist, however, and the perceptive poet or novelist can assimilate and fashion them. The places a writer shows us may exist first in the mind, yes, and in the work of poetry or fiction; but it exists to some degree independently as well. If we examine the created place, and if we see the landscape in the actual world of which it speaks, we recognize the features: the color of corn-silk in an Iowa field, the taste of dust on a Chicago street. North Dakota is everywhere, and Dublin, and Walden.

NOTES:

(1) William Blake, "Auguries of Innocence".

(2) Wendell Berry, "An Anniversary". *The Country of Marriage* (New York: Harcourt, Brace Jovanovich, Inc., 1973).

(3) Tom Montag, "A Local Habitation". *Margins* no. 16 (January 1975), p. 41.

(4) "Milton, Manfred, and McGrath: A Conversation on Literature and Place". *Dacotah Territory,* no. 8/9 (Fall Winter 1974-75), p. 23.

(5) Mark Vinz, "Poetry and Place: An Interview With Thomas McGrath". *Voyages to the Inland Sea*, 3. John Judson, editor. (La Crosse, Wisconsin: Center for Contemporary Poetry, 1973), p. 33.

(6) *Voyages to the Inland Sea*, 3. John Judson, editor. (La Crosse, Wisconsin: Center for Contemporary Poetry, 1973), p. 62.

(7) William Kloefkorn, *Alvin Turner as Farmer*. (Lincoln, Nebraska: Windflower Press, 1974).

(8) Kloefkorn, *Uncertain the Final Run to Winter*. (Lincoln, Nebraska: Windflower Press, 1974).

(9) Ibid., p. 18.

(10) John Stevens Wade, *Gallery*. (London: Poet & Printer, 1969).

LITTLE MAGS: SOME COMMENTS

The results of Leonard Randolph's recently conducted NEA survey of little magazine editors raises two primary and some secondary questions. My first areas of concern are: 1) the attention to non-profit/tax-exempt status for little magazines; and 2) the attention to college- or university-based littles. Further, I will discuss distribution, "regular" publication, and the lifespan of the little magazine.

Non-Profit/Tax Exempt Status

The questions about and the discussion of non-profit/tax exempt status are, of course, necessary because the National Endowment for the Arts' enabling legislation does not permit *direct* funding of organizations without such status. To sidestep this problem, the Endowment has funded the Coordinating Council of Literary Magazines and charged it with the responsibility of making sub-grants to the little magazines. Other programs of the National Endowment for the Arts, as the Literature Program does, fund "channeling" organizations which, in turn, fund individuals, organizations or projects. Information on the non-profit/tax exempt status of little magazines seems needed, for two reasons: first to determine how many and what kind of magazines do not have or will not be applying for NP/TE status; and second, to use this information in determining what kinds of programs for the indirect assistance of magazines seem necessary.

If the Literature Program of the National Endowment is intent on uncovering ways to assist little magazines indirectly, and it would seem from the discussion of "bulk purchase of subscriptions or single copies for distribution" that this is the case, then the lack of non-profit/tax exempt status by 113 of the magazines responding to the survey is a significant and useful piece of information. I would not, however, want to see the questions about NP/TE status interpreted as indication of special concern on the part of the Literature Program for the magazines with such status. I would not want to see a trend toward NP/TE status for little magazines. Such a trend might do damage to the literature of our country. In this context, I think of Ezra Pound, who was associated with various little magazines in the early part of the century; I'd be interested in his reaction to the fact that 42 little mags have, and 12 more are seeking, NP/TE status. Pound knew what was involved in the process of making literature; I rather doubt that he would encourage magazine editors to seek such standing. I hope that what appears to be emphasis on NP/TE status in the Literature Program will be seen only as attention for the sake of information, and will lead to the creation of mechanisms for indirect support to little magazines, whether NP/TE or not.

College- or University-Based Magazines

The attention given to college- or university-based little magazines might seem, on the surface at least, to be undue. We are already aware that many supposedly intelligent and well-educated readers in this country believe "little magazine" refers exclusively or primarily to college- or university-based quarterly journals. Nothing could be farther from the truth, of course. The survey itself shows that 41 of the responding magazines are so associated, while 128 are not. Three times as many "independent" little magazines as university-affiliated journals publish regularly; if this information can be disseminated widely, there may well be changes in the thinking of many American readers, including the officials of private foundations and state arts councils. The survey reveals that 96 little magazines claim staff of one to three people; 64 claim four or more. I suspect that many of the magazines with staff of four or more are university-affiliated and that many of the others with the larger staffs are cooperative ventures. Policies and programs which would serve the greater portion of the little magazines community would necessarily make substantial provisions for the journals with three or fewer people working on them: 96 to 64. The journals with three or fewer people are also, I suspect, largely without NP/TE status.

It would be a mistake, I repeat, to establish firm policy which ill-considers the smallest, most independent of the littles—those without NP/TE status, those with staff of three or fewer. It is these magazines, I think, which have been too long neglected already by those discussing "American literature".

Distribution

Another area of the survey-results which should have our attention is that dealing with the distribution of little magazines to bookstores and newsstands. At present, 87 magazines sell no copies through a distributor, and 127 sell 100 or fewer copies that way. At the same time, only 21 show no interest in obtaining a distributor, and all but 24 are interested in selling 100 or more copies on newsstands or in book stores. I think such expectations are unrealistic in the face of lack of interest on the part of distributors, book stores, and book store customers. At least at present, most little magazine editors are misplacing their concerns when they emphasize the need for bookstore distribution. There is some value, certainly, in getting little magazines into bookstores, but not at high cost, in terms of the time and energies of the editors, and not while little magazines continue to be shabbily displayed once in the bookstores. Literature Program funds would be better spent on bulk subscription orders to individual little magazines than on distribution schemes. A good deal of money could be invested in the attempt to create a workable distribution system, but it would be money wasted if bookstores and bookstore customers still showed little interest in the magazines. A magazine, I think, is in general an item which comes in the mail. Bookstore distribution can be useful, but should not be an urgent concern of editors, nor of the Literature Program of the National Endowment.

"Regular Publication"

We ought to be aware that most of the magazines surveyed, and most of those responding, are publications which appear regularly, periodically, three or more times a year. When the National Endowment makes policies regarding little magazines, it would do well to include at least some provisions for little mags which appear less often (i.e., once or twice a year); or sporadically (i.e., once one year, three times the next, twice the following). My reasons for saying this are: 1) publications which are intended to appear three times a year may face editorial, financial, or production problems which slow the appearance of an issue or a number of issues; 2) literature cannot be required to meet a production schedule. Concern for meeting a publishing schedule can lead an editor to publish material somewhat beneath the standards he would like to maintain.

If policies regarding even indirect funding of little magazines have rigid requirements about regularity, they may encourage the publication of more bad literature than is already appearing; if, on the other hand, there were a mechanism for assisting the work of deserving editors whose magazines appear less often than three times a year, literature in this country would be the better for it. Financial considerations, I fear, can very noticeably affect editorial vision.

Lifespan of the Little Mag

There is one particular item of information revealed in the survey-results that ought to be well-considered in the formulation and implementation of programs to lend indirect assistance to little magazines; 90 magazines responding to the survey have been publishing five years or less; the other 70, for more than five. The life-span of the little magazine is lengthening, it would appear, as Randolph noted in his analysis of the survey-results.

A principle which ought to be considered, however, and one that seems evident from my own reading of little magazines, is that the first issues of a journal are generally its most exciting; in the first several issues of a magazine, the editors come to the task with fresh vision, with high intentions, with a good deal of spirit. They have not yet fallen into formula. They have not yet repeated themselves. There is excitement with new blood. The caveat I wish to offer is this: if the goal is to assist the emergence of the best of our literature, we cannot afford to neglect the newest of our magazines, those publishing five years or less. Lengthening the life span of a particular little magazine is not, of itself, a worthwhile endeavor, if the magazine does not have any special reason to continue publishing. *More* and *longer*, in literature, are not necessarily virtues. Continuity and longevity have value, certainly, but only in the context of the literature a little magazine is publishing. "Quality" is not a commodity to be surveyed with a questionaire to editors. This we ought not forget.

**As I have said about the survey-results, the information provided is important and useful. I would, however, caution against the encouragement of a trend toward non-profit/tax exempt status for little magazines; literature is not made, generally, in tax shelters, and we should not believe that NP/TE status standing will ultimately be of much use to our "literature" itself.

**I am grateful that the survey makes clear the fact that there are at least three times as many "independent" little magazines as university-affiliated journals. This, and the fact that 96 little magazines claim staff of one to three while 64 claim staff of four or more, are clear evidence that the process of literature, the publishing of literature, is largely a very individualistic, independent, lonely enterprise.

**I believe the editors surveyed showed misplaced concern when 92 of them indicate they would like to increase bookstore distribution to 100 or more copies per issue.

**We ought to be wary of defining necessary little magazines by the standard of regular publication three or more times a year; any policy or program implemented by the Literature Program of the National Endowment ought to be flexible enough to assist worthy magazines not so-defined.

**Finally, we need to be careful not to think that longevity, for little magazines, is either necessary or valuable. I am not entirely sure that any little magazine deserves to reach old age, whatever its merits.

SOME NOTES ON FREEDOM AND FORM

For the contemporary poet, the choice is not between *freedom* and *form*. The formal aspects of poetry—if the written or spoken work is to be art—are far and away more crucial than concerns about *content* or even about mere "technique". The formal properties of pieces of art in any medium determine to a large degree whether what we are viewing is art or whether it is babbling, rambling or dabbling. Poetry must have form. However, the question of form is not simply one of traditionally recognized forms (versions of the sonnet, villanele, or whatever) versus newer principles of measurement. Concern for traditional forms very often becomes concern for "technique" only, at the expense of the formal principles truly proper to poetry; likewise, concern for new units of measurement can distract one from the poem's inherent form. Certainly the poet today has a great deal of freedom in terms of the range of formal alternatives open to him, from the truly formal qualities of traditional verse to fresh and unusued principles for structuring that which is poetry. John Cage's strangest musical creations are music, rather than noise, precisely because he works from what are rigorous and appropriate principles for structuring a musical piece. A poem without structural principle is no poem at all.

Believing this, however, we must recognize that methodologies proper to poetry are virtually endless, and can succeed if carefully and rigorously applied. We may speak of *breath* as one formal component of poetry, for instance; or *line;* or *space;* or *silence;* or *idiom.* To rigorously apply any structural principle to poetry, however, is not to superimpose something extrinsic to one's materials upon those materials; rather, it is to uncover and reveal the true form inherent in the materials at hand; to make the poem an objective entity, revealing in one's materials what is actually there awaiting clear expression. A sense of form frees one from the overbearing need to carry a carpetbag full of techniques, tricks. Michelangelo needed to know how to hold the chisel and hammer, how to chip away irrelevant stone in order to free his David, yes; technique in poetry is simply knowing how to hold the chisel to one's materials—knowledge we must assume the competent poet has. The *sine qua non* of poetry, however, is recognizing the inherent David.

There ain't no such animal as free verse—and I wish the proponents of traditional forms would realize this: either you have verse, measured by some principle or other, or you have babbling. One's principles of measurement can be inappropriate to one's materials, dooming a poem to failure; we would not set down our gravest somber thoughts to a horse gallop rhythm and expect to be taken entirely seriously. Yet, without relying on obviously traditional principles, a poet like William Carlos Williams in his "Poem" about a cat stepping into an empty flowerpot, can produce a formal construct fully appropriate to his material. At first glance, Williams' poem seems to be little more than a visual image that works; the poem describes, simply and starkly, the careful movement of a cat. But the reader is left with a very clear sense that the poem is *true,* true to the physical realities of the cat, its muscle and bone and nerves in motion. That something of the cat's physicality has been captured and held in language. The aural and rhythmic qualities of the poem seem carefully modulated to fit our sense of the motion of the poem's cat, and our sense of cats in the world. Williams effectively translates *cat* into language. Michelangelo revealed his David, Williams his cat.

That no traditional poetic form could depict the particular cat, and particular movements of that cat, as effectively as Williams is able to in this (as some would label it) "free verse" poem ought to be evidence enough for the skeptics: we have to have structural principles operating in our poetries, but they need not be traditional poetics. Only those techniques—iambic foot or breath line—which effectively reveal the true form of one's materials are appropriate in any particular instance.

TOUCHING THE ESSENTIALS

The name Alan Swallow, to poets, publishers and lovers of
the printed word, symbolizes the best tradition of an American literary culture. It is a name that suggests to many people
a man who remained apart from the commercial claques of
his day and sensitive to the needs of writers in a way that
will probably not be matched by another publisher with his
long-range objectives. For Swallow was determined to print,
publish and distribute books widely on an independent basis—a virtually one-man attempt to make an impact on his
times in the precarious and often perverse world of publishing.

—William F. Claire
in the "Introduction"

Publishing in the West: Alan Swallow (The Lightning Tree, Inc.),
edited by William F. Claire, is—if anything—a fitting tribute to Alan
Swallow, Publisher. Swallow, poet, teacher, and critic, as well as publisher, offered his first "trade" book in the fall of 1940; he supported
himself by teaching until August of 1954, at which time he began devoting "full-time" to his publishing activities. He died at age 51 on
Thanksgiving Day, 1966, in Denver. As publisher, both before and after his full-time involvement, Swallow worked hard to bring into print
some of the most significant titles of our time. *Publishing in the West:
Alan Swallow* is, in large part, a selection of Swallow's letters and
"newsletters" to some of his authors and interested people. Anais Nin
contributes an appreciation of her sense of the man; James Schevill discusses "the three hands of Alan Swallow". There is also a short biblio-
graphic note on Swallow, and a list of the books Swallow had in print
at the time of his death. Nin's and Schevill's contributions are not sen-
timental remembrances, rather fond recollections of a singular figure in
American publishing. Of course Swallow's own letters here, and his
"newsletters" to his authors, reflecting his many interests and his concerns as an editor and publisher, speak for themselves, and for a spirited
and energetic man, one driven it would seem by the same devils which
move at least some of those in small publishing today.

Anais Nin says of Swallow:

I never saw Alan Swallow waste a moment of anger at commercial publishers. He simply thought they were mistaken
in their own self-interest. Shortsighted. He was more intent on creating his own structure which would embody his
earthy wisdom. . . The commercial publishers were ultimately destroying the very source of their wealth. Writers suc-
cumbed first of all to a false dream of wealth which only a

few would attain, then to a hothouse forcing of their talents, then to a star system which continued to publish the
most mediocre work of any writer who had attained a reputation. This meant that the sytem was destructive to the
life of writing itself. Good writers were caught in an absurd
race for quick sales, false publicity, and if they failed to pass
the first harsh test of economic exigencies they were considered failures. Some of these writers came to Alan Swallow. He made minimal demands on them. He was patient
with them. They continued to expand and develop and several among them were recognized as valuable by Big Business later.

Here was a dedicated man, a considerate man, a man with foresight and
his own vision of how literature ought to be published. Swallow's publishing was beset with difficulties, not the least of which was his own
poor health, but he continued, always the optimist. His booklist at the
time of his death is impressive, certainly, but his contribution to the literature of this country is even greater. James Schevill grasps the gist of
it:

> Looking back at my association with Swallow, I know that
> he taught me an invaluable lesson about life and literature in
> this country. They are inseparable and each one of us is re-
> sponsible for the connections we make between our daily
> lives and the spirit of imagination that creates the value of
> the printed page. The example of his integrity made it im-
> possible for anyone connected with him not to recognize
> the dangers and hopes of literature in this strangely power-
> ful and chaotic society.

Often these days I think how far in the wrong direction small press
may be moving. Instead of creating the alternative structures we truly
need, we often seem to imitate commercial publishing's methods at
smaller scale. We strive again and again to make "pretty" books while
slipping editorially; we try to "sell", and often, to create literary "stars".
Could anyone say of us, as Schevill does of Swallow:

> To him the printed language is supreme, a way to pass on
> high standards, to maintain traditions, to continue the heri-
> tage of humanity. Alan Swallow was such an idealist of the
> word. Sometimes the books he published tended to be ra-
> ther plain in appearance, but the fact is that he was more
> concerned with publishing a variety of important work than
> with the way each book appeared.

I would hope that there are still such publishers. My recommendation is that any of us seriously interested in continuing small press publishing look again at what Alan Swallow achieved. Swallow's example, of course, will not teach us everything; we will, however, learn some of the essentials we might be overlooking.

SOMEONE ELSE'S ODYSSEY: SELLING BOOKS

My own gut prejudice remains: if I'm publishing something—book or magazine—that someone wants, needs, or is interested in, he or she will ask me for it. As much as I see the need to make contemporary literature accessible and generally available, to get it to those readers beyond the initiated small-press/little-mag devotees, I am still wary, sometimes even hysterical about, machinations which reach towards *Promotion,* toward the commercialization of literature, toward the selling of a product. Literature is not a pair of shoes. Literature is not a beef-steak. We are compromised by treating it as such.

If a publisher is kicking out the literary jams, so to speak, publishing new and important writing, he or she cannot afford to scheme financially or to waste any energy selling the goods. The American Society of Schemers has as its motto: "Never scheme for money." Amen. Small press publishers ought not scheme for money, nor should they scheme to *sell* their books and magazines. Good literature and fast talkin' seem to me to be incompatible.

One terrible bind of contemporary literature, of course, is this: new, creative literature is vital to American culture(s), yet it has not been able to compete in the marketplace with the commercialized literature New York publishers are programming via marketing research. Literature perhaps doesn't belong in the marketplace. Mr. Pound, alas, wouldn't fit very neatly onto a computer print-out, nor Dr. Williams. Yet we read them, and we read new literature.

Perhaps we remain literature junkies in a culture fattened on other luxuries. Perhaps we are the perverts in our society, twisted specimens of humanity slavering over the printed page. Whatever the case, the audience for contemporary literature is astoundingly small for a country as large and diverse as ours. I can say it here—25,628 people in this country are interested in "literature." We, the small press editors and publishers, must begin to realize, it seems to me, that our puny efforts towards the promotion and distribution of new writing are not going to enlarge its audience to any great degree, if at all. Heroin junkies physically need the stuff. Some of us, maybe, need literature in order to carry on day after day, but the need isn't physical; that doesn't set our cells to screaming. Then, too, the dealer ain't coming around dangling a bag of junk in front of our eyes; ain't no pushers for poetry, folks, getting us hooked. Ain't no one hanging around the schools, passing out samples. Folks just plain don't *need* it; yet we know that in the long run our culture couldn't survive without it.

We ought to realize by now that if we're intent on *selling* books, we're in the wrong part of the book "business". If you want to sell books, sign a contract with the next Harold Robbins and promote him. Or get into porno (though even porno dealers are complaining about poor sales these days) and get distributed by the Mafia. But don't publish *literature*. The stuff just don't sell. Sometimes you can't even give it away.

No small press publisher, I submit, can or should hope to become commercially viable. Red blood in our veins, red ink in our ledgers. The integrity of the vision of the small press editor-publisher, in some part at least, seems dependent on the fact that each book he or she produces will lose money out-of-pocket, will take groceries off the table. We could wish that it were otherwise, we could bust ass trying to improve our condition, but the fact that each item released by the small publisher costs him or her personally—in terms of time, energy, money—helps, in its small way, to insure some measure of quality, some measure of vitality in our literature. I think, in this context, of Russian samizdat literature; the only manuscript I would risk Siberia for, the only one I'd spend endless hours typing, would be one I believed in. The same can be applied, to some extent, to small press publishing in this country. As beneficial as grant programs for little magazines and small presses seem to be, and are, we have to recognize, I think, that such funding can sometimes encourage the publishing of second-rate, fattened literature. I'm not calling for an end to grant programs; rather, I'm asking that all concerned be clear-eyed enough to see the inherent dangers.

Len Fulton and Ellen Ferber made a book-selling odyssey across the country in the summer of 1974. Fulton for many years has been a prime mover in small publishing in our country; he is publisher of Dustbooks, which produces the *International Directory of Little Magazines and Small Presses* annually and *Small Press Review* monthly. He looms as a large figure in the recent history of small publishing, a knowledgeable and insightful man. Ellen Ferber became associated with the Dustbooks' projects in recent years. The story of their trip is reported in *American Odyssey: A Book Selling Travelogue* (Dustbooks).

The maverick of the west, Len Fulton, heads towards the east, towards New York, on a book-selling tour; that could startle one. But Fulton lived and worked for a while in New England. Part of this odyssey, at least, was a trip back home. And part of its purpose was to get Fulton and Ferber to the New York Book Fair where Dustbooks set up shop with other small press publishers in a culture-boggling book affair. The book-selling was done along the way, from Paradise, California, to

New York, one route, from New York to Paradise, another route.

For the most part, bookstores bore me. And the thought of anyone stopping at, or attempting to stop at, nearly every bookstore they happened to pass traveling cross-country is something more than I can comprehend. I know the location of several good bookstores across the USA, and these are enough for me. They have not been, however, enough for Fulton, apparently, a glutton for punishment.

Having read *American Odyssey,* I still cannot comprehend why anyone would make the gruelling trip that Fulton and Ferber made, but certainly I have a better sense of the authors, and some sense of the condition of booksellers across the country. Fulton and Ferber show us the thoughtful book dealers who love books and literature; they show us the slick butcher-counter attendants serving up the latest ground beef; they show us the variety of bookstores in between. There is an appendix, an "annotated list of bookstores" at the end of *American Odyssey* which sets down impressions of the stores visited (or not visited, as the case may be). The list might be useful information for anyone interested in the condition of American bookselling.

However, despite the fact that *American Odyssey* is a book selling travelogue, the best of the story lies elsewhere. Fulton and Ferber have put their fingers to the pulse of this country in a way few others have been able to. The character sketches, the quickly-drawn impressions of city, town, country-side, the careful details, hung together on the narrative of a drive across the USA, present a vivid sense of our lives as we spend them day-to-day. It is for this picture of America that I value *American Odyssey;* the book is enjoyable, intriguing, fast-paced. *This* turn of phrase, *that* surprising comment, *the other* notes on America— these pull you into the narrative and carry you along.

Still, I'm afraid *American Odyssey* is going to be read by small press folks chiefly as a guide to bookstores in America; that some of us may look to it only as a report on an experiment which proved itself successful. It was an experiment, certainly, and it was—we could say—successful. Fulton and Ferber sold $1333.08 worth of books on the trip, visiting 275 stores in 42 days. They were hurried out of some stores, they were offered coffee and talk in others, they made sales in about one-third of the shops they visited. Dustbooks, though, is one among hundreds of small publishers in this country; if most small publishers attempted a similar American Odyssey, booksellers would soon learn to spot us at a glance, more quickly learn to show us the door. The *American Odyssey* is a *story,* about one publisher's trip, it is *not* an answer to the distribution problems many small publishers feel they face. It is not the game-plan for the next assault on American readers.

To return to an earlier metaphor: if Fulton and Ferber were, in the course of their trip, playing the part of the junk dealer, the heroin pusher in literary context, they failed miserably. As pushers, they sold a total of 636 books worth $1333.08 in dealings with 275 bookstores which served cities with populations totaling 4,963,700 people. These figures indicate that we can expect one person out of every 7804 to buy a Dustbooks title under the best circumstances. 25,628 out of the 200,000,000 people in this country (extrapolating from the 1 to 7804 ratio) are interested in the kind of literature Dustbooks is producing and seem willing to spend about a nickel apiece. Any junkie willing to spend only $.05 for a fix ain't a real heavy user, I wouldn't think.

The point is this: there ought to be a more efficient way to reach those interested in new literature than through an American Odyssey. As a summer trip, it's a pleasant enough idea if you're the kind of person who can meet and deal with people at the pace such a bookselling tour would require. But as a distribution venture, on any scale larger than one or a few presses, the attempt would have to be doomed—the market *is* only *so* large; we've known that for years, but have largely failed to recognize it, preferring to bash our heads against the walls, scheming distribution and sales.

I am *not* saying, abandon efforts towards the distribution of small press materials; I am saying—put distribution problems in the larger context of what small press publishing is about. Our intent, we would probably say, is to set down the important literature being written today, to pass it along to those who are interested in seeing it, to keep the pot of culture bubbling in our own small way. Our first responsibilities, as editors and publishers, are to ourselves and our integrity, to our writers and their integrity, and to that class of American reader who need the stuff we're doing. Our attempts to interest a larger audience in new literature ought to be a secondary. Recent figures indicate that nearly 20% of the American population is functionally illiterate. Will we try to sell them poetry? When will we feel the audience is large enough? Or do we now recognize the fact that some new pieces of writing ought to appear in editions of 50 copies, a hundred copies, a hundred and fifty—that as much as we might admire the ordinary citizen, most of what we're doing as publishers does not touch him where he lives today, though it makes possible, in some small sense, any hope for a cultural tomorrow. Some forty years hence, yes, the monolithic Norton anthology will press some of the writers we're publishing today between its pages. For now, we simply need to publish the literature, to sell it to those readers we can without selling it out, without commercializing it.

THE LITTLE MAGAZINE/SMALL PRESS CONNECTION: SOME CONJECTURES

In the past, the study of American literary publishing has tended to center on the history, significance, and influence of the "little magazine" and to neglect the role of the small literary press. Works such as Frederick J. Hoffman's *The Little Magazine: A History and Bibliography* have been widely acknowledged and used as resources in the study literature; other studies, such as the annotated bibliography included as part of *The Little Magazine in America, 1950 To the Present,* serve to update and expand Hoffman's classic work and, sometimes, to emphasize the little magazine at the expense of the small press. It is only recently, with the publication of Hugh Ford's *Published in Paris* (Macmillan, 1975), that any full account of particular literary presses (those in Paris earlier in this century) has been readily accessible. Numerous studies of "fine presses" are available, but such books have been concerned primarily with the art of book-making rather than with the dynamics of literary publishing. Because Ford's *Published in Paris* presents considerable factual material about the operation of small presses, despite the boundaries of its concerns, the book will enable those interested in the processes of literary production to begin making considered and well-balanced assessments of the historical importance of the small literary press. Ford's book, we might hope, will spur similar research about past and present American literary presses. To date, however, the intense interest in the little magazine has meant, largely, the neglect of the small press. In part, this may stem from the fact that the little magazine is more readily researched and studied than the press. A little magazine can be indexed, its editorial vision can be analyzed, its sphere of concern over a period of years can be assessed; the nature, concerns, and editorial vision of a good small publisher, by contrast, may very often be difficult to ascertain: first, the small press editor does not have the convenience of "editorial notes" in which to set down his literary tenents; second, the publisher may present diverse kinds of writing which are dissimilar in all respects except for that intangible called "quality," something not easily described; and third, students of literature generally seem more interested in the development of particular writers (and hence, in the bibliographies of particular writers) than in the larger dynamics of literature (to which the bibliographies or "lists" of publishers are relevant). The editor of the little magazine can and often does explain his editorial position in the pages of his magazine; the small press editor can do so at the risk of irritating readers who buy a particular book in order to read the writer, not the writer's editor. In addition, an editor's concerns are more quickly apparent in a little magazine by virtue of the number of selections presented during a year's publishing; the book publisher usually presents considerably fewer writers and therefore fewer examples of his editorial interests in the same span of time. Further, the "lag time" between a decision to change editorial direction and the implementation of that decision is less for the magazine than for the press. The critical vocabulary necessary for discussing the common "quality" of several kinds of writing is available, but when a long-lived small publisher's list becomes extensive, such discussion may be highly intricate and complicated. Recurrent editorial patterns are more readily discernible for the magazine than for the press—again, because the magazine presents a greater number of selections in a given period of time than does the press. Although the needed critical vocabulary may be available, we have only limited understanding of the dynamics of literary interrelationships and influence; Hugh Kenner in *The Pound Era* presents the first comprehensive "model" for grappling with complex interactions of writers, writings, and emerging literary currents. Literature is studied so often in terms of "writers" alone and so seldom in terms of "processes" that we are not yet accustomed to considering the significance of the multifarious literary interrelationships that book publishing entails. We can, further, speak about the editor of the little magazine in terms similar to those we use for writers—we may discuss his "vision," for instance, as we would talk about the vision of a novelist or poet. The editor of a good little magazine seems to be more "visible" (though not obtrusive, in the best cases) than the small press editor, although each may be exercising the same tight editorial control. Because researchers' interests have tended to focus on little magazines, the study of small presses has been neglected and the detailed factual information and analysis needed for an understanding of the broader literary processes small presses are a part of has not been gathered and made. The relationship between the small literary press and literature is only beginning to be examined. When factual material about literary publishing in America since 1950 is finally collected and analyzed, the significance of the small press might well prove to be greater than the current neglect by students of literary publishing would indicate.

That the editor of a little magazine is frequently also the editor of a small literary press should not surprise us; the concerns of the two enterprises are similar and interrelated—literature and readership—however different the magazine and the press may be in practice. An editor may found a little magazine only to discover that magazine-format is confining and does not permit all the kinds of publishing one would like; in such cases, the press is an outgrowth of the magazine. An editor might feel, for example, that one or more of the contributors to his magazine needs more substantial exposure than magazine publication would permit—i.e., that a particular writer would be better served by the presentation of a large collection of work in one place than by the publication of the same work in a number of issues of the magazine or in several different magazines. Such circumstances may serve as the most common impetus for the founding of a press out of a magazine.

Depending in part on the editor/publishers' financial resources, and in part on how frequently the editor sees the need, books may be an occasional or regular supplement to the magazine operation; the magazine itself remains the center of activity while books are viewed as adjuncts. *Gallimaufry* (formerly of San Francisco, now of Arlington, Virginia), for instance, continues as a literary journal on newsprint, but the editors have established a "Gallimaufry Chapbook Series" and are publishing 40-48 page collections of work by writers who have been, often, contributors to the magazine. *Manroot* (South San Francisco, California) has instituted a Manroot Book series; unlike *Gallimaufry*, however, *Manroot* has been changing its editorial policies and scope of concern, to become less an eclectic gathering of work and more a tightly focused thematic publication; the *Manroot* Jack Spicer issue (no. 10) is evidence of this altered direction.

In some cases—and we have seen this more frequently in the past five years—the editor of a little magazine chooses to publish a book, the work of a single writer, and simply calls it a "special issue" of his magazine. The editor of *Road Apple Review* (Oshkosh, Wisconsin), for example, presented William Kloefkorn's *Alvin Turner as Farmer* in 1972 as Volume IV, Number 2, despite the fact that *Road Apple Review* and Road Runner Press are related enterprises. Windflower Press (Lincoln, Nebraska) re-issued *Alvin Turner* as a book two years later. *Painted Bride Quarterly* (Philadelphia, Pennsylvania) recently published a title by John Giorno as an issue of that magazine. *December Magazine* (Chicago, Illinois) has probably made more frequent use of this type of special issue than most other little magazines: since 1967, five novels and two books of stories (with another collection of stories forthcoming) have appeared as *December*s. The reason for such a decision could be financial—i.e., money is available for the magazine but not for the press; or the editor could be attempting to conserve his energies by producing a "book" without interrupting the flow of his magazine-centered activities—he may fear, for instance, that time and energy devoted to the production of a book will disrupt his magazine's publishing schedule; or the editor may conclude that a book appearing as an issue of his magazine will have better distribution than otherwise—subscribers to the magazine, at least, will receive a copy of the book immediately, while remaining copies can be promoted and marketed in the same way book publishers handle their titles.

A variation of the "special issue" book by one writer is the magazine appearance of what are essentially chapbooks by two, three, or more writers. Writers are sometimes allotted as much as 20-30 pages; depending upon the editor's selection skills and intent, the work presented may have the wholeness and integrity associated with a good chapbook or small book. *Salthouse: A Magazine of Field Notes* (Manchester, Michigan), for example, will soon be publishing an issue given over entirely to the work of two poets. *Stations* (Milwaukee, Wisconsin) devoted each of its first two issues to fairly lengthy selections from the works-in-progress of six writers, with extensive statements by each contributor about the work he is doing. Each issue of *Stations* is, in effect, a tightly edited and carefully orchestrated anthology. Other magazines, which may regularly have eclectic or "grab-bag" policies, have also been known to publish anthology-like issues containing large swatches of work by relatively few contributors. Thematic "special issues" which present work by many writers around a single topic also have the appearance of anthologies. The *Manroot* Jack Spicer issue, mentioned previously, is one example; poetry, appreciations, and criti- cal essays by a range of writers center on Spicer, with many contributors acknowledging "literary debts" to Spicer the poet. Both *Dacotah Territory* (Moorhead, Minnesota) and *Scree* (Missoula, Montana) have published "Native American special issue" anthologies. *Dacotah Territory* also recently produced (as no. 11) a "Minnesota Poets in the Schools Anthology."

The occasional special issue devoted to the work of a single writer and the anthology numbers of little magazines indicate that there is a strong impulse among the magazine editors to produce titles which are characteristically book-like in terms of editorial stance and literary intent. The *Ironwood* (Tucson, Arizona) special issue devoted to George Oppen is a book, and is edited as such, regardless of its appearance in a serial sequence. The several issues of *Vort* (Bloomington, Indiana), each presenting essays and commentary on one or (more frequently) two contemporary writers, are also book-like collections of criticism. Although subscriptions to *Vort* are encouraged, I suspect that the magazine does better single-issue than subscription sales to individuals simply because one might be particularly interested in some of the poets whose work is discussed but not in all of them. Two issues of *Truck* magazine (Carrboro, North Carolina), no. 13/Landscape and no. 14/Explorations, are also books centered on particular thematic considerations. A book, we might say, can stand alone with its own particular literary identity and a clear, self-sufficient reason-for-being, independent of any larger design on the part of the editor. With the eclectic magazines which do not, or only seldom, publish special issues, the reader must become aware of the editor or editors' peculiar stamp— the special nature of the editor's vision which marks his magazine over the course of its existence—for unless a magazine which purports to publish "the best contemporary literature available" has a clear editorial intelligence behind it, it can easily end as a hopeless, unfocused hodge-podge of contradictions, as a citadel of dullness. The "grab-bag" magazines are significant in one crucial respect—many of them are the first places that new, unknown writers can publish; but these magazines need a vitality, a unity, a vision that is too often lacking, to the detriment of the better pieces of work presented.

Some magazines steer clear of the hodge-podge effect by devoting themselves to particular kinds of writing: *Interstate* (Austin, Texas) is decidedly experimental in its emphasis; *Kayak* (Santa Cruz, California) is devoted to surrealistic poetries; *Alcheringa* (Boston) concerns itself with ethnopoetics; *Salthouse* presents historico-geopoetic work; *Assembling* (New York City) publishes "the otherwise unpublishable." The strength or weakness of magazines which have clearly defined boundaries of concern lies in the skill of the editor, in the excellence of his eye. A magazine publishing bad examples of experimental writing, for example, or one presenting the worst surrealistic poetry being written, does no service to the particular kind of writing it purports to be interested in, and no service to literature generally. By contrast, a well-edited magazine with special concerns benefits not just its particular kind of writing, but all writing. Further, such magazines frequently function as "continuing-anthologies" or "active-anthologies" and can be used in the same way anthologies published as "books" are used.

The number of special single-author, thematic, or anthology issues of little magazines and of "special interest" literary journals seems to have grown considerably in recent years. Where formerly an editor may have been content with a series of eclectic issues, more frequently now he seems to feel the need to produce singular issues with distinctive and clear-cut concerns. The magazine editor is beginning to view his role as similar to that of the "writer," in terms of vision, balance, rhythm, and style in the work he is producing as editor. An issue of a little magazine is becoming, more and more, a personal artistic statement on the part of the editor. The magazine becomes a clearly-stated aesthetic proposition the way that a well-written and well-assembled book of poems or stories or a novel is. The present tendency is to infuse each issue of a magazine with the wholeness, the unity or integrity we are accustomed to finding in good works of art and good single-author collections or well-edited anthologies.

The fact that magazines in the past tended to arise from or to form around themselves a community of writers served to given even the most grab-bag of them some measure of wholeness and unity. *Invisible City* (Fairfax, California), *Kayak, Wormwood Review* (Stockton, California), and *Vagabond* (Ellensburg, Washington) continue this tradition, serving identifiable communities. Other magazines publishing today, e.g., *Blue Cloud Quarterly* (Marvin, South Dakota), *Center* (La Honda, California), *Mojo Navigator(e)* (Oak Park, Illinois), and *Montana Gothic* (Missoula, Montana) are distinguishable and identifiable on the basis of each editor's interests and taste. Still other magazines, such as *Aspect* (Somerville, Massachussets), *Caim* (Baltimore, Maryland), *Lake Superior Review* (Ironwood, Michigan), and *New Collage* (Sarasota, Florida), have no strong editorial presence and appear to serve no community in particular; magazines of this sort are often anonymous entities. All too frequently the lack of any community of writers means a magazine drifts aimlessly, selecting material almost at random, and getting virtually no notice and readership. The trend towards issues of magazines with the integrity of books, of course, is an encouraging sign: if a magazine is not useful to one particular community of writers, at least it can be of service to certain sets of ideas or kinds of writing (which implies, perhaps, a community of concerns).

Possibly, one key distinction between a devoted magazine editor and the small press editor is this: the best little magazine editor situates himself within a literary community and uses his magazine to capture, reflect, and shape the energies of that community and to facilitate communication with those beyond the circle of writers; the small press editor, in contrast, is primarily interested, with each title he produces, in presenting a substantial, integral work by an individual writer (or in the case of anthologies, a carefully edited selection of writings). Certainly the small press can serve a literary community, and many of them do; as with some magazines, there is the danger that small presses may publish only the clique of writers around them; other presses, especially those which are outgrowths of healthy magazine endeavours, serve a vibrant, already-existing community. Perhaps the small press editor who brings out a highly influential and significant work intends, however slightly or secretly, to hitch his wagon to a star, to immortalize his name (or at least the name of his press) by being associated with a particular artist who comes to be regarded, either immediately or over the long haul, as a "major" writer. That the small press editor's impulse is necessarily any more aristocratic or elitist than the magazine editor's is doubtful; many magazine editors feel they are publishing the most select, excellent writers of a particular generation and are part of an aristocratic literary tradition. Indeed, the editors of some little magazines (*Partisan Review, Paris Review, The Hudson Review, The Iowa Review,* and many university quarterlies in general—with the notable exception of *New Letters* and *Cut Bank*—come to mind) are notoriously snobbish in their editorial selections, though not for any discernible literary reasons. Even magazines which are established to serve a particular literary community may be governed by aristocratic principles, if the group of writers being published is viewed as a special elite. Certainly the editors of some small presses, such as Black Sparrow (if we stretch definitions to count Black Sparrow a small press), the Fiction Collective, The Elizabeth Press, and others in varying degrees seem interested in publishing that acknowledged first-rank of poets and fictioneers and intend the books they produce to endure as particularly remarkable contributions to the literature of the world. This is not to say that the editors of less aristocratic small presses, e.g., New Rivers Press, Gallimaufry, Pentagram Press, Alice James Books, and others, believe they are publishing inferior writing; rather, perhaps, they feel there is more exciting, serious writing appearing today than we have been led to believe; we do not have many Walt Whitmans and Ezra Pounds among us these days, but then we are not living in an age of giants. Or at least there are many ex-

cellent small press editors, I'll wager, who will argue that the giants are
extremely rare and that the task of the contemporary editor is simply
to discover the best works of the generation, be they "major" or "minor."

A distinction between the little magazine and the small press might
be drawn in terms of the immediacy and topical characteristics of the
magazine in contrast to the artifactual nature of the published book.
Magazines can have an impact and topicality which binds them to a literary era, but if art is art it transcends those boundaries and endures;
the best of the poems and stories in a little magazine will stand the
weathering of time, although for a full sense of a particular poet or
story-teller's range and vision we will need to see other work in other
magazines or full-length collections. Little magazines, by publishing
single poems or stories, are issuing, perhaps, "interim reports" on the
state of a writer's development or the progress of a particular extended
piece of work. As more and more editors turn to the small chapbook
as a particularly useful way to present a writer's on-going work, however, the immediacy of the magazine's "report" will be somewhat dissipated; the chapbook can be an excellent way to document and present
evidence of a particular writer's continuing development. Some editors
have gone so far as to issue boxed numbers of their magazines, the boxes containing various pamphlets and chapbooks by individual writers.
Kirby Congdon's *Magazine 5* (New York; 1972) and the most recent
issue of *Some* (New York City; no. 7/8, 1976) are excellent examples
of the melding of small press/little magazine concerns. We have the
sense that these two boxed issues are balancing the magazine tradition
and the press tradition, to initiate a new style of publishing. We have
also seen, sometimes, that small presses offer subscriptions to broadside or chapbook series; the publisher may desire to have the extended
contact with readers which magazine subscriptions provide. Some editors who have both a magazine and a press, such as John Judson of
Northeast/Juniper Books (La Crosse, Wisconsin), offer a subscription
to the magazine alone and another subscription to the magazine and the
chapbook series. Others, such as The Alternative Press (Grindstone
City, Michigan), provide copies of all work produced in the course of a
year for a flat subscription fee. Some libraries have begun to deal with
small presses the way they deal with little magazines, by providing
standing orders for all of a press's work. Such an arrangement helps insure that the libraries will receive titles they wish to have without the
risk that a book will be published and go out-of-print unnoticed. Each
small press book or chapbook retains its "artifactual" nature, in such
cases, yet the series it is part of is perceived by the subscriber/reader as
an on-going enterprise similar to the little magazine by virtue of its ex-
tension through time. The chapbook, by its very nature, and the subscription to a press's work lend small book publishers' lists some of the
immediacy more often associated with little magazines. The pamphlet

or small chapbook can also be used to present topical material, of course; literary history provides innumerable examples of the pamphlet being used this way, though the percentage of works so produced surviving as art is relatively low. Whatever distinctions are drawn between the magazine and the press begin to break down as magazine editors strive to create a sense of wholeness within each issue of a magazine and small press editors begin using little publications to provide ongoing reports on the state of literature.

Some magazines never develop an accompanying small press; many such magazines are edited by people not responsible for the publication financially—university literary quarterlies, for instance, very seldom if ever found small presses, although they may publish special issues devoted to individual authors. The vision behind such institutionally-sponsored magazines may very well be that of a particular editor, and the publication may be clearly stamped with his concerns, yet in terms of the economics of literary publishing such an editor is not free to expand his goals beyond prescribed limits. Those magazines from which we see small presses emerging are more frequently the work of an editor or group of editors who find themselves responsible for all aspects of the magazine's existence. Often, the magazine and the newly founded press are serving a clearly defined literary community, the press being viewed as an added service to the member-writers. There are, certainly, magazines which are clearly intended to remain magazines, never to evolve into or to develop a small press. Other magazines are at the service of what editors see as their most urgent needs—if a different kind of publishing seems appropriate to changing circumstances, the magazine operation can be adapted accordingly. There are also small presses which are clearly small presses only, whether designed to serve a specific literary group or the more intangible interests of "literature." Theoretically, at least, the editor of an existing small press can establish a magazine to facilitate communication with a larger literary community or to deal with certain situations he may face, but in my experience such occurrences are rare; after some research, I remain unable to name a significant magazine which emerged from an established small press—a great deal more research in this area needs to be done, however. As a general rule, it appears that a little magazine and a literary press are founded simultaneously, or the press emerges from the magazine operation.

Partly because sufficient factual material about the operation of small literary presses remains ungathered, a full examination of the role of small publishers cannot be made; we do not know enough yet to understand how publishing influences literature and how literary circumstances require the evolution of different kinds of publishing. And partly because researchers interested in literary publishing have studied the little magazine isolated from its small press counterpart, we have seen very little data on the interrelations between the two enterprises. The preliminary conjectures offered here are made in order to identify and argue at least some of the correspondences binding the magazine and the press together as related and interdependent endeavours. Students of publishing need now to verify or disprove these tentative conclusions by proceeding to collect and analyze sufficient information to allow the full examination which will provide insights into the dynamics of literature in America today.

PASSING ON THE LITERATURE: SOME REMINDERS

An excellent book—such as Ted Kooser's *A Local Habitation & A Name* or Jaimy Gordon's *Shamp of the City-Solo*—comes along to remind us: the business of literature is literature. The small presses which are now publishing solid literature, writing that will endure, are doing it for the sake of the art, not for commercial or personal gain. We accept that as granted. Serious questions arise, however. More and more books are being published by more and more small presses. To all appearances, the small press today is as lively as or more lively than it has ever been. But is small publishing, at this moment, fundamentally healthy? We might begin to wonder. Instead of creating the alternative structures truly needed to ensure the publication and dissemination of new literature, we often see small presses imitating commercial publishing's methods at a smaller scale. We see "pretty" books being made, books which have little literary merit, however wonderful the book-crafting. Small press books are "sold," and sometimes "sold out," aren't they, as literary *stars* are created, the small audience for new literature being hustled. Hit-and-run, "guerrilla" publishing is dead, isn't it; instead we hassle grant-money and grant request forms, quarterly budget statements and invoices in quadruplicate. Getting review space in the "trade" journals and shelf space in the bookstores, these have become paramount concerns for many small press publishers. The now old-fashioned (has the revolution passed so quickly?) hand-to-hand, or by mail, free "underground" method of passing literature around has fallen into disfavor and disuse, alas. The world of the small presses now has small press service organizations—although some of these have already become dinosaurs, intent on protecting their arse-ends. Small presses are flocking to bookfairs. More and more, we seem to be in the business of selling books.

Fundamentally, I cannot object to many of these developments in independent publishing, in perspective: the audience for new literature is miniscule, and persistent attempts of many kinds ought to be made to expand that readership. Craftsmanly book-making does, perhaps, enlarge the audience for a particular piece of writing, though we can't really say, since adequate clinical and/or in-the-field studies haven't been done to provide any substantial evidence one way or the other: because the books published by commercial houses "sell" and because they are "competently" crafted, we seem to assume, without recognizing the hard-sell promotion involved, that our competently crafted books will "sell" also. If the question is one of "which book has more readers, or more interested readers," I'm tempted to answer that many of the mimeo books of the sixties—by "craftsmanly" standards perhaps barely deserving of the term "book"—stirred up fire in a good many more readers than nine out of ten of the well-produced books appearing today. Were readers in the sixties, in the heat of the "counterculture" phenomenon, more intent on the writing itself than on the package it came in? Were they merely glowing around the "anti-establishment" campfires? or were they just damn glad to put their eyeballs to fresh ink, period? Certainly, I cannot provide any definitive answer— but I do offer the questions as fair territory for writers trying to dream up projects. Many readers in the sixties, touching that new literature as the tide was starting to come in, obtained the mimeo books and mags free or by swap. The books were cheap enough to make that they could be *given away,* they could reach an audience. We have forgotten, I think, that books can be made that way, that vital literature can be passed on and passed around hand-to-hand, without the exchange of money. D.r. Wagner's poetry, appearing in editions of 100 or 250 copies, is—very fortunately—still with us, if we know where to find it; it has not been "lost" in mimeo, and Wagner remains a very discernible influence even now, several years since his self-imposed silence on the scene. He has not been—and god forbid that he should be—lionized in the universities, although his is a lyric poetry which stands among the best of this or any age. How much of the writing appearing now has such power? There is, to be sure, much competent poetry, and these days even some good fiction, being published by the small presses. There is, indeed, a good deal of excellent writing being done. In the midst of the distribution-review-promotion machinations on the part of many small publishers, however, the fact of the *writing,* or the quality of the writing, often seems almost incidental. That is what I am objecting to.

If distribution schemes and critical notices in the review journals and grant money for literary projects and bookstore distribution don't in some integral fashion help to create and support (in a sense larger than the financial) and enhance literature itself, these are entirely wasted efforts. For what point is there to either a good or bad-mouth review of a book unless some writer—either the author of the book himself or another—assimilates something of value from the review, unless the interested reader gains new insight. A critical notice in a poetry or review journal is or ought to be intended as more than a cog in the promotional machinery of small publishing. The well-written essay or review ought to inform and educate, as well as entertain and (maybe) sell books. But, alas, you know it's just so nice to have those coupla good puff sentences to slap onto promo flyers, ah. I mean, you know, that's why we do it, so readers will know what kinda book it is anyway, whether they should get their mitts on it or not, right? Maybe so, maybe so, he said, shaking his head from side to side, quietly.

I've been of the opinion for some time that small press publishing, unlike much commercial publishing, is a *service* to *literature*. I recognize that literature has to have an audience at some point—if the tree fell in the middle of the forest with no one to hear it, would there be sound? If our poets and fictioneers went silent now, whose loss would it be? Ah, he said, taking notice, some generations from now, the academics would have no fodder, would they? And with that cynical remark he went silent again. But he thought about all the trees falling in the forest and all the energy expended in order to make new literature available. He thought about Emily Dickinson. And he wondered if perhaps there weren't a better way: what if, he thought, what if writers unilaterally stopped offering their work to publishers and instead deposited copies of manuscripts in local, regional or national archives for storage? Ah, then "reviewers" (if there were to be any) would be disinterested, wouldn't they, intent on discussing the literature, with nary a thought to selling the book. Writers would no longer have to spend considerable time and energy hustling publishers, and publishers could go back to being businessmen, if that were their inclination, or turn their efforts again to writing, if that is what had been sacrificed for the sake of publishing. But then he thought, no, no, that's not realistic, is it? I mean, we live in a world of egos and dollars.

Still, the business of literature is literature. The audience for literature ought to be interested in good writing. The writer ought to be writing, the editor editing. The critic ought to lend his insights, the keys he has found (and he ought to entertain, surely). The publisher ought to publish, to make physically accessible. The small press person often finds himself or herself in strangely contorted positions: for the audience of the new literature is often the writer of the new literature who is also the editor, the publisher, the critic (to say nothing of distribution, promotion, grant-hounding, record-keeping, or sweeping up). Many hats for many roles; often the literature gets lost in the shuffle.

I would not argue unrealistically that each person in small press ought to have one task and one task only, though such a division of responsibility would alleviate some difficulties: the poet who is also critic, for instance, would not be in the position to puff a bad book from a press with whom he may be attempting to place a manuscript; writers who are their own editors are notoriously blind; further, anyone who has dipped into the world of small publishing very long has heard the complaint that the readers of little magazines are the editors of other little magazines, each feeding on the other. I would argue, rather, that we begin a thorough reassessment of what we are about, recognizing that what matters, ultimately, is the writing which gives impetus to all the other of our varied activities.

As editor of *Margins,* a monthly review of little magazines and small press books, I see much of what small presses are producing today. And like most others in small publishing, I have my biases and blind spots; one commentator has pointed out, for instance, that in the past *Margins* has reviewed considerably more "pretty" books than mimeo productions, irrespective of the quality of the writing in either, that the literature which interests most of the reviewers writing for *Margins* is that which appears in well-crafted format. This is a common blind-side bias, of course, but certainly one that is inexcusable if our concern is for the writing. Similarly, small publishers are aware that in order to get shelf space in bookstores, i.e., in order to compete in the marketplace, small volumes must have perfect bindings; hence, better than sixty percent of the books being published today have square-back, lettered spines. And to what purpose? to get the book on the shelf? The binding of a book is usually irrelevant to the quality of the contents, of course; letterpress production versus offset versus mimeo cannot alter the quality of the literature, only the quality of the artifact; perhaps books of poems which look like the books of poems to which we have become accustomed will more readily stir a reader's interest: do we read artifacts or do we read literature? Have we become book collectors? Our bias shows; I'm as guilty as any, I'm afraid, but I'm now conscious of such discrimination, and attempting to work away from it. Because those of us in small publishing often try to compete with industry publishers for audience, we find ourselves imitating industry methods: distributors and bookstores; review journals; trade organizations; book fairs.

If we start with the premise that new literature cannot "compete" in the marketplace, then we can begin to see distribution to bookstores as a peripheral concern. Most bookstores are meat markets, and most bookstore patrons are looking for juicy steaks. There are, of course, the "small press" bookstores whose purpose is the furtherance of new literature; these are worthy and honorable undertakings, and publications placed therein may be considered well-placed. If, however, one intends to "recoup publishing expenses eventually," to place books with chain stores such as Dalton's or Walden, one had best go into another line of work. New literature and business-as-business simply remain incompatible. Blame New York, blame Culture, blame our education system, blame any handy scapegoat: the fact remains.

The new "visibility" of the small press in recent years appears to be increasingly counterproductive. We begin to chase the illusion that small press publishing can be successful "eventually." To this end, the prices of chapbooks and small volumes of poetry have been raised, almost to the point that anyone paying cover price for a first book by an unknown poet is a fool; unless the new poet is destined to become a honey-child of the book collectors, such an investment is logically unjustifiable. All this is said, of course, without respect for the writing itself. If bookstores are to get their forty percent for selling the book, and the distributor his ten or fifteen percent, the prices on small press books must go up; further, the marked bias among book "handlers" against books (and broadsides) which cost less than a dollar is so pervasive that inexpensive books will sit boxed in the basement until they mold; they mold and go unread. The most vocal members of the Committee of Small Magazine/press Editors and Publishers seem continually to call for distribution ideas and distribution projects and grant money for distribution, distribution, distribution. That concern has been voiced for several years now, and many of those elected to the COS-MEP board of directors continue to list *distribution* as a paramount item on the docket. Past efforts towards distribution have brought few fruits, it would seem, and energy expended thus far goes only to further the dream that we can make a success of small press publishing with traditional methods. We cannot.

I have been tempted to do, and may still end up doing, a mimeographed issue of *Margins*. *Margins* has readers who respect what the magazine is attempting; but I wonder how many would understand the purpose of a mimeo issue, or a newsletter issue similar to *Margins* no. 1, no. 2, and no. 3. Would the image of *Margins* fall in readers' estimation if, instead of the present newsprint format, it appeared in mimeo—even if the nature, the quality, and the quantity of contents remained unchanged? I fear that *Margins* in such a format wouldn't be taken very seriously.

And, to be honest, I have been tempted to discontinue the magazine entirely, for "philosophical" reasons, whatever the sad state of the magazine's finanaces. If and when *Margins* folds, financial reasons could be honestly cited as cause of the demise; many of those interested in *Margins* and the small press scene generally would understand. Money talks, yes, and when we explain the death of a magazine in financial terms, readers can more readily accept the discontinuation. If, however, I were to say that I am beginning to view *Margins* as part of the problem rather than part of the solution, that I am beginning to think *Margins* is a co-conspirator in continuing the illusion that small publishing can "make it," that our efforts towards covering the small press scene may sometimes be counterproductive, such explanations I would expect to raise a hue and cry. I am reluctant to shoot the 20-some issue horse right now, however, because I think *Margins* does, in some limited way, aid the creation of a healthy and useful "community" of small publishers and it does provide an outlet for healthy criticism of the contemporary literature almost universally ignored elsewhere. A sense of "community" is, I think, important to the work of the small publisher. As publishers, we most often labor in isolation, alone with a strong sense of our aloneness. The knowledge that others are carrying on in situations similar to our own can serve to give us strength. The fact that new criticism has few other outlets is not and will not determine whether *Margins* continues or folds, since I have become increasingly interested in publishing both large and small books of criticism and commentary, and have several in mind or in actual preparation. Such books will serve to expose new criticism; and because the publishing of books will entail fewer editorial problems for me than the publishing of a critical journal, the temptation to do books only is attractive. Thus, if I find sometime in the future that there is little reason to attempt to foster a sense of community among small publishers, *Margins* will have few essential reasons for continuing. *Margins* may or may not sell books; selling books is irrelevant to its first concerns. *Margins* may or may not make books accessible; accessibility may only help to foster the false notion that we can "sell" our books.

The concerns I have with *Margins,* I think, are related to those of many small press publishers today, though certainly many would disagree with personal positions I've taken—for instance, I know very few publishers who categorically reject CCLM or NEA grant monies as possible sources of funding their projects. I know few publishers for whom distribution is not a paramount concern. Disagreements are probably healthy. Some arguments are undoubtedly "gentlemen's arguments," interesting ways to pass some time. Others, however, involve root problems facing small publishers. Not the "problems" of grant funding or distribution, which I consider peripheral, but the quality of our literature, the nature of our sensibilities, the extent of our feeling; these ought to have our primary attention. If our interests lie elsewhere, then we are not involved with literature, but with publishing as a business or with literary entrepreneuring, or with star-gazing. If we are not interested in literature, let's not pretend we are.

I do not intend to say here that we ought to be producing only mimeographed books and magazines, nor that we have no business attempting to place books in sympathetic bookstores, nor that we ought not send out review copies to book review journals, nor that we ought not form small press service organizations, attend small press books fairs, or whatever. What I do intend to say is that we ought to concern ourselves first and foremost with the writing, the literature, which informs our many activities. That, first and last, to remember.

I would like to have the sense, once again, that those of us involved in small press publishing are doing essential work, that we are carrying on the best of our literary tradtions and are creating new "traditions" to carry into the future. I lose that sense as I see small presses make central "problems" which ought to lie at the edge of what we can see. We have to involve ourselves with the politics of literature, yes, and we probably have to hustle our literature if it is to find an audience. But if our first concern is not the literature itself, we are wasting ourselves, our lives.

SMALL PUBLISHING, IN YOUR BLOOD

It gets in your blood. Small press publishing gets in your blood; and once it does, there is no turning back. Or, five years as a small publisher have convinced me that there is a demon on my back, driving me. I don't know that all small publishers have demons driving them; nor that they're all crazy. I do know that once you've assumed the role of small publisher, your perspective on the world begins to change; you sense that very often you can do without "necessities," that sometimes you can use even the grocery money to publish literature and still survive. If you are a husband, you need a patient and understanding wife; if you are a father, you need children who are indulgent about your work schedule, your crankiness, your "things." I know. However much Monday Morning Press or *Margins* or Margins Books are my creations, they would not be possible without the cooperation of my wife and two daughters. The three of them are, we might call them, unindicted co-conspirators. When Mary married me in 1969, I was writing poetry—the disease hadn't spread any farther than that. Little did she know that within two years the small press infection would touch every aspect of our lives; that everything we decided for ourselves would in some way also concern Monday Morning Press and *Margins* and vice versa. Mary has lived patiently with my need to have two or three cups of coffee and read my mail in the morning before speaking; she has lived patiently with the folding of broadsides, the collation and stapling of books in the middle of the living room, with the poetry readings, with writers and publishers dropping in from California, New York, Australia. She's lived patiently with review copies under the bed and on the dresser and scattered across our living room, with bundles of *Margins* and piles of books stacked in the living room, in the hallways, in the attic. She has time and again allowed money to be drained from our savings account to ransom whatever happens to be at the printer. This madness wasn't covered by any clause in our marriage contract, but Mary has patiently accepted the strange state of affairs that small publishing creates. Human beings cannot be expected to live with small press publishers, but some do—and thank God for that.

My first contact with small publishing was in summer, 1971, at Green's Bookstore on Downer Avenue in Milwaukee, where I discovered some Albatross Press "Roadmap Editions," then being published by Martin J. Rosenblum. Here was work by people my own age, in print: it was a revelation. Later that summer, I met Rosenblum, who was serving as poetry editor for the *Bugle American* (an alternative newspaper in Milwaukee) and who had accepted some of my work for his poetry page. Talking to him about Albatross Press, I saw that I could establish a press of my own: another revelation. Monday Morning Press was founded in fall, 1971. In its most active phase (fall 1971-fall 1972), Monday Morning published 13 folded broadsides, four chapbooks, and one 80-page book.

By fall, 1972, however, *Margins* had been established and began drawing my time, energy and money away from Monday Morning Press. I had been familiar with Len Fulton's *Small Press Review* nearly a year when, in July, 1972, Dave Buege (who had founded, that spring, *Harpoon* magazine and Harpoon Press) and I began talking about the need for review space beyond what *Small Press Review* was providing. The impetus behind *Margins* at that point was not that Buege and I were dissatisfied with *Small Press Review;* rather, we felt that because of the welter of small press activity in the country more review space, more discussion of new publications was needed, urgently. We had no ambitions towards a 72-page monthly journal, nor 216-page triple issues. Our first issue (August 1972), in fact, consisted of six legal-size pages, printed on both sides, stapled in one corner. (I wonder how many current *Margins* readers have seen that very modest first issue.)

We intended, in the beginning, to distribute *Margins* gratis to libraries and bookstores, hoping (as we said in our editorial in No. 1) "to present the audience of *Library Journal* with a scope of materials comparable to *Small Press Review. . .*" Our rationale: "There is a healthy abundance of small press material presently available; the future seems to promise even more. No one, most particularly perhaps book-store buyers and acquisitions librarians, can pretend to keep up. *Margins* is a new review of little magazines and small press books that intends to sift through and evaluate as much of this material as is humanly and financially possible." No. 2 (October 1972) and No. 3 (December 1972) were similar in size and format to No. 1.

The scheme to use advertising instead of subscriptions to support *Margins*—workable in theory—fizzled because few small publishers were interested in or could afford advertising, even at our ridiculously low page-rates. Further, our production and mailing costs rose from an incredible $29 for No. 1 (I still think the printer miscalculated on that one) to about $100 for No. 3. (By comparison, a triple issue in 1975 cost me $1500 to print and $450 to mail.) By December, 1972, I was also beginning to itch for a more substantial journal than the newsletter *Margins*. Dave Buege was deterred from continuing as co-publisher of *Margins* by the additional costs magazine format entailed; he elected to assist with layout and production and serve as a contributing editor for a while. Production costs by No. 4 were seven times what they had been for No. 1, advertising revenue had not increased substantially, and I began to think some changes were in order. Although *Margins* continued to carry some gratis subscriptions for another year, we started charging libraries for the magazine. The subscription rate was increased to cover the enlarged magazine version of *Margins*. Advertising rates, however, were kept at the same low level, as a service to small publishers—if they could not afford $20 for a full page, they could not afford higher rates either.

Neither advertising revenue nor subscription monies were sufficient to keep *Margins* solvent, however, chiefly because I seemed to insist at every turn that the magazine expand physically. No. 4 was a twenty-page issue (8.5" x 11" pages); No. 5 was forty pages, as were No. 6 and No. 7. The press run increased from 400 for No. 1 to 600 for No. 4 and 800 for No. 5. With No. 6 (press run, 1,000), I started printing with Port Publications in Port Washington, Wisconsin—some 20 miles north of Milwaukee.

Not only did Port Publications offer the best printing rates I'd found, and not only did they have a web offset press suitable for *Margins'* page-size and for newsprint (which I wanted to publish on), but this printer had my respect as well: Port Publications had printed the Milwaukee underground paper *Kaleidoscope* when no one else would. Simply printing that paper cost them dearly. One issue of *Kaleidoscope* in particular created trouble—it was deemed obscene in court and a local businessman instigated an advertising boycott against the weekly newspapers owned by Port Publications and published for small communities north of Milwaukee. The boycott was effective; Port Publications lost at least two of its community newspapers. Bill Schanen, who owned Port Publications, insisted that "freedom of the press means freedom of the press, *Kaleidoscope* included." Schanen died of a heart attack in the midst of the dispute over *Kaleidoscope* and the advertising boycott. His son, Bill Schanen III, now capably manages Port Publications, continuing to provide hassle-free printing for Milwaukee's stranger publishers.

I found "newsprint" *per se* an attractive medium for *Margins,* for two reasons: first, newsprint costs less—that attraction is obvious; and second, as the title of *Margins* is meant to imply, reviewing is not a be-all and end-all activity. Reviewing is peripheral to literature, supportive of it but not central to it. Good literature survives both the praise and the condemnation. Thus, what *Margins* does is at the edge of serious literature; thus, also, the appropriateness of newsprint, immediate and accessible, without pretense.

Margins No. 6 was the first newsprint; *Margins* No. 7, the first issue prepared on an IBM Composer rather than a typewriter. In the summer of 1973, having lost all other visible means of support, I began working as typesetter for the *Bugle American.* One little-sung skill in the world—and a skill poets would do well to pick up, to support themselves—is the ability to type 60-80 words a minute. (Being able to work a telephone switchboard doesn't hurt either.) One fringe benefit of the *Bugle* job was the use of the paper's IBM Composer; I was able to set *Margins* Nos. 7 through 13 on that machine. I'm not one to damn technology: the IBM Composer (and here I'm bowing towards a giant which doesn't need me to puff it)—and contrary to George Mattingly's nasty-minded, disparaging assertions about the machine in the COSMEP Production

Design handbook—has proven to be an invaluable piece of equipment and a friend; quite simply, without it *Margins* as conceived from August 1973 through the end of 1976 could not have existed. The Composer enabled *Margins* to expand its coverage considerably without increasing the number of pages per issue, and to present a somewhat professional-looking journal at low cost.

In the summer of 1974, I gave up the *Bugle* work in favor of a free-lance editing gig for The Institute of Ecology/National Science Foundation project, *The Urban Ecosystem: A Holistic Approach* (ed. Forest Stearns and Tom Montag; Stroudsburg, Pa.: Dowden, Hutchinson & Ross, 1975), which paid rather handsomely; but I was left without a Composer. The quotations for typesetting *Margins* I'd obtained indicated that the average cost per 72-page issue would run better than $900. I decided to invest in a machine of my own. After six or seven issues, I reasoned, the machine will have paid for itself. And I've found it has: by summer of 1976, my machine was used to typeset better than 1100 pages of *Margins,* five Margins Books (all prose), nearly all the recent Membrane Press books, and all the Pentagram Press books to date—in addition to various brochures, pamphlets, and flyers for strange and worthwhile enterprises in Milwaukee. It has also brought in some money now and again, when I've done typesetting for magazines ranging from *Minnesota Review* to *Ecology* (its most recent 20-year index, 250 8.5" x 11" pages with 2-column eight-point type!). Of course you have to *pay* IBM for the machine if you want to keep it, and a $4800 investment is a frightening proposition for someone who simply started out as a writer and found along the way that other tasks needed doing. But freedom of the press belongs, in part, to those who set the type.

Of course, I simply assumed in the beginning that a small publisher would do his own design, layout, and paste-up. Unfortunately, my education—B.A., English, 1972, after seven and a half years in college, off and on—didn't quite prepare me for design and production work. As with my typing skills—adequate in school, but greatly improved during my year-long stint with the *Bugle American,* getting out an issue every week—one simply learns these things as he needs them. The first issue I did the actual lay-out and paste-up on was No. 6. That issue is marred not only by my obvious ineptness at lay-out, but also by the feeble-mindedness of the typewriter I used to set the copy. I finally ditched that mental defective early in 1976. Our first newsprint issue looked pretty bad. The lay-out on No. 7 was equally inept. By No. 8 (October-November 1973), I was beginning to catch on; and the physical appearance of *Margins* continued to improve for some time, settling at the present level of competence about the middle of 1974. My skills at design, lay-out, and paste-up are not remarkable—simply, I hope, adequate.

Margins appeared as a bi-monthly publication from its inception in August, 1972, until December, 1974, a total of 15 issues. In that time, the magazine had grown from a 12-page newsletter to a 72-page journal (with one 80-page and two 88-page issues thrown in during 1974 for good measure). At the end of 1975, I decided that a 72-page *monthly* publication was feasible, both financially and in terms of my energies. How naive. *Margins'* income from issue to issue remains fairly constant—what publishing monthly would mean is that we would lose no more per issue than we had been losing, but twice as much over the course of a year. The financial loss I could deal with—I had been robbing Peter to pay Paul for some time already; I could handle a little more fancy shuffling. There was enough good material reaching *Margins* to warrant the increased frequency of appearance; I wasn't worried about having suitable material to print. What I didn't realize, when I made the decision, was how much additional energy publishing monthly would require. One plus one does not equal two, I can assure you; it equals three or four or five. A magazine which in the beginning had taken at most ten hours of my time each week started taking, by January 1975, 70 or 80 hours. Although Mary was proofreading *Margins,* and although she was able to keep pace with my own production speed, my workload consisted of correspondence and editorial responsibilities, typesetting, lay-out, and paste-up, filling orders, maintaining subscription lists, and mailing out the issues when they appeared. *Margins* started appearing monthly, yes; and I was seen less and less frequently outside my basement office. Hence my nickname in the family: The Mole.

In late 1971 and early 1972, I was writing my first reviews of small press publications, for *Bugle American* and *Small Press Review.* I found that I both enjoyed and learned from the process of reviewing. I also found that I could write more reviews than either *Small Press Review* or *Bugle American* could publish. When Dave Buege and I were discussing the possibility of *Margins,* I saw it as an outlet for my own reviewing energies. Buege himself was more interested in helping create the "reviewing space" than in actually doing much reviewing (and in fact his only review for *Margins* appears in No. 2). Two young smart-ass punks from Milwaukee were establishing a review mechanism; neither had very much experience doing reveiws and neither knew many commentators interested in writing for the magazine. A magazine—albeit very modest—without a stable of writers; without many "review copies" on hand; without a list of subscribers. Doing things bass-ackwards— starting at zero and developing naturally rather than designing a complete editorial vision with a printed prospectus—was *Margins'* way of succeeding.

Contributors to *Margins* No. 1 were Martin J. Rosenblum and Tom Montag; Rosenblum reviewed the first two volumes of *Voyages to the Inland Sea* at some length; Montag did two reviews and a "little magazine round-up." Reviewers for No. 2 were Dave Buege, John Jacob, Diane Kruchkow, and Montag (unloading eight reveiws). No. 3 saw Karl

Young and Kirby Congdon added to the list of contributors; plus 12 reviews by Montag. Brian Salchert and Paul Portland did short reviews for No. 4; Montag checked in with 14 pieces. Where does this guy get off, anyway? The fifth issue was better balanced: of the eight feature pieces, two were by Montag, one each by Jay Bail, Felix Pollak, Diane Kruchkow, Kathleen Wiegner, Karl Young, and John Shannon. The short "In the Margins" reviews in No. 5 were written by Jeffrey Woodward (2), John Jacob (1), Brian Salchert (1), Kirby Congdon (1), Terrance Ames (2), and Montag (6). *Margins* No. 6 was less well balanced than No. 5, but thereafter the reviewers appearing in *Margins* were numerous and diverse. By the end of 1975 (No. 27), pieces by 304 different contributors had been published. (If *Margins* is a clique, as has sometimes been alleged, it's a damn big clique—and getting out of hand). The "staff" of *Margins* grew slowly—new, reliable contributors would often recommend other writers to me as possible reviewers. As one reviewer lost interest, another would sign on. And so before very long, that little blaze in Montag's and Buege's eyes was a raging inferno. Well, at least—to change horses in midstream—it was a healthy tempest in its tiny teapot. Or the frog that ate Milwaukee.

There are undoubtedly as many ways to edit a review journal as there are editors. My own policy, whenever possible, has been to include rather than exclude; to notice, rather than ignore; to make a judgment of some sort rather than remain silent. I have seen my role as editor of *Margins* as one of gatherer or funneler of energies: to channel, rather than to rewrite or revise a writer's words or vision. In its first four and a half years, *Margins* was intended to be a platform from which a diverse array of commentators could be heard. I have never consciously sought to push any party line nor shore up any particular writer's "reputation." I do accept editorial responsibility for all pieces which have appeared in *Margins,* but agree with and personally stand by only those articles appearing under my name (and that of Crusader Rabbit). Those reviewers whose views I disagree with have a right to be heard in *Margins;* such openness is a policy I will argue until the cows come home. The risk of an open editorial policy, of course, is a diffuse and unfocused magazine. The benefits, however, seem worth the risk. A "gathering" vision can allow the reader to glimpse the richness of the various literatures appearing today. It can help insure that many contemporary literary concerns are given the attention they deserve, that all the wheat is harvested.

Admittedly, my open policy has meant that some "bad" writing has been published—dull or pretentious or wrongheaded or ungrammatical pieces can be found in nearly every issue of the magazine. Admittedly, some areas of contemporary literature have been slighted. Experimental writing, for instance, has not been given its full due in our pages, less because of any prejudice of mine against such literature, more because there are so few critics both qualified and willing to write for *Margins.* Likewise, beyond the fine special focuses we have published, I believe that women's literatures have been rather shabbily treated in *Margins;* the magazine's discussion has been insufficient in terms of coverage, inadequate in terms of perceptive analysis, and insubstantial in terms of judgment. Black small press literature has been covered only randomly, on a hit-and-miss basis. Examination of translated works is seldom made in *Margins'* pages either—a state of affairs very likely due to my conscious prejudice against translations. Certain "schools" of writing have not been discussed at much length, again because of my prejudices—I have very little patience with cheap surrealism, immanentism, and modularism, with second- and third-generation New York school work, with the gaggle that waggles behind Charles Bukowski, etc. etc. The deliberate omissions I make no apologies for; the unintentional neglect of various literatures is a more serious flaw, frequently caused by circumstances difficult to change. It is, very often, not possible to gather the best reviewers and critics in a particular area to be explored; nor is it always possible when making an assignment, to gauge a particular writer's critical acumen on the basis of reputation or the recommendation of others. And sometimes, the sheer bulk of work to be done has meant that I haven't been able to do the editorial work needed to turn a so-so article into a good, readable piece; that I have let pass into print sentences which are ungrammatical and judgments which are untenable. Whatever *Margins'* various shortcomings, however, I think one can say that the magazine has surveyed current literature with a sweep and plumb few other magazines have managed; that *Margins* will stand as a better index of the literature 1972-76 than most other single sources.

My boasting is not *at all* intended to puff myself or my abilities as an editor. Without the fine writers who have gravitated to *Margins* over the years, the magazine would be nothing. I'll take some credit for sending sparks into the tinder, yes; but it has been *Margins'* contributors, issue after issue, who have carried in the logs, who have lent the magazine whatever blaze and brightness it has had. Had *Margins* never existed, some critics writing today might never have turned to critical work; and some of those that have would surely find greater difficulty getting their criticism and reviews into print. Although the enthusiasms of *Margins'* contributors may not be contagious, I trust they have led some readers to literatures otherwise neglected. No issue of *Margins,* nor *Margins* as a whole, has had the best imaginable balance of viewpoints and enthusiasms. But at least some substantial discussion has taken place; that much seems undeniable.

Perhaps *Margins* has raised a little hell—some would say it has not been enough, others that it has been too much. Hell-raising is part of the function of the effective review journal. If you count the number of books advertised in *Margins* that have been given bad reviews, you'll find, I think, that advertisers have not been a sacred cow. If you read my position on grants as set down in "Some Polemics, Practical Considerations or a Modest Proposal" (*Margins* No. 14, pp. 14ff), you may understand that we have not been beholden to any funding agency. If you examine the "Letters" column over several issues, you should discover that *Margins* has not surpressed negative criticisms. It has been my policy, in fact, to publish negative rather than positive reactions to the contents of *Margins*. I have the whole large canvas of the magazine on which to paint; it seems only honest and appropriate to use the "Letters" section for contrary opinions. Further, I am generally skeptical about magazines which find it necessary to print flattering letters—these appear to be crude attempts to bolster the editor's self-esteem and I find the practice distasteful. The publication of disturbing or controversial material has not been intended to create noise only, but to generate substantial discussion of the issues at hand. In the American literary establishment there are so few platforms from which minority reports can be read that it has seemed unquestionably necessary for *Margins* to present the dissenting viewpoints. Certainly, there are those who would say that, in doing so, we have hindered rather than helped literature. However, I believe that literature is more gravely harmed by the stifling of dissent, by the glossing over of questionable practices, by the neglect of what ought to be examined in the light of day. True, I sometimes wonder how an Iowa farmboy ended up in the middle of literary-political battles; and true, I sometimes wonder if all the smoke is worth the heat; and yet I'm convinced that reasonable men and women are entitled to draw their own conclusions—once they've heard the discussion. They must hear the discussion; they must see a little hell raised and harvested.

At the beginning, as the magazine was initially conceived, *Margins* was intended to be a selection tool for librarians and booksellers, as well as a journal of information and opinion for interested individuals. Critical judgments were to be made, but succinctly enough to be useful to those intent on acquiring the books. *Margins* was to serve primarily as an access resource. As my conception of *Margins* changed, however, the idealized reader has changed. Although the magazine is still useful as an access tool, the articles and reviews have gotten longer and have become more concerned with problems of literary form and technique and with literary-political questions. Such discussions are, probably, not particularly useful to those chiefly interested in buying books; they are of more interest to the person concerned with the shape and direction of contemporary literatures generally. Further, the exploration of literary-political problems—placing literature in one of its larger contexts—and of the possibilities of form and technique probably concern the writer as writer more immediately than the general reader, although such discussions—by indicating which way the winds are blowing—help to keep the larger audience informed about literature's predicaments and developments. That *Margins* is partly focused on problems of prime concern to writers does not mean that the magazine's intended audience is only or primarily a circle of writers or a community of small press publishers.

In *Margins* No. 4, I indicated that "much of the energy [in the small press community]. . .flows in a circle." I urged small publishers to "break out of [their] closed circle & begin to direct [their] energy outward. There is material of value in small press, but inbreeding & elitism keep it here. The task is to get small press materials before the reading public: I am still so naive as to believe that once the public has access to it, they will appreciate its value &, we hope, lend it support."

Whether *Margins* has successfully helped to enlarge the audience for small press materials I cannot say. I do know that there are readers who do appreciate the information and views which *Margins* makes available. That my interests as editor have moved from access information to substantial critical discussion is nowhere more evident than in the *Margins* "Symposium Series" under the general editorship of Karl Young. In his "A Note on Symposiums" in *Margins* 28-30, Young very judiciously described the information/criticism duality inherent in *Margins,* and our efforts to meet two sets of responsibilities:

One of *Margins'* major functions is to further discussion of contemporary writing. In the three years of its existence, it has grown and tried to adapt itself to a large and often mercurial literary scene in which hundreds of new writers come forward each year and old hands keep changing as their work evolves. For the most part, this large body of writing has been discussed on a one-to-one basis: one reviewer reviewing one book or magazine. This has been a valuable approach and has proved itself flexible enough to explore a large range of new work. But we feel that contemporary writing should be approached intensively as well as extensively, vertically as well as horizontally. We feel that multi-voice responses provide the best vertical, intensive examinations of current writing and that such responses can best be encouraged and directed through the symposium form.

As Young makes clear, *Margins* has been challenged to survey a wide array of literatures—the breadth of the scene—and to plumb the depths with solid critical discussion at particular points of interest. As a reading of *Margins'* "Letters" column will indicate, we have not always succeeded to everyone's satisfaction. Sometimes the choice of subjects for discussion is disputed by correspondents; sometimes, merely the perceptions and insights of particular contributors. Other readers hold that the special attention the "Symposium Series" focuses on particular writers can be risky: that now is not the time to give any contemporary writer so much attention. Others see the Series as a valuable idea, but headed in the wrong direction. Some—not regular readers, certainly—believe that critical discussion of any sort is a waste of time. Surely critical judgments about current literatures need to be made, though perhaps the perceptivity of those judgments cannot be assessed until some future date. The success of our critical discussion of current literature, in the Symposium Series and throughout the magazine, perhaps should not be measured only by comparison to present opinion, but also with the perspective time will bring.

Margins' shift to more substantial discussions is a reflection of a change in my sense of our literary circumstances. In 1972, the most urgent need was to make current writing known and accessible; this need could be met by providing relevant information, by serving in a "review" capacity. More and more, however, it becomes clear that information is not enough, that simply to "review" new books may be detrimental to literature. Partly because I reject the notion that small presses must "make it" in a financial sense, and partly because I see reviews starting to serve a promotional rather than a critical function, I have become increasingly less interested in publishing reviews *per se* in *Margins.* Essay-reviews which deal with complex matters inherent in the work under discussion are another matter; when assumptions and working principles are explored, when a particular book is related to its tradition and is placed in the context of other literatures today, when the essayist seeks not to hastily sketch his impressions, but carefully examine the full implications of particular writing, the essay-review moves far into the realm of criticism, with value beyond the immediate announcement of a book's existence. If you are not part of the solution, you are part of the problem; and as more and more small publishers begin to invest large amounts of time and energy in promotion and marketing, when what they should be worrying about first is *literature,* I tend to think *Margins* has become part of the problem. A review journal with the size and scope *Margins* has had can help perpetuate the illusion that small presses can and ought to compete with commercial publishers. What is more urgently needed than a review-promotion mechanism, in the face of the swarm of new books appearing every week, is a larger and more encompassing sense of what current literature is and where it is heading. Single book reviews, by and large, cannot offer a sense of the broader ranges of contemporary writing. Sometimes even examination of the corpus of a single author provides few clues. Not many journals are attempting to make this larger kind of sense out of the various activities small presses are involved in, and—since review space in other publications has increased—I have elected to move my publishing in the direction of essays and essay-reviews.

It has been with some dismay that I find myself more frequently identified as the editor of *Margins* and a critic rather than as a poet. My work as editor and critic is more widely circulated than the poetry, yes; but I have had eight poetry titles published (*Wooden Nickel, Twelve Poems, Measures, To Leave/This Place, Making Hay, Making Hay & Other Poems, Ninety Notes,* and *Naming the Creeks*) and I would expect that people who've heard my name would also have heard of my poetry. Such has not been the case; that I write poetry at all comes entirely as a surprise to some; others simply consider my work as editor and critic to be the more significant. However, in my own mind, I am a poet who took on additional tasks which needed doing. Neglect by others of one's creative work is, perhaps, the price one pays for achieving some measure of success in other areas. In part, the impression that I am first editor and critic stems from this: my editorial-critical duties have taken so much time and energy that I have abandoned my creative work for long periods; between October, 1973, and November, 1975, in fact, I wrote no poetry at all, but edited 18 issues of *Margins,* wrote nearly 100,000 words of essay and review, and mailed out countless letters. I justified the shoving aside of my creative work on the grounds that the world needed a review journal such as *Margins* a good deal more than it needed another poet. By November, 1975, however, I had returned to poetry with a vengeance, writing regularly for the next six months by stealing time from other commitments.

Has the fire—through the years—been worth the fuel? Who's to say? I've found it difficult to envision a life without *Margins*-like work to do; the creation of a useful critical-review journal has been satisfying, though it has not been without its headaches, its endlessly difficult problems. Just as women frequently suffer "post-partum depression," so I get my post-issue bluez every time a *Margins* goes in the mail. There have been several extended periods of grave dissatisfaction with *Margins,* usually caused by the various pressures inherent in the work, by lack of money, by the need to work at other jobs in order to support the magazine. Periodically the projects have reached a "critical-mass" stage and have exploded in my face, to be put back in order when the debris has cleared away. Sometimes, the cost of literature has seemed too high a price to pay; literature, after all, is not all of life. Which hat are you wearing today, Mr. Montag? Husband? Father? Friend? Poet, critic, editor, publisher, typesetter, layout artist, secretary, shipping clerk, janitor? Or which combination? Are you going to be civil to your family, or go for the juglar? Are you going to stop being a fanatic and start being human today? Have you lost your perspective? Have you found Jesus? Despite the ragged days and the long hours, the work continues to feel worthwhile, necessary. Despite the bluez, the pressures, I think I've managed to keep at least one foot on the ground; that has seemed to be enough.

I might bitch, but I keep working. That should prove something.

INDEX

An asterisk following a page number indicates that the entry is discussed at some length.

Addresses for most of the small presses mentioned in *Concern/s* can be found in the *International Directory of Little Magazines and Small Presses,* available through Dustbooks, PO Box 1056, Paradise, California, 95969.

<u>Pentagram Press is</u>

Michael Andre: My Regrets
David Clewell: Room to Breathe
Harley Elliott: Sky Heart
Theodore Enslin: The Further Regions
Doug Flaherty: Near The Bone
John Jacob: Making Play
John Judson: Routes From The Onion's Dark
William Kloefkorn: ludi jr
Ted Kooser: Not Coming To Be Barked At
Richard Kostelanetz: 'The End' Appendix
Steve Lewis: Exits Off A Toll Road
William Matthews: Sticks & Stones
Tom Montag: Concern/s: essays & reviews 1972-76
—————— : Making Hay & Other Poems
—————— : 90 Notes
Robert Peters: Shaker Light
Martin J. Rosenblum: Scattered On: Omens & Curses
Michael Tarachow: Into It
————————— : as editor, Toward A Further Definition
Diane Wakoski: The Fable Of The Lion & The Scorpion